Surviving
Your Child's
Adolescence

*D...*

*Thank you so much
for your help and
support,*

*Best wishes for
the summer,*

*Sanjay Sharma*

# Surviving Your Child's Adolescence

### How to Understand, and Even Enjoy, the Rocky Road to Independence

Carl Pickhardt, PhD

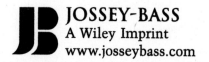

**JOSSEY-BASS**
A Wiley Imprint
www.josseybass.com

Published by Jossey-Bass
A Wiley Imprint
One Montgomery Street, Suite 1200, San Francisco, CA 94104-4594—www.josseybass.com

Jossey-Bass books and products are available through most bookstores. To contact Jossey-Bass directly call our Customer Care Department within the U.S. at 800-956-7739, outside the U.S. at 317-572-3986, or fax 317-572-4002.

Wiley publishes in a variety of print and electronic formats and by print-on-demand. Some material included with standard print versions of this book may not be included in e-books or in print-on-demand. If this book refers to media such as a CD or DVD that is not included in the version you purchased, you may download this material at http://booksupport.wiley.com. For more information about Wiley products, visit www.wiley.com.

Library of Congress Cataloging-in-Publication Data

Pickhardt, Carl E.
  Surviving your child's adolescence : how to understand, and even enjoy, the rocky road to independence / Carl Pickhardt. – 1st ed.
       p. cm.
  Includes bibliographical references and index.
  ISBN 978-1-118-22883-8 (pbk.); ISBN 978-1-118-41934-2 (ebk.);
  ISBN 978-1-118-42122-2 (ebk.); ISBN 978-1-118-43386-7 (ebk.)
  1. Parent and teenager.   2. Parenting.   3. Teenagers.   4. Adolescence.   I. Title.
  HQ799.15.P53 2013
  305.235–dc23
                              2012038559

Printed in the United States of America
FIRST EDITION
PB Printing   10 9 8 7 6 5 4 3 2 1

*To all those parents and teenagers who manage to keep their relationship together while adolescence is growing them apart, as it is meant to do*

# Contents

Acknowledgments      ix

About the Author      xi

Author's Note      xiii

Introduction      xv

Voices of Parents Past      xix

1    Preparing for the Inevitable      1

2    A Road Map to Early and Mid-Adolescence      21

3    A Road Map to Late Adolescence and Trial Independence      49

4    Parenting Adolescent Sons and Daughters      83

5    The Complexities of Spoken Communication      105

6    The Use and Abuse of Conflict      127

7    Discipline That Does and Doesn't Work      149

8    Informal and Formal Education      175

9    Problems with Peers      197

10    The Power of Parents      227

Epilogue: Climbing Fool's Hill      249

Recommended Reading      253

Index      255

# Acknowledgments

I thank *Psychology Today* for the opportunity to write the weekly blog Surviving (Your Child's) Adolescence, which provided the inspiration for this book. Special thanks need to be given to all the parents at workshops over the years who have taught me so much as I was trying to teach them a little; to my four grown children, who each introduced me to a new path through adolescence; to my agent, Grace Freedson, who keeps managing to find publishers for my parenting books; and of course to Irene, who is a wonderfully supportive writer's wife.

# About the Author

**Carl Pickhardt, PhD,** the author of fourteen parenting books as well as works of adult and children's fiction and of illustrated psychology, is a writer, graphic artist, and psychologist in private counseling and public lecturing practice in Austin, Texas. He received his BA in English and MEd in counseling from Harvard, and his PhD in counseling psychology from the University of Texas at Austin. He is a member of the American Psychological Association. He has four grown children and one grandchild.

Pickhardt has written newspaper, magazine, and Internet columns about adolescence, family life, and adult relationships. For the past four years he has been writing a weekly parenting blog for *Psychology Today*, Surviving (Your Child's) Adolescence.

Pickhardt gives frequent public lectures about parenting and adolescence to PTAs, church congregations, and mental health groups, and is often interviewed by print media about diverse aspects of child development, parenting, and family life. More information about all his books can be found on his website: www.carlpickhardt.com.

# Author's Note

Unless otherwise attributed, all quotations and case examples used in this book are fictional, created to reflect concerns and to illustrate situations similar in kind but not in actuality to those I have heard from clients over the years.

# Introduction

> Given what I've heard from other parents with
> teenagers, I'm dreading our child's adolescence.
> They make it sound like such a hard time—harder
> to get things done, harder to get along, harder on
> everyone. My child and I have been such good
> company up to now. Can't we just remain friends?

Despite whatever alarming accounts you may have heard, you
are not destined, or even obligated, to go through agony when
your child enters *adolescence*, a relatively recent concept that
dates back to the early 1900s when psychologist Stanley Hall first
popularized the term. Adolescence describes the transitional
time between the end of childhood and the onset of early adulthood, a period that has lengthened in this country over the years,
thanks in part to child labor laws, compulsory K–12 education,
and a growing discontinuity between the generations because of
increasingly rapid social and technological change.

From what I have seen these many years in private family
counseling practice and speaking with parents at workshops,
about a third of young people go through adolescence without
making much of a ripple in family life, growing and changing
well within the home rules and tolerances of their parents. These
are the *easy adolescents*. Another third intermittently pushes
some family limits, but these episodes are usually successfully
confronted and resolved so that life goes forward without any
major disruption. These are the *average adolescents*. And then

there is the final third of young people, who break significant family boundaries or stumble into serious unhappiness, and it is the parents of these who usually seek counseling help. These are the *troublesome* or *troubled adolescents*. If you have multiple children, a single "easy" adolescent is all you are likely to get, so don't automatically expect such smooth parental sailing with the next or the rest based on your harmonious experience with one. Even with an easy adolescent, however, there will still be some normal adjusting to do.

Adjusting to what? This is the question parents need to be able to answer if they are to be adequately prepared for the teenage years. To effectively keep up with an adolescent, it helps to stay ahead of the growth curve by anticipating what common changes, tensions, problems, and conflicts will typically arise as the process unfolds. Confusing to parent and teenager as adolescence may seem, it is a developmental process, orderly in its larger outline. Most important for parents to accept at the outset of this transformation is that an adolescent is *not* a child. They need to understand and work with this change, not fight against it. In adolescent parlance, they must "get used to it!" *Surviving Your Child's Adolescence* is intended to help parents do just this.

Chapter One helps parents prepare themselves for the inevitably changing relationship to their child that adolescence brings. Chapters Two and Three present a road map to four stages of adolescence through which young people must grow on their way to young adulthood. In Chapter Two, I map out early and mid-adolescence and the transformation from childhood. In Chapter Three, I map out late adolescence and trial independence, and the challenges of your child acting older. Chapter Four distinguishes the adult-adolescent relationship depending on whether one is mothering or fathering a teenage daughter or teenage son. Chapters Five through Ten each describe a significant focus in the parent-adolescent relationship: communication, conflict, discipline, education, peer relationships, and the power of parents. Last is an Epilogue that provides some perspective on the journey of adolescence through which parent and teenager have traveled together.

An adolescent is an adult in training, a young person on an arduous ten- to twelve-year journey of transformation that begins in late elementary or early middle school, and doesn't usually wind down until after the college-age years, in the early to mid-twenties. During this process, the dependent child, learning from parental preparation, from peer association, and through experimenting with new experiences, gathers enough power of knowledge, competence, and responsibility to finally claim independent standing as a young adult.

Compared to childhood (up to about age nine), adolescence is the *harder half of parenting* because now the parental job becomes a more unwelcome one—for both adult and adolescent. Why? The general answer is that it is difficult to stay as closely and influentially connected with a child once adolescence increasingly puts parent and teenager at cross-purposes over matters of freedom and starts causing them to grow apart.

Adolescence is not just a simple passage from childhood to young adulthood. It is a revolutionary process that changes the child, and the parent in response, and redefines their relationship. It is also a ruthless process. Adolescence begins with the loss of childhood, proceeds through increased conflict over freedom, and ends when the young person moves out and empties the family nest. Along the way, parent and adolescent learn to tolerate increased distance, differences, and discord as more independence is established between them. Fortunately, this abrasiveness is intermittent, not constant. There is still the caring they feel for one another, the enjoyment they have together, and the future family connection they count on being able to share.

Adolescence is a moving and fascinating time. Parents get to see their child transform from a little girl or little boy into a young woman or young man by journey's end. I hope this playbook for parents, based on many years of counseling families with teenagers, will help you find a loving and constructive way to participate in this exciting period of your daughter's or son's growing up. As you do, remember this: parenting adolescents is least of all a science, more of an art, and most of all an adventure. So hang on, hang in there, and enjoy the ride!

# Voices of Parents Past

"Maybe adolescence is a child's way of getting even with her parents."

"If there's two of us and only one of him, how come we feel outnumbered all the time?"

"She's allergic to work. It irritates her mood."

"He said he'd do it in a minute, and it's been over an hour."

"She said it isn't lying if she only tells us what we think to ask."

"He said we never said he couldn't, but that's because we never thought he would!"

"She said she wouldn't have gotten into this trouble if she hadn't been caught."

"The furthest he can see into the future is now."

"The only time she's considerate is when she wants something from us."

"He'll argue with us about the time of day!"

"She says we used to be such great parents, but now we've changed."

"No matter how much freedom we give him, it's never enough."

"She doesn't care what we think, but she hates being criticized."

"He said he's just going to hang out with friends, will be back later, and for us not to worry."

"All she's asking for is enough support so she can live independently."

"He promised we'd never catch him doing drugs, and we never have."

"She doesn't want to be included, but resents it when we leave her out."

## Chapter One

# Preparing for the Inevitable

The change seemed to happen overnight—that suddenly! Through elementary and middle school, our only child was easy to be with, but now with him at high school it's more difficult to stay as close. We don't talk as much, and we argue more when we do. Used to be we could do no wrong, but now it seems we can do no right. Gone is the happy threesome that we used to be. Now he wants to spend his time alone or with friends. We're just not fun to be around anymore. What did we do wrong?

Of course, the entry into adolescence doesn't actually happen overnight, but for many parents it can seem that way. In hopes that they and their child would escape the discomfort of her teenage years, they may have denied small changes they didn't want to see until the unwelcome signs were finally too numerous and intense to be ignored. Thus it's their sudden awareness and admission that happens overnight. Now is when the parental questions begin. What's going on? What happens next? How should we prepare? Suddenly there's a lot that parents need to know—not just about how to manage their changing child but about how to manage themselves. Parents tend to think that the primary challenge with adolescence is how to affect the teenager's conduct when in fact the first order of business is how to maturely conduct themselves. Just as the first injunction for medical doctors is "Do no harm," for parents of adolescents the first command is "Govern thyself wisely." To do this, some adult reorientation is required that necessitates changing parental attitude, understanding parental disenchantment, resetting parental expectations, making parental adjustments, and accepting why most parenting goes unappreciated, particularly in adolescence. It all starts with your attitude.

## Parental Attitude

Consider *four important changes in attitude* that you can helpfully make when your son or daughter separates from childhood in late elementary or early middle school and begins to act more abrasively adolescent.

1. *Don't take your child's adolescence as a personal affront.* Your son or daughter is not acting like an adolescent to "get you" or to get you upset. They are acting adolescent for themselves, for their own interest, mostly unmindful of you. Inconsiderate adolescents often are, but calculating they are usually not. They are simply too self-centered on their own development to think about the effects of their changing behavior on you. For example, irritating though leaving the snack dishes unwashed, the lights on, the door open, the radio playing, or the faucet flowing may be, these are not deliberate provocations. These are thoughtless behaviors. To maintain a viable relationship, you have to keep perspective while also specifying and insisting on the terms of family consideration you need your adolescent to observe. Just remember that if other parents were put in your place, your teenager would be acting much the same. The parental job is to understand that although adolescent changes affect you, they are not about you. They are about your son or daughter.

2. *Don't punish your child for acting adolescent.* Adolescence is a process of growth. Just because you find some of the changes

offensive doesn't mean you should treat them as an offense. For example, you don't ground or otherwise sanction an adolescent for becoming more moody, less communicative, more argumentative, or less organized. You accept the process, but hold the young person accountable for choices made as the process unfolds. Thus don't penalize your child for the messiness that comes with increased disorganization, but still demand that he pick up after himself, and keep after him until he does. The parental job is to impose sufficient structure, set sufficient limits, and make sufficient demands so that the adolescent acts in ways that work within the needs of parents and family.

3. *Accept that adolescence is a more combative age.* A healthy adolescent is supposed to contest family limits and push for more freedom to grow. Healthy parents are supposed to withstand that push for the sake of ensuring safety and insisting on responsibility. This opposition unfolds throughout adolescence over many common areas of disagreement—adequate communication, household help, social freedom, school performance, and family rules among them. Increased conflict gradually builds up the teenager's determination to live on her own terms and be independent. More conflict does not mean something is wrong with your relationship. Conflict is the process used to broker increasing differences between you and your teen, a necessary part of how you get along.

4. *Understand that adolescence is meant to break the spell of childhood.* What spell? At the outset, parents feel as smitten by the newborn child and little girl or boy as that little person is by them. Add ten years to the child, and that enchantment has begun to lose some luster for both teenager and parents as more opposition and diversity develop between them. The mutual adoration that begins with infancy and that develops into close companionship

in childhood becomes mixed with more frustration and strained by more separation in adolescence and that's okay. After all, if parents and young people were to get through adolescence as enchanted with each other as they began, neither would ever let the other go. This mutual disenchantment does not signify a loss of love, but is founded on other losses experienced on both sides of the relationship, as described in the next section.

## Mutual Disenchantment

Parenting an adolescent can stand in painful contrast to parenting a child, and the name of that pain is *loss*. It is loss that creates the disenchantment that grows between parent and adolescent. Consider a few common losses about which each can complain.

Parents often have complaints like the following:

- The child wanted time together with parents, but the adolescent wants more time apart with friends.
- The child was admiring (even adoring) of parents, but the adolescent is more critical.
- The child wanted to tell parents everything, but the adolescent wants to be more private and less confiding.
- The child was compliant with most of what parents requested, but the adolescent is more actively and passively resistant.
- The child liked to please parents, but the adolescent seems to court more disapproval.
- The child was proud to be seen with the parents, but the adolescent often considers this public association an embarrassment.
- The child wanted a lot of physical affection with parents, but the adolescent prefers to have less loving touch.

The adolescent can have complaints like the following:

- Parents who used to be calm and relaxed are often more worried and tense.
- Parents who used to be trusting are often more questioning and suspicious.
- Parents who used to be more satisfied and accepting are often more critical and disapproving.
- Parents who used to be playful and fun to be around are often more serious and demanding of work.
- Parents who used to enjoy doing for you, often want you to start doing more for yourself and them.
- Parents who used to encourage freedom of expression and activity are often more intolerant and restrictive.
- Parents who used to be interesting company often become more boring to be around.

Now their mutual admiration society begins to turn into a mutual irritation society as each increasingly rubs the other the wrong way. The other party, who used to do no wrong in their eyes, now seldom seems to do much right. So who's to blame for this abrasive turn of events? That's what they all want to know. "You used to be such a great kid. What happened to you?" ask the aggrieved parents. "Well, you used to be such great parents. What happened to you?" retorts the aggrieved adolescent. Blaming each other is not the answer, as the real culprit is adolescent change. Better is to understand that come adolescence, both parent and teenager have more in common than they like to think, actually sharing many of the same complaints:

"You never listen to what I say."
"You don't do what I ask."
"You keep putting me off until later."
"You don't appreciate all I do."

"You're always criticizing."

"You always want something more."

"You stay in a bad mood."

The change is hard on them both. To bring parental adjustment to adolescent change a little closer to home, consider it in metaphorical terms.

## When Your Dog Becomes a Cat

Years ago, a parent tried to explain to me how disenchanting the adjustment to her child's adolescence was by giving me a metaphor that has stayed with me. Describing how hard it was when her warmly affectionate child started acting like a more coolly distant middle school adolescent, this parent asked, "How would you like it if your affectionate and loving dog started acting like your standoffish and irritable cat? That's the kind of change I mean. What happened to my beloved dog, is what I want to know. I miss my companionable and cuddly dog!"

After our conversation was over, I started playing with the metaphor she used, and was surprised where her comparison led my thinking. For openers, the dog can be demonstrative, friendly, empathetic, compliant, social, close, playful, predictable, communicative, and constant. The cat can be aloof, moody, apathetic, detached, solitary, distant, watchful, unpredictable, inscrutable, and changeable. Then I tried to amplify the differences:

The dog welcomes attention most of the time. The cat wants to be left alone a lot of the time.

The dog comes when called. The cat comes when it wants.

The dog walks on a leash. The cat walks by itself.

The dog is more even-tempered. The cat is more temperamental.

The dog is easier to read. The cat is more unreadable.

The dog likes to do what you like to do. The cat likes your doing what it likes to do.

The dog seems more under your control. The cat seems more committed to its own agenda.

The dog wants to please and works not to displease. Sometimes it can be hard to tell if the cat really cares.

The dog is always glad to see you at the end of the day. The cat may or may not be interested. (This comparison reminds me of Nora Ephron's wonderful line from *I Feel Bad About My Neck: And Other Thoughts on Being a Woman*: "When your children are teenagers, it's important to have a dog so that someone in the house is happy to see you.")

This "child to adolescent–dog to cat" comparison was only an analogy, but the parental adjustment the mother suggested was real enough. Could she still love her teenager as "cat" the way she did her child as "dog"? Yes, but the relationship had become more challenging than it was before. A particularly frustrating part is when the adolescent behaves more like a cat-dog. Consider the conflicted, mixed messages a parent can be given. Sometimes the adolescent acts as though she wants to be treated like a dependent "dog," and sometimes like a more independent "cat":

| | |
|---|---|
| "Help me." | "I can do it myself!" |
| "Talk to me." | "Don't talk to me!" |
| "Show me how." | "I can figure it out!" |
| "Pay me attention." | "Leave me alone!" |
| "Give me a hug." | "I don't like being held!" |
| "Tell me what to do." | "Don't tell me what to do!" |
| "Take me along." | "Why do I have to go with you?" |

Which way does the adolescent want it? Both ways: the child (doglike) part of her wants to stay the same, but the adolescent (catlike) part of her wants to become different.

Of course, the adjustment challenge is on both sides. This adjustment from child to adolescent, from dog to cat, is hard for the teenager as well. And as she struggles with the change, her old pet's-eye view of her parents alters as well. Sometimes the kind masters act like mean rulers. Sometimes the favored companions become a social embarrassment. Sometimes the approving adults become disapproving critics. Sometimes the interested confidants become unwelcome inquisitors. Sometimes the authorities who were mostly right are often wrong. Sometimes parents who used to understand her so well, now act as though they haven't a clue. No wonder the teenager feels conflicted—wanting to be adolescent and act more grown up, but regretting the loss of all that went with being a child, including how wonderful parents once were.

So, what I told the parent who gave me this disenchantment metaphor was this: "It's all right to miss the familiar ways of your child as 'dog,' but don't let that loss get in the way of appreciating the more mysterious ways of your teenager as 'cat.' And don't forget, when your child starts changing into an adolescent, you start changing in response, which takes some getting used to for your teenager." The antidote to disenchantment is acceptance, which is where the power of expectations comes in. What doesn't work is for parents to expect their child to continue acting doglike during his or her more catlike adolescence. They have to reset their expectation to accept and fit the reality of adolescent change.

## Resetting Expectations

Most parents, particularly with a first or only child, or with a second child if the first has been particularly "easy," are unprepared for that young person's adolescence. They consciously try not to think about it because all they've heard about it scares them, or if they do think about it, they often assume that these unwelcome changes will happen to other people's children, but not to one of their own. However, denial is not a good coping strategy. In fact, denial is the enemy in hiding. By refusing to consider what they do not want to have happen, parents are unprepared when their son or daughter lets it be known that he or she is no longer content to be defined and responded to as just a child. "I'm not your little girl anymore, so stop treating me that way!" snaps the sixth-grade daughter refusing to laugh at her dad's playful joke, the kind he was fond of making to cheer her up when she had a sad day in elementary school. She is putting him on notice that this kind of humor is no longer fun or funny.

It behooves parents to develop a realistic set of expectations about the harder half of parenting, the adolescent years. A primary expectation to begin with has to do with duration. Today's parents can generally assume that adolescence will commence around ages nine to thirteen in late elementary or early middle school, and not to wind down until the early or mid-twenties, a little after the college-age years. Must it last this long? In most cases, the answer seems to be yes. It takes a lot of psychological and social growth to gain sufficient knowledge, skills, confidence, and maturity for stepping off on one's own, taking charge of one's life, supporting oneself, and making one's way in the world as an independent young adult.

So why are expectations psychologically important? Think of them this way. Expectations are mental sets we choose to hold (they are not genetically endowed) that help us move through time (from now to later), through change (from old to new), and through experience (from familiar to unfamiliar) in order to anticipate the reality we shall encounter next. To appreciate the power of expectations, consider being in a circumstance where you have no idea what to expect. Ignorance tends to beget feelings of anxiety: "I've never faced a situation like this before!" "I don't know where to go, what to do, or what to say!" "I have no idea what the results will be!"

Most parents usually appreciate the importance of clarifying expectations when it comes adjusting their child to change. They see the preparatory role that expectations can helpfully play. So when it comes to helping the child make a geographical move, start a new school, or get ready for a medical operation, for example, they take the time to realistically anticipate what these new experiences are going to be like in order to smooth the way. "Even though rehabilitation after the operation will be tough, it's better for you to know that there will be discomfort and work for you to do to get better." Parents understand that anticipated hardships are easier to deal with than those that are unexpected because they have been denied.

Unpreparedness is emotionally costly and, where it is unnecessary, not worth the expense. This is the case where parents are blindsided by the adolescent transformation in their son or daughter because they chose to expect that he or she would continue behaving like the darling little child they had always comfortably known. Now see what happens. Consider three kinds of expectations parents can hold—predictions, ambitions, and conditions—and consider the outcome when they don't fit the realities of adolescent change.

*Predictions* have to do with what parents believe *will* happen. "My adolescent will be as openly confiding with me as she was as a child." But come adolescence, many young people for the sake of independence tend to become more private and less disclosing to parents. Now, when their prediction is violated, parents can feel surprised and anxious in response to the diminishing amount of communication. "We're hardly told anything anymore!"

*Ambitions* have to do with what parents *want* to have happen in adolescence. "We want him to continue to be as academically conscientious as he was as a child." But come adolescence, many young people suffer an "early adolescent achievement drop" (see

Chapter Eight) when homework and school performance suffer from a lowering of motivation. Now when their ambition is violated, parents can feel disappointed and let down in response to the falling effort. "He doesn't seem to care about making good grades anymore!"

*Conditions* have to do with what parents believe *should* happen in adolescence. "She should continue to keep us adequately and accurately informed about what is going on in her life." But when adolescence begins, many young people become more deceptive with parents, sometimes lying about what is going on for illicit freedom's sake. Now when their condition is violated, parents can feel betrayed and angry in response to more dishonesty. "We're not told the whole truth as often anymore!"

Unrealistic expectations can have emotional consequences for parents. Feeling surprised, disappointed, or betrayed by a normal adolescent change, parents can overreact with worry, grief, or anger, thereby "emotionalizing" a situation and making it harder to resolve effectively. This doesn't mean that parents should just accept it when a young person cuts off communication, stops doing schoolwork, and acts dishonestly. *Expect does not mean accept.* Parents must address these new behaviors to let the young person know that they still need to be adequately informed, that performance effort at school still must be maintained, and that there must still be truthful communication. But if these parents had anticipated the likelihood of these changes, a rational discussion and not an emotional encounter would have ensued.

This book is meant to help you create realistic expectations about the journey of your child's adolescence. Parents who are adequately informed about some of the normal changes, tensions, conflicts, and problems that typically unfold during adolescence are best positioned to cope with these challenges in appropriate and effective ways because they expected that these unwelcome issues and alterations might arise. By way of additional example, consider what can happen for parents emotionally when they fail to set realistic expectations about how normal adolescent change may alter their traditional relationship to the child.

- The parent who predicts that the adolescent will continue to prize parental company more than any other is rudely awakened when the young person now prefers spending time with peers instead of time with parents. *This parent cannot make peace with this loss of companionship.*

- The parent whose ambition is to enjoy the same interests with the adolescent that were shared with the child is rudely awakened when differentiation from childhood and parents causes that similarity to be lost. *This parent cannot make peace with this loss of common interests.*

- The parent whose condition is that the adolescent should continue to look up to and want to please the parent as in childhood is in for a rude awakening when the young person becomes more critical, even putting Mom and Dad down for what they don't know. *This parent cannot make peace with this loss of approval.*

These parents can certainly choose to maintain these unrealistic expectations, but they will do so at an emotional cost—feeling abandoned, rejected, and disparaged. It would be better for them to adjust their expectations to fit the new adolescent reality. Protest normal developmental alterations they cannot change, and they are in danger of overreacting when times get hard. In addition to resetting expectations, many parents have some hard adjustments to make.

## Adjusting to the Five Realities of Adolescence

Not only does adolescence challenge the child to change; it challenges parents to change as well. They must adjust to some hard realities in relationship to their teenager that can be difficult for them to accept and that can require some hard adult growing up to do. As their son or daughter acts less like a child and more like an adolescent, parents struggle to make five major adjustments—to ignorance, estrangement, abandonment, control, and conflict. These adjustments can be more difficult when tied to unresolved issues of a similar kind that parents themselves carried into their adulthood. For example, a parent who grew up in an abusive family may feel frightened when the adolescent becomes more easily frustrated and emotionally intense in conflict. In this case, it becomes more difficult for the parent to cope in the present because memories of past anxiety are being revived by a normal adolescent change. Let's look at these adjustments in detail.

## Ignorance

Adolescence causes the child to become more private and less forthcoming as one way to define and defend a growing independence. Thus the adolescent is often less communicative with parents than was the child. As their son or daughter spends increased time with peers, away from home, and out in the world, parents have a higher need to know about what's going on, while their son or daughter has a higher need for his or her actions not to be known. The emotional consequence of this parental ignorance is more worry from knowing less when they want to know more. Those parents who have a very high need for information, perhaps from growing up in families with a lot of instability or unpredictability, can find their child's erratic adolescence particularly scary. When in ignorance, they are prone to become frightened and anticipate the worst. *The challenge for these parents is to prevent imagination from exploiting ignorance to fearful effect.*

## Estrangement

Adolescence causes the boy or girl to differentiate from how he or she was as a child and from how his or her parents are in order to establish a more unique and individual identity. Thus, for parents, the teenager's experimentation with new and varied interests, images, tastes, and friendships can create a degree of unfamiliarity that did not exist before. Sharing less in common with the adolescent than with the child, they feel they know the teenager less well. The emotional consequence is a degree of parental discomfort with the adolescent, whom they feel more awkward to be with and who fits less well into the family. Now it becomes more difficult to communicate and to connect. Those parents who need high similarity with their adolescent to feel close can feel more alienated at this time. And if they experienced significant alienation from their parents during their own adolescence, this difficulty in relating to a teenager of their own can feel very sad. *The challenge for these parents is not to be put off by what seems unfamiliar, but to keep bridging emerging differences by expressing interest, and not to pull away.*

### Abandonment

Adolescence ordains more separation from parents as the young person asserts social independence of family, now preferring to spend more time with peers, and more time by himself or herself when at home. This growing apart means that parents have a harder time competing for the teenager's attention, and they may miss their son's or daughter's company. The emotional consequence is a degree of loneliness made worse if they have lost a best buddy or constant companion—a child who wanted nothing more than to be and do things with them. Those parents for whom this young companionship was most rewarding can feel most bereft come adolescence. And if they prized closeness with the child the more so for having grown up with an unavailable or absent mother or father, parents can deeply miss the old, close relationship to the child. *The challenge for these parents is to accept that less contact does not mean less love, to sincerely appreciate and mourn the passing of how things were, and then to forge independent relationships to satisfy their unmet companionship needs.*

## Control

When a son or daughter separates from childhood and enters adolescence, wanting to please parents tends to diminish, and willingness to displease parents in service of asserting more independence becomes the new order of the day. Thus, for parents, there is some loss of traditional authority when adolescence arrives. The emotional consequence of having less power is more frustration when the teenager questions or challenges a parental decision or deliberately resists or disobeys. Now it becomes more difficult to get the teenager to fit or follow the adult's agenda. Those parents who grew up identifying and complying with strict parents can feel very angry when they discover that their ruling power now depends on the teenager's willingness to cooperate with what they want. *The challenge for these parents is to accept that although they can't control their son's or daughter's choices, they can inform them, asserting influence through communication they make and stands they take.*

## Conflict

Adolescence causes the teenager to become more abrasive and difficult to live with. Now he or she contests more parental decisions, disagrees more with what parents have to say, and pushes against old restraints to gain more freedom to grow. Thus begins the long process of opposition to liberate the teenager from parental rules and requirements and claim independence at last. The emotional consequence is increased disharmony between parents and teenager. Now parents find themselves dealing with a young person who has become more of a pusher and less of a pleaser to live with and who is more prone to argument than agreement, creating a relationship in which there is more tension and stress. If parents grew up with little exposure to conflict or in families where conflict was an interaction to beware, they may feel threatened by a teenager who regularly takes them on, in the moment treating them more as enemy than as friend. *The challenge for these parents is to calmly engage in conflict as a normal communication process through which they can constructively broker disagreements with their adolescent.*

Parents having the hardest time making these five adjustments are those who are unable or unwilling to let go of the child relationship so that the adolescent one can unfold. These adults often identify themselves through statements they make. About ignorance: "I must know everything that is going on." About estrangement: "We are going to stay as close as we were in childhood." About abandonment: "I will always be my child's best friend." About control: "I should not be challenged or resisted." About conflict: "I can't stand for us not to get along." I believe that these parents to varying degrees have some of their own growing up to do. This requires that they make the following five adjustments in their reaction to their child's adolescence:

- *They will be inadequately informed:* "I must get by on less information than I would ideally like to know."
- *They will be less compatible:* "We do not share as much in common as we once did."
- *They will be left more alone:* "I am no longer my child's favored company."
- *They will be less in charge:* "I have less influence to get my way."
- *They will be more in opposition:* "We have more cause for disagreement between us now."

Then, of course, there is the additional adjusting to a fall from grace, whereby the adolescent is less appreciative of his or her parents than was the child. Let's consider this adjustment next.

## Lack of Appreciation

Adolescence can be a reminder of how most parents feel unappreciated most of the time, tending to the needs of a young person who doesn't want such tending to. Here are some of the things parents of teenagers often hear: "Leave me alone!" "I don't want to talk about it!" "You never let me do anything!" "You're always on my case!" "You never understand!" "Why do I have to?" "I'll do it later!" In the adolescent's defense, it's truly hard to value parents when their demands and restraints keep getting in the way of all the freedom one wants at a more independent-minded age. This is why adolescence is the age of *thankless parenting.* For the sake of their child's best interests, responsible parents must take unpopular stands against what the adolescent wants, and they do not receive gratitude for their efforts.

Parents of adolescents are frequently ignored, taken for granted, discounted, tolerated, criticized, resented, and resisted, so they often feel that they are being treated as people their children are barely able to put up with, not caregivers who are sacrificing self-interest on a daily basis to help their son or daughter grow. What recently brought this neglect to mind was the complaint of one hardworking mother of two adolescents: "Most of the time I feel like I'm invisible for all I do!" Except that this is not really a problem, I suggested. It's a reality. Most parents labor in obscurity because invisibility of effort is simply an unrewarding condition of parental life, a condition that gets worse once one's child enters adolescence. Years ago, I put this in writing when working with a group of parents who had teenagers.

## Thankless Parenting

All parents labor in obscurity,
The work they do too ordinary
To be recognized by the society
That depends for future citizens
Upon the preparation
Parents give.

The endless daily tasks
Are too many to enumerate,
Too small to notice and too transitory
To be remembered by the beloved beneficiaries,
Grown children unable to recount one nth of all the effort
Made on their behalf when parents set themselves aside,
Home from the job still working to provide,
Did it all when all their energy was spent,
Responding to an infant's crying need,
Sacrificing to fulfill a child's heart's desire,
Rushing to meet an adolescent's dire emergency.

Just suppose on graduation into adulthood,
Grown children got a printout listing
Every act of care taking
Received since birth,
A million pages
Itemizing each parenting decision,
Necessary and discretionary service,
And painful problem-solving deliberation,
The more mundane the better:
"Nineteen eighty-one,
On the fourteenth of May
I kept you home with a fever,
And wiped your nose eleven times today."

*Surprised,*
*The young adult*
*Politely scans the document*
*Promising to look it over later,*
*But never does since daily parenting*
*Makes for such dull reading,*
*Wondering:*
*"Who would want to know all this?"*

*No one.*
*That's why parents labor in obscurity.*

Parenting is an inequitable arrangement, particularly with adolescents, because parents invest far more of themselves in their self-preoccupied teenager than their teenager ever invests in them. However, lest you consider this inequity unfair, think of it this way. Parenting is a great privilege. It is the only job that matters so much—accepting primary responsibility for nurturing and preparing the next generation of human life. Given the importance of the work, the self-sacrifice is worth it, particularly when the investment is made with love.

Preparing for the inevitable, parents need to ready themselves for the harder half of parenting that the adolescent years begin. "Harder" doesn't mean bad or worse or unhappy. It means different and more demanding and more complex. It also means more rewarding as they get to witness and participate in the growth of their child into a young adult, in the development of their daughter or son into a young woman or young man. In the next two chapters, I propose four stages of adolescent growth, a roadmap to help parents anticipate normal changes along the way.

## Chapter Two

# A Road Map to Early and Mid-Adolescence

I tell you what: this isn't Kansas anymore, not the way our kid is acting now! And sometimes I'm not so sure about me, how I'm reacting back. Used to be I knew what to do as a parent because I knew what our daughter was going to do. But she's become so unpredictable. My wife and I, sometimes we feel we've lost our way. What happens next? Where do we go from here?

Although the process of adolescence is often a confusing experience for parents and teenager, I believe it is orderly enough to be broken down into a sequence of four descriptive stages, each encompassing a range of specific changes and problems. For example, common problems like the academic achievement drop in early adolescence (ages nine to thirteen), more conflicts with parents over social freedom with peers in mid-adolescence (ages thirteen to fifteen), unhappy dating relationships in late adolescence (ages fifteen to eighteen), and credit card overspending in trial independence (ages eighteen to twenty-three) all seem to unfold in a predictable progression. By keeping a rough map of adolescent growth in mind, by being able to anticipate normal alterations and upcoming issues along the way, parents can be more prepared for what may come next. I believe that preparation counts for a lot in the effective parenting of a teenager.

With a map in mind, you have a greater sense of what might occur and so are in a stronger position to respond rationally.

When an unwelcome but anticipated possibility does occur (incidents of shoplifting in early adolescence, more lying in mid-adolescence, more social substance use in late adolescence, or flunking out of college in trial independence, for example), parents who are adequately informed about the adolescent passage are less likely to emotionally overreact and make a hard situation worse.

So in this and the next chapter, I offer a brief "roadmap to adolescence" of my own making, a general overview of four developmental stages that I conceptualized to help parents locate where in the overall process they are with their teenager, what they should understand now, and what they may anticipate next. Each stage has a function, and with each stage comes a different set of challenges for adolescent and parents as well. The following are brief descriptions of the four stages:

- *Early adolescence (ages nine to thirteen)*. The function of the first adolescent stage is to accomplish *the separation from childhood*. The parenting challenge during this stage is to tolerate more personal disorganization, a more negative attitude toward their authority, and more testing of family limits, without taking these changes personally or reacting negatively in return. *During this period when the young person is experiencing loss and disorder from growing out of childhood and frustration with parental restrictions on freedom, parents must keep a positive attitude during a more off-putting time.*

- *Mid-adolescence (ages thirteen to fifteen)*. The function of the second stage of adolescence is to establish an *independent "family" of peers*. The parenting challenge during this stage is to provide loyal opposition to the young person's push for more social freedom with friends when it appears unwise or unsafe, without resorting to coercion or censure to settle disagreements. *During this more contentious period, when the young person urgently needs to be connected with companions, parents must maintain a healthy family structure and use the increased discord to teach how to manage conflict in a constructive and healthy way.*

- *Late adolescence (ages fifteen to eighteen).* The function of the third stage of adolescence is to *experiment with acting older* to get ready to operate on more adult terms. The parenting challenge during this stage is to allow more grown-up freedoms while imparting the necessary knowledge and insisting on the commensurate responsibility needed for successfully mastering the next level of independence soon to come. *During this period when independence from family is imminent, parents must safeguard increased freedom by providing adequate preparation and insisting on accountability.*

- *Trial independence (ages eighteen to twenty-three).* The function of the fourth and last stage of adolescence is to practice *operating on one's own.* The parenting challenge during this stage is to let go of authority yet still be there to provide helpful advice and problem solving when asked, without rescuing or criticizing when the young person makes a serious mistake. *During this period when some aspects of adultlike freedom usually prove too much of a good thing for the young person, parents must let go of managerial control while giving encouragement and offering mentoring support.*

This chapter outlines the general features of early and mid-adolescence, and the transformation from childhood. Chapter Three outlines the features of late adolescence and trial independence, and the challenges of acting older.

## Early Adolescence (Ages 9–13)

The opening stage of adolescence can pose an unwelcome adjustment for parents lulled by their daughter's or son's compliant and harmonious childhood, as they suddenly see their daughter or son fall apart in one way and start what one sad parent described as "the change for the worse" in another. The mother was describing how the early adolescent had become more scattered and more resistant to authority than before. These are the twin signs that the separation from childhood and the adolescent journey to independence have begun, signs of change that begin for many children in late elementary school and are under way for almost all students by middle school.

The loss of childhood and loss of their old companionship is hard on both children and parents. As the child changes, parents change in response, and their relationship is never again the same. Ask parents, and they will testify: "Our child used to be loving, obedient, hardworking, helpful, cheerful, and talkative, and now he's become more inconsiderate, resistant, unmotivated, uncooperative, moody, and uncommunicative." However, ask the early adolescent, and he will tell you how parents have changed: "They used to be understanding, patient, supportive, trusting, relaxed, and fun, but now they've become demanding, impatient, critical, questioning, tense, and serious all the time."

Underlying their shared irritation with each other is a mutual sense of loss. Now the early adolescent knows she can't go back to the security and familiarity of childhood again and will never enjoy the pure delight of parental company that used to be so central in her life. And parents are painfully coming to accept that they are at a point of no return with their daughter as well. Parents will never again have their daughter as adoring and adorable child—as "best buddy" or "constant companion." Rather than treat the passing of the young person's childhood as a cause for their recrimination, parents should take time for mourning, for acknowledging how they will miss that golden time in their relationship, and for expressing gratitude for what they have been given. Nothing "wrong" has happened on either side of the relationship. Adolescence, a more contentious period in their relationship, is under way. Now the predictable phases of early adolescence are beginning to unfold: personal disorganization, a more negative mind-set, and early experimentation. It may help to know that each of these phases has a function in the adolescent's growth.

- The function of *personal disorganization* is to loosen the grip of childhood functioning to create opportunity for more a complex system of self-management to develop. Through words and actions, the young person demonstrates that the old simple way of operating is no longer adequate to cope with the new period of growth that has now begun.

- The function of the *negative mind-set* is to create dissatisfaction that provides the motivation to begin adolescent change. Through words and actions, the young person lets it be known that he or she doesn't want to be defined and treated as "just a child" any longer and is prepared to resist parental authority to act on more independent terms.

- The function of *early experimentation* is to gather more worldly experience to grow. Curious about what the world of experience beyond childhood is like, the young person tests parental and social limits, showing that new freedoms, some associated with older activities, are now subject to his or her interest and exploration.

Let's examine each of these phases in more detail.

### Personal Disorganization

In the words of one dad, the first sign of adolescence that he noticed in his sixth-grade son was "how the wheels have started coming off the truck." By this the man referred to a general breakdown in the boy's normal functioning. Used to be the child remembered his commitments, but now the adolescent is more *forgetful* of his obligations, like doing what he was supposed to for school and family. Used to be the child generally kept track of his things, but now the adolescent is constantly *misplacing and losing* them. Used to be the child lived in a reasonably well-ordered personal space, but now the adolescent lives in *messier* surroundings littered with a clutter of belongings. Used to be the child was able to concentrate on tasks at hand, but now the adolescent is more easily sidetracked and *distracted*, finding it harder to pay attention, listen, and follow through.

Why the disorganization? The answer: because adolescence accelerates growth in multiple ways. For example, there are hormonal changes that come with puberty, there are psychological changes that come with redefining one's identity, there are family changes that come with asserting more independence at home, there are educational changes that come with entering secondary school, and there are social changes that come with more challenging peer group membership. Adolescent growth is toward more complexity of psychological and social functioning. In the process, the early adolescent must learn new systems for self-management. What she discovers at first is that her simpler child ways of functioning are insufficient to cope with the more complex demands that come with learning to act more grown up, hence the disorganization that usually accompanies the beginning of the adolescent process.

At this juncture, parents should not become impatient or irritated or punitive when the child struggles to catch hold. They should assist the young person in learning how to develop the organizational skills needed to cope with the new complexity. For example, parents need to help the young person develop sufficient self-management skills for remembering what's important, for keeping track of belongings that matter, for maintaining adequate personal order, and for paying sufficient attention. For young people with attention deficit issues on top of early adolescent disorganization, this parental assistance is particularly important. Keeping the bedroom a simplified and ordered space, for example, can help a young person feel more focused and in control, just as moderating involvement with swiftly changing, high-stimulation electronic entertainment may help discourage more distractibility.

If there is one issue that is emblematic of early adolescent disorganization, it is the *messy room*. At first, the scattered living space is like a psychological mirror that reflects the young person's disorganized internal state. In this sense, it illustrates the growing disarray brought on by more growth change than the young person can immediately master. Soon, however, what began as a by-product of psychological disarray can become coupled with the need to assert more independence by announcing that he should be able to live in his own space in his own way.

To parents, the messy room can feel like an affront to domestic order, representing "disrespect" for the more neatly kept home they value. Adult expression of disapproval in response usually becomes an affront to the adolescent, who sees a power issue worth fighting for. It represents "personal freedom" to live on his or her terms. Thus a specific disagreement over order becomes a symbolic struggle over who's in control. "It's my room!" declares the early adolescent. "I should be free to live in it any way I want!" "Wrong," counter the parents. "It's our home, and you will live according to the standards of household order that we set!" So the battle lines are drawn for a conflict of mess up versus clean up that can unfold over many years.

For the early adolescent, there can be a lot at stake in asserting the right to a messy room—issues about independence, individuality, and opposition to parental rules. The young person may be making a statement of independence: "I should be able to live in my own space as I wish!" The young person may be making a statement of individuality: "I am now a different person than I was as a child!" The young person may be making a statement of opposition. "I'm going to live my way, not your way!" So do you want to let the messy room go? Do you want to just accept it as an anarchic by-product of this more disorganized and rebellious age? Or do you want to make a supervisory response instead?

My advice: let the messy room go, and you may do so to your cost. You may end up adjusting to what you don't like and then blame the adolescent for your unhappiness. Better to hold yourselves responsible for not adequately supervising what matters to you. If you want your child to do the maintenance work to keep his or her room picked up, you are going to have to do the supervisory work to get that cleaning up to happen. This supervision has not only a specific objective but also a larger message to convey. By insisting on regular room cleanup, you let it be known that your child must live on your terms so long as he or she is dependent on your care. She can live on independent terms only when she is on her own.

For example, on a weekly basis, you could conduct a room inspection and pickup visit to see that the young person's space is put back in working order (order that satisfies you and usually works better for the adolescent). You can simply make the weekly pickup a condition that must be met before weekend freedom is allowed. You can even help in the process if you and the adolescent wish. In either case, you do not do this with complaint or criticism, or in anger. You just make it a part of the regular housekeeping that parents are committed to do that your adolescent grudgingly comes to accept as normal household routine.

Why is the matter of the messy room so important to you? Because a "trashed" room causes you to feel that your home is being trashed, and, because your home is in extension of yourself, you are feeling trashed as well. Further, because you work to keep a home and keep it up, you feel that the work you do to create a home is being devalued. The messy room is a good example of why "Don't sweat the small stuff" is bad advice when it comes to supervision. If your child knows that you will keep after the small responsibilities, such as cleaning up a messy room, he or she also knows that you will be keeping after big stuff, like obedience to major rules.

Now your early adolescent has a suggestion. "Just close the door and keep out, and the mess won't bother you." Don't accept this self-serving offer. If you allow the mess to keep you and your supervision out, your child may start keeping things in the room, and conducting activities in the room, that you do not want in your home or in the child's life. At the age of awakening curiosity about the grown-up world, such freedom can be abused—as license to explore and experiment with the forbidden. As for your child's statement, "This is my room, and you can't come in without my permission," your answer needs to be "Yes and no." Yes, you should knock before entering if the door is closed. Yes, you should allow the room to reflect the changing identity of your growing child (decoration within your tolerance for acceptable expression). And yes, you should value this decoration as a window into understanding your child's changing interests and identifications as he or she continues to grow.

---

### The Limits of Privacy

Having said this, I also believe that you have to state conditions under which you will say no to the right to privacy. As with freedom on the Internet, with a cell phone, with allowance, with driving a car—with any significant freedom—so with personal space: privacy remains a privilege, not a right. So long as that freedom is exercised within the limits of mutually agreed-on responsibility, you will respect that privilege. Use privacy to conceal what is forbidden, however, and the privilege is lost because personal freedom is being abused. Now another right comes into play, and it is your right of search and seizure if you are being denied adequate information for understanding what is going wrong in your child's life and why. For example: inexplicably, grades are down because homework is not kept up. You are being told lies instead of truth. There have been instances of sneaking out. Strange home phone calls

*(continued)*

come in for your child, and the callers refuse to identify themselves. Your child's physical appearance looks more wasted. And your child's mood is sullen and withdrawn. What's going on? So in search of explanation you go through your child's room, only to discover notes, letters, and a diary outlining a double life you never suspected, the second life posing substantial danger to your child's welfare. The only thing you can't understand is why your child left incriminating evidence so easily found. The answer usually is that the child was desperate to be found out, but lacked courage to tell you directly. Many children who are caught in continual wrongdoing, who are taking more freedom than feels safe, are glad to be caught, because now they can get parental help getting their lives back in constructive control again.

There is another point to keep in mind about disorganization and the messy room. Unless you contain the messy room with supervision and police the rest of your home, the mess will spill out into other rooms. Teenagers are extremely territorial. They leave belongings out and don't clean up after themselves to mark and claim additional area to convey that they are now taking up more space within the family. By insisting on cleaning up and maintaining order, parents are letting it be known that the teenager will be expected to live on parents' organized terms in their home.

## Negative Mind-Set

In addition to more disorganization (distractibility, messiness, and forgetfulness), what notifies parents that early adolescence has begun is the young person's more negative mind-set, or what they often say is his "bad attitude." At this juncture, parents wonder what has happened to the child who was full of enthusiasm all the time and such a pleasure to live with. Now it's as though someone pulled the plug on the young person, and all that positive energy for fun and constructive activity has been drained away. One parent described this change poetically: "developmental lumphood," she called it, by which she meant that all her son wanted to do was lie around and complain about having nothing to do because whatever he used to enjoy doing wasn't worth doing anymore. And the parent was correct.

Now the old childhood interests, activities, and entertainments no longer satisfy because he no longer wants to be defined and treated as a child. He wants something different, something older, something more, he doesn't yet know what, and until he finds it he is filled with discontent, the name for which is *boredom*. Feeling bored for the early adolescent is not a trivial emotion. It is really a painful expression of loneliness—the inability to connect with self, with others, with the world in any good-feeling way. There is the sense of being unoccupied, undirected, and at loose ends, hence the complaint: "There's nothing to do!" But when parents suggest some work around the home that needs doing, the adolescent just gets angry. "Oh, leave me alone! You don't understand! I'm too tired!" The parents wonder, "Tired of what?" The answer: of not knowing what to do with himself. He knows what he doesn't want to do (like being told what to do), but he has no clear vision of what he does want to do. When it comes to motivation, he increasingly feels he's running on empty.

The basis for the negative mind-set is the early adolescent's rejection of herself as a child. The problem is that although the young person knows how she doesn't want to be, she hasn't yet developed a good-feeling alternative. This self-rejection is costly because she can't reject the child she was without rejecting part of herself. And that hurts. One way to manage hurt from self-rejection is to turn it into criticism of those at home. She can get down on other members of the family, particularly younger siblings; but what parents often don't see is how she can get down on herself. "I can't stand how I am!" At this vulnerable age, the self-consciousness of puberty doesn't help. "And I hate how I look!" In a mood to reject everything and everyone, she can strive to bring other people down to her unhappy level. That adage "misery loves company" was made for the early adolescent age.

Rather than acting offended by the negative mind-set, parents need to be sufficiently sensitive to it to assess how badly the young adolescent is actually feeling about himself. They often have to infer this emotional state by how he is behaving, because that is how unhappiness is likely to be expressed. For a minority of young people, there is a risk of self-harm at the outset of adolescence, when extreme negativity about self leads to a painful sense of inadequacy, inferiority, or worthlessness. These feelings flow from the negative mind-set at its worst, and they can be managed self-destructively. For example, parents have to keep a weather eye out for such punitive actions as scratching or cutting oneself, falling into despondency or anxiety and socially withdrawing, developing an eating disorder, self-medicating with early substance use, engaging in dangerous risk taking, or committing serious rule breaking. Self-harm is the exception, not the rule, in early adolescence; but it does happen, and when it does, outside counseling help should be sought. When an extreme negative mind-set is combined with being on the receiving end of significant social cruelty (teasing, exclusion, bullying, rumoring, ganging up; see Chapter Nine), acts of violence to self or others is more likely to occur.

Why is the early adolescent so miserable? Rejecting his child self and much of value that went with it is emotionally costly. As he casts off the child he used to be, he must give up some cherished trappings of childhood. For example, because he doesn't want friends coming over and teasing him about playing with Lego and sleeping with stuffed animals, he feels he must wean himself of these childhood attachments by throwing them away. He doesn't want to accept parental affection, but he misses his parents' loving touch. Because his grandparents still treat him as a child, he pulls away from them, all the while missing how they love to cherish him for how he was. Growing up takes giving up; and loss from what is given up is sad. He may also give up historical interests, hobbies, activities, or sports in which he has invested himself over his young years, things he still enjoys and is good at but that he feels should now be outgrown. "I'm too old to do that anymore!" So he renounces what he once loved to do.

Parents are often confused about whether or not to protest when a child gives up a much-loved activity. They need to be clear. Because these involvements are often pillars of self-esteem, before letting kids quit something previously of great importance, parents should suggest a delay on giving them up. "Why don't you wait and see how you feel about playing soccer in a couple of months? If you still feel the same, let's talk again." And if after an agreed-on extension of time, he still wants to quit, set a condition: a replacement activity must be chosen. You don't want him to go from something to nothing at this empty age; you want him to go from something to something else. If he protests about attending the new activity you both have agreed on, complains to you about attending, but then enjoys the experience and is grudgingly willing to go again, accept your thankless parental role and tell him he has to go. Now he can save early adolescent face by blaming you for making him attend, and gets to enjoy himself once he gets there. His instinct is to disengage from what he loves; the parental responsibility is to keep him adequately engaged.

What additionally feeds early adolescent negativity at this time is intolerance of parental demands and limits that now stand in the way of the new freedom that the adolescent wants, even though she doesn't know precisely what she wants to do with it. So a sense of grievance, a chip on her shoulder, develops. As a child, she didn't mind parental authority so much, but as an early adolescent who wants to break out of the boundaries of childhood to create more room to grow, she resents the demands and limits parents impose. So she belligerently demands, "What gives you the right to boss me around?" She is more resentful, resistant, and rebellious.

People do not rebel without grounds for doing so, and the negative mind-set gives the early adolescent adequate grievance to support a sense of just cause. Now there is resentment at unfair restrictions by parents that justifies resisting what they want and when they want it. Often parents think this rebellion is against them, but it is primarily not. It is actually directed against the old definition of being a child, being compliant and dependent. To overthrow this definition, the adolescent rebels against it and in the process rebels her way out of childhood. *Early adolescent rebellion is opposition against old self-definition acted out against parents for transformation's sake.*

Parents should remember that the antidote to rebellion is challenge. Rebellion is actually an act of dependence. The person rebelling is choosing to define himself or herself in opposition to what those rebelled against expect and request. Challenge, in contrast, is an act of independence, choosing to pursue a goal or engage with an activity because it develops one's capabilities in ways one wants to grow. To discourage rebellion, don't fight against it. That will only provide more fuel for opposition. Rather, encourage challenge by supporting the development of existing interests and opening doors to possible new interests and experiences to which the young person may be inclined. I've seen parents turn an indoor adolescent into one who loves outdoor adventures, and help an aimless adolescent open up her creative, artistically expressive side.

Rebellion itself takes two forms: active and passive resistance. *Active resistance* has to do with dispute and disobedience. The adolescent will argue about anything. "The A in adolescence stands for argument," an embattled dad told me. Why? Because by contesting parental wants, she starts creating her own agenda.

Specifically because something is what parents want done, she will chose to do the opposite, or at least not comply without objection and complaint. *Passive resistance* has to do with procrastination and delay. Here, timing is of the essence. A prompt response means operating on parental terms, but a postponed response means operating on her terms. The longer she can put parents off, the more they have to wait on her and the more she is calling the shots. A ten-minute task, well managed by a passively resistant adolescent, can take several hours to get done.

Of course, parents weary of argument and delay. However, they might want to remember this: an early adolescent who demonstrates strong power of resistance with them is more likely to have adequate resistance when it comes to withstanding forceful friends than a child who is utterly compliant at home and is a social pushover with peers. Resistance to parents can strengthen the capacity to speak up and stand up for oneself with others.

Ultimately, both kinds of resistance serve the same growth need. They help the early adolescent serve notice to parents that they must accept her on more independent terms. And resistance works. To some degree, on some occasions, parents will be too distracted or too tired to follow up a request or demand. They will allow the adolescent's resistance to back them off for some period of time or entirely. "More freedom" then becomes the name of adolescent power gained.

The negative mind-set in early adolescence is multiply determined. It is partly based on the loss of childhood, on the self-rejection of childish ways, on not yet finding how to redefine oneself, on not knowing what to do with oneself, and on antagonism toward parents who often stand in the way of freedom wanted now. More negativity is a necessary condition for adolescence to begin, because people, young or old, do not generally transform themselves unless they are discontented with how they are. The early adolescent is developmentally dissatisfied. The negative mind-set signifies that she is done with childhood and now feels ready to grow on to something more. Early experimentation is the way.

### Early Experimentation

With some measure of new freedom gained from how the negative mind-set has fomented discontent and rebellion, the early adolescent now has room to experiment with more risk taking, to learn about the forbidden, and to test limits to see what can be gotten away with. "Which rules are firm, and which are not?" is the question the early adolescent feels impelled to ask, testing to see which rules are backed up and which will be let go. At this age, the adolescent probes to determine parental consistency. Where parents forget what they asked, give up asking, or don't follow through with what they asked for—that is a place where more social freedom from rules and requests is apparently allowed. The more inconsistent parents are, the more they send a double message: "Sometimes we mean what we say, and sometimes we don't." Receiving that message, the early adolescent will bet on "don't." Then, the more escape from a requirement an early adolescent is permitted to get away with, the more unmindful of social rules she becomes. As one parent put it, "When parents waffle, adolescents win." So the watchwords for parents at this stage, particularly with a strong-willed child, are "mean what you say, stick to your word, follow through with what you want, and back up the conditions you set."

This is the age when experimentation with acting older can begin to be expressed in ways that parents do not support. There are things like using harsh language when tough-talking with peers and perhaps trying it out at home; pushing to see R-rated films that some friends have already been allowed to see; creating a "cool" identity on the Internet and social networking; experimenting with smoking cigarettes and maybe inhalants and alcohol; showing more interest in the dark and violent side of life, and playing computer and video games where those themes can be simulated and acted out; seeking out sexual information, which can include reading romance novels or watching pornography; expressing more desire to dress older in a non-childlike way; and spending more time listening to popular music that speaks to the angst of one's older age. All of this experimentation and more have to do with engaging in experiences that help the adolescent feel less of a child and more grown up.

Then there are emerging interests in the adolescent that were not present in the child and are not shared with the parents. This is when parents can feel at a loss as to how to relate to the adolescent. The daughter, for example, no longer wants to attend sporting events with her dad (his passion) because now the adolescent's dominant interest has shifted to online communication with friends. So the dad says, "Since she's given up on sharing my love of sports, we don't have any good way to be together anymore." What this dad doesn't understand is that the time has come to *reverse the flow of interest* with his daughter. When she was a child, responding to his interest was a way to bring him close. Now that she has entered adolescence, however, it is his turn to respond to her new interests if he wants the two of them to stay connected. He can show interest in her interest in online communication, inviting her to teach him about what this new kind of socializing is like. The rule for relating is this: *with the child, there is a desire to share the parental interest; with the adolescent, the time has come for the parent to reach out to understand what interests his older son or daughter.*

This experimental age is a time for parents to normalize the discussion of alcohol and other drug use, because even if there isn't experimental experience at this young age, there is experimental interest. After all, to seem more grown up, one is supposed to know more about grown-up topics, particularly of the forbidden kind. What friends are saying and the media is portraying provide entry-level understandings—and, more important, misunderstandings—about substances and substance use. Starting in middle school, hearsay from peers about drugs can be harmful. What your son or daughter learns from these trusted informants may include "Tobacco is harmless," "If you only sniff a drug, it won't hurt you," "You can't get drunk on beer," and "Pot is not addictive." If you don't weigh in with your own knowledge, powerful misunderstandings are allowed to stand. However, unless you have opened the topic up for normal conversation, you won't have the chance to share more accurate information. So start by explaining that your adolescent is at an age when he will hear a lot of information and misinformation about drugs. You hope that he will share what he hears so that you can provide another perspective to consider. You are not trying to change his mind or control his thinking, only to give additional information as he forms his own opinions.

Then there is limit testing to challenge what is socially forbidden. This is the age when three kinds of social violations commonly occur: pranking, vandalizing, and shoplifting—risktaking usually in the company of adventurous friends to see what can be gotten away with. Some parents write this early experimentation off as "innocent mischief" and leave it at that, but such permissiveness is not a good idea. It's better to close the loop of responsibility and cause the adventurous adolescent to confront the consequences: confess to the victim of his experimentation, get to hear how the victim felt, and then make restitution to the victim for damage done. Let these violations of early experimentation go, and more serious limit testing and rule breaking are likely to follow. At this experimental age, parents need to patrol violations not only at home but also out in the world.

Finally, early adolescence opens up interest in what's happening outside of family and beyond childhood, a threshold vision of a scary world where dangers lurk and violence can happen to anyone. If so expressively inclined, young people may depict these fears in words or pictures. When they do, at school for example, teachers will sometimes get upset by the dark poetry and drawings of bloody mayhem that some students create. Do these alarming creations signify that the boy or girl is mentally deranged? Not usually. By such expressions, early adolescents try to tame the dangers they fear. This is partly why they gravitate to more scary movies—to see how much fear they can stand by watching or doing what feels alarmingly exciting. The other side of fear is fascination with what they dread. Make it a subject of interest, and the adolescent can bring it more under his control. And now he looks for peer companions with whom to share the daunting journey of growing up that lays ahead, which shows good sense. Adolescence is no time to socially go it alone, and mid-adolescence is when consolidating that group usually begins in earnest.

## Mid-Adolescence (Ages 13–15)

Come their child's mid-adolescence, parents tend to be more ambivalent about her competing family of friends. On the good side, this companionship can provide her with a lot of social support; but on the bad side, they can get her into a lot of trouble. So how parents relate to this tighter group of more influential friends is very tricky, and very important. In general, you need to support those close friendships that seem to serve your son or daughter well, including these young people in family circle activities where your child wants. It's for the best to come to know your child's friends well, to create a welcoming home your child wants to invite them into, and to build a valued relationship with them, in the process becoming a source of influence with them. Parents who with disapproval cut themselves off from the early adolescent's friends not only disenfranchise themselves as a positive influence but also encourage ignorance from lack of contact, which in turn provokes their fears.

What do you do if you believe that the influence of certain friends at this impressionable age is detrimental? Don't criticize the friends, because that will cause your adolescent to feel criticized and to defend them against you. Instead, specify your concerns in terms of behaviors the friends engage in that you don't want your child doing. Say something like this: "I want you to be able to select your own friends, but I also want some say over what you do and don't do with those friends. I know from what you have said that they like to smoke and sometimes go around tagging buildings. I can support your friendship with them so long as you do not join in those activities. If you can't keep from going along, then I need to limit your hanging out with them to over here where I will welcome getting to know them better, of course expecting them to respect our home rules."

On some mysterious occasions, a parent (usually the mother, from what I've seen) will have a sense of distrust or discomfort with her adolescent's new friend, and won't really know why. Should she share that vague distrust or discomfort with her child? I believe she should, confiding the feeling for what it is. She could say, "I have no data to actually support this, and I know your new friend hardly at all, but some kind of alarm bells went off inside of me when I met her, so I would like you to be particularly aware and careful in her company." When this information is shared in a concerned and not a controlling way, I have seen adolescents put it to vigilant use.

Mid-adolescence begins a period of more frequent and intense conflict between parents and teenager. Why? First, the separation from childhood that was accomplished by early adolescence has inspired the young person to push much harder for independence and more room to grow. Second, the opportunity to be out exploring the world in the company of friends matters to the adolescent more than ever before. The power of this collective company increases how hard the mid-adolescent is willing to fight for the social freedom she wants. To experiment with new experience and to socially belong, she wants to keep up with her peers and wants the support of her peers. Independence from parents may be prized, but independence from peers is not. Now her social standing and emerging self-definition are closely tied to the group she runs with, and social cliques exert compelling pressure on members to conform. (It's no coincidence that youth gangs find mid-adolescents to be of prime recruiting age because of their need for affiliation.) The social identity equation is *we = me*. When "me" feels small and insignificant, being part of a "we" is extremely empowering. This is why belonging to a group, clique, or gang has so much attraction at this age. The danger is that in the company of peers, an adolescent will engage in risk-taking and wrongdoing he or she would never do alone.

In early adolescence, protesting parental restrictions on personal freedom was primarily a matter of principle. The young person questioned and protested parents' right to place such restrictions. Her ongoing arguments against this unfairness nourished a grievance that justified actively and passively resisting parental authority. In mid-adolescence, however, the issue of freedom has become much more socially compelling. If her friends are allowed to do something, she believes she should and must be allowed to do it too. So she puts her parents on the spot by asking for last-minute permission to see a movie, doing so in front of friends who have already been allowed to go. This is when parents, to avoid this social extortion, need to offer to take her into the next room to privately discuss the outing while her friends wait. Now she is suitably outraged. "If their parents allow them to go, that should be enough for you!" But her parents hold their ground against the double dose of peer pressure she has organized against them—from her impatient friends and, by implication, from their permissive parents.

She is truly maddened. When she was a child, she could leave the house to play with friends, and her parents told her to have a good time and be back by a certain time. But now that she is older, and believes she should be allowed more unquestioned freedom to come and go, they have grown more cautious and controlling. She feels she should have a longer leash, but they keep pulling her up short. The questions they ask, assurances they extract, agreements they make, arrangements they check, and limits they set all get in the way of what she wants to do right now. Nothing matters more than *freedom now*: "My life will be ruined if you don't let me go!" However, distrustful of her brash social agenda, parents may decide that her plans sound unwise. "It's not safe for you and your friends to wander the mall after the movie. We'll pick you up as soon as the show gets out. Stay there and be there. And no popping out early to roam around." But the mid-adolescent dismisses these concerns as unnecessary cautions based on exaggerated worries. "You're being overprotective!" Her risk-taking is downplayed by denial. "Nothing bad is going to happen to me. I know how to take care of myself. Don't you trust me?"

What the parents really don't trust is how group pressure and the desire for excitement can override individual judgment. What they don't trust are dangerous exposures and accidents waiting to happen that lurk in the larger world outside of family. And what they don't trust is how their adolescent is changing in mid-adolescence.

### The Shell of Self-Centeredness

Now parents are up against a young person who often seems to function in a more self-serving way. Feeling liberated from the shackles of childhood definition that early adolescent disorganization, negative mind-set, and early experimentation have broken, the mid-adolescent becomes urgently preoccupied with three priorities: freedom to focus on *self*, to have *fun*, and to gratify wants *now*. It's not the parents' job to argue with the mid-adolescent's personal priorities in order to change his mind, but it is their job to insert a more responsible set of their own to which he is expected to adjust. So parents let it be known where they stand. "Focusing on yourself is fine, but we also expect you to consider the welfare of others, like what the younger kids may need." "Having fun is fine, but we also expect you to do some work first, like completing chores before going out." "Wanting things right now is fine, but we also expect you to delay some wants until later and even do without, like not going with your friends so that you can be here to see your relatives." Indulgent parents who don't insert their own priorities at this extremely self-preoccupied stage are at risk of encouraging a young person to grow forward holding the belief that self, fun, and now are all that matter in life. Not only can this sense of entitlement make the next stage of adolescence more difficult for parents, but sooner or later, harsh social reality will provide lessons to the young person that parents neglected to teach. Other authorities will be less inclined to be so forbearing and tolerant.

### Evasion of Responsibility

In service of this mid-adolescent mind-set, what eventually happens is that the young person, focused only on his three personal priorities, will make a decision that violates a commitment to parents or compliance with a family rule. Now what he fears is that his parents, in disciplinary response, will take away what feels most precious at this age—social freedom—at least for a while. So what should he do? Confess and give up what matters to him most, or see if he can somehow evade responsibility? Mid-adolescents frequently choose the second option. And it is one for which they have a variety of escape (from responsibility) strategies at their disposal. So when confronted, the teenager may use *denial* ("It didn't happen; you are mistaken"), *excuses* ("I was tired, and I forgot"), *blame* ("It was my friend's fault"), or *lies* ("You never said I couldn't, so I thought I could"). Parents who don't confront these evasions of responsibility can foster the mid-adolescent's belief that when he gets into trouble, rather than own up and accept the consequences, he should deny, excuse, blame, or lie his way out.

Why would parents not confront these escape strategies? The answer often is that they are reluctant to provoke conflict with their more combative mid-adolescent. After all, at this age, she believes that freedom for self, fun, and now, particularly in the company of friends out in the world, is a right worth fighting for. And if she is abusing substances at this time, her mind-set will be only become more determined, while her use of these evasive strategies will only be more practiced and effective. For parents, mid-adolescence is the age when thankless parenting truly begins. Now, as they take stands for the teenager's best interests against what she wants, parents get rewarded with more criticism and conflict for their efforts. The mid-adolescent does not say, "Thanks a lot for keeping me in and not letting me go." Now there are more end runs. There is the *single end run* when your teenager goes over to a friend's and both sneak out from over there. And there is the *double end run* when each tells her respective parents that she is spending the night at the other's home, and now both are free to skip out for a night of adventure. So parents particularly need to check sleepover arrangements at this age. And if your mid-adolescent sneaks out after hours for some forbidden freedom (which happens more frequently at this age) and if you have an idea where she is, go after her. To have your parent unexpectedly show up in front of your friends, ready to escort you back home, is a socially embarrassing example of parental vigilance and pursuit that is not soon forgotten.

The mid-adolescent wants social freedom more strongly than she has ever wanted it before. The job of parents is to keep a secure family structure in place around her as she increasingly pushes against the safeguards they have in place.

### Intolerance of Restrictions

*Five pillars of social authority* support family structure. Each can hamper the teenager's freedom, so there will be times when he contests them all.

1. There are *demands* parents make: "This is what you must do."
2. There are *limits* parents set: "This is what you must not do."
3. There are *questions* parents ask: "This is what we need to know."
4. There are *confrontations* to be made: "This is what we need to talk with you about."
5. There are *consequences* to allow or apply: "This is the outcome of choices you have made."

Come mid-adolescence, dispute is not the only kind of communication, but there is usually more of it. The adolescent is contesting parental demands, limits, questions, confrontations, and consequences that parents, for the sake of the teenager's safety and developing responsibility, are called on to assert. In the face of increased disagreement, parents must model the constructive conduct of conflict they want the teenager to imitate and learn in response.

And they must be prepared for *protective belligerence* at this irritable age. When there is something important they want to discuss with their teenager, there never seems to be a "good time" to approach her because she is either on the computer, texting, watching a program, busy doing something, busy doing nothing, in a bad mood, too tired, or on her way out the door. "Not now—later!" is her constant refrain. Given this reality, parents have to brave her irritation, because as far as the adolescent is concerned, there is no good time to discuss their question or concern. So they might as well choose a time that suits them and expect it to be inconvenient for or unpopular with her.

And when it comes to granting freedom, parents must drive a hard bargain. One good way to do this is to hold your teen to a *conduct contract*, like the example here. This conduct contract comprises six articles of agreement that the teen knows must all be lived up to in order for freedom requested to stand a chance of becoming freedom given.

1. There must be *reliability*: the mid-adolescent has been giving parents adequate and accurate information about what he did, is doing, and is planning to do.
2. There must be *predictability*: the mid-adolescent has been faithfully keeping all promises and agreements made to parents.
3. There must be *responsibility*: the mid-adolescent has been taking good care of business at home, at school, and out in the world.
4. There must be *mutuality*: the mid-adolescent has been living on two-way terms with parents, doing for them just as they do for him.
5. There must be *availability*: the mid-adolescent has been willing to discuss parental concerns when these needs arise.
6. There must be *civility*: the mid-adolescent has been willing to discuss with courtesy and respect whatever parents want to discuss.

When the mid-adolescent has been meeting all the terms of this pact, parents are more likely to grant his next request for freedom. However, if he has been lying to them, breaking his word to them, getting into trouble away from home, only thinking of his wants, refusing to talk when they want to communicate, and speaking to them disrespectfully, they are less likely to give permission. Freedom at this expansive age must be conditionally given—conditions must be met before permission is approved. Parents who fail to support their family structure with firmness in mid-adolescence will find the next stage of adolescence more difficult to manage.

Most important, if parents aren't firm about giving their teen conditional freedom, their mid-adolescent is deprived of a support he needs: *the protection of parental prohibitions*. At this age, the adolescent knows he has more freedom than is good for him because parents can't actually "make him" do what he doesn't want or "stop him" from doing what he does. He knows that what freedom he takes is up to him, and this is scary. What secures him is a family structure he can depend on when a social need arises, such as when he is urged by friends to do something he doesn't want to do, but is afraid to step up and say no on his own behalf. So he can turn a parental prohibition to personal use by blaming parents for his refusal to go along with peers. "They'd ground me forever if I did what you guys want me to do. It's not worth it!" This is of course a lie, but it saves face with peers. I once heard a dad turn this dynamic into an explicit offer to his young teenager: "Always feel free," he said, "to blame me for refusing when you need to stay out of trouble that friends are urging you to get into."

The map to early and mid-adolescence has a lot of "bumps in the road"—more disorganization, resistance, testing of limits, peer influence, lying, and conflict, to name a few. Now the process of parenting gets less pleasurable as the object of your concern becomes less appreciative of your efforts on his behalf. With the first two stages of adolescence, the separation from childhood has occurred and the age of thankless parenting has arrived. In the next chapter, I describe the final two stages—late adolescence and trial independence—that are about preparing the young person for acting more grown up.

## Chapter Three

# A Road Map to Late Adolescence and Trial Independence

Just because we want our teenager to grow up doesn't mean we want him to start acting all grown up, at least not yet, and that's where we butt heads. He tells us that in a couple years he'll be on his own, so why not learn about those freedoms now? That's when we feel caught between a rock and a hard place, not sure when to hold on and when to let go.

Here the road map continues from the previous chapter as I describe the last two stages of adolescence, late adolescence and trial independence, when the adolescent agenda turns to meeting the challenges of acting older. Compared with parenting during the first two stages of adolescence, now the parenting job becomes more complex.

## Late Adolescence (Ages 15–18)

The period of late adolescence accelerates independence by encompassing powerful new activities that are all associated with acting older, such as the entry into high school, driving a car, social dating, part-time employment, and managing an allowance. We'll also look at what the parental agenda needs to be during these crucial years and why, with so much going on, late adolescents often seem "lazy" to their parents.

## Entry into High School

Coinciding with the high school years, the third stage of adolescence is impacted not so much by what is formally taught by teachers as by what is learned outside of class. Consider the lowly freshman, at the bottom of an age heap of more seasoned upperclassmen who are models, messengers, and mentors embodying more grown-up freedoms. The learning curve of growing up becomes steeper, and the climb is faster, when an underclassman is brought into significant association and inclusion with upper-grade students, contact that feels exciting, but also scary. Consider how flattered and anxious the mature-looking freshman girl feels when receiving dating interest from a junior or senior guy. His attention can be really difficult for her to resist, and soon she is feeling out of step with her peers, pressed to act as old as she can as fast as she can to fit in with the older company she is now striving to keep.

Whether the freshman is academically advanced, is athletically talented, or just physically looks or socially acts much more mature, being thrust into the company of older students creates pressure to act above his or her age. Older students are not interested in growing back down to you; you are expected to grow up to them, which makes refusing their invitations very hard to do. So the first watchword for parents of a late adolescent who is entering ninth grade is to encourage same-age association this first year as much as possible. Also encourage your freshman to join some extracurricular school activity or organization. Such membership can lower the likelihood of being befriended by fringe or alienated older students trolling for lonely entrants eager for somewhere disaffected to belong.

At first glance, parents and a high school–age teenager appear to share the same objective for her: to learn to "act more grown up." However, on closer examination, they have very different definitions of what that phrase intends. For parents it means shouldering additional responsibilities to demonstrate more self-sufficiency. For the teenager it means having adventures that certify she is now officially grown enough to act "older." "High school feels like freedom city," was how one freshman described the excitement of starting ninth grade. "I can't wait to be a senior and be at the top of the heap! Seniors rule the school!"

In a short forty-eight months, the incoming freshman will (both she and parents hope) be a graduating senior, only to discover some sadness at separating from friends and anxiety over moving on to whatever happens next. Both sadness and anxiety will dampen a lot of the senior year triumph she expected to feel. For some seniors, the final year of high school becomes "the last blast" of freedom while still living at home, a time to celebrate (at parties) a long good-bye to the family of close friends with whom they shared the teenage years. For other seniors, the agonizing process of completing college applications is painfully drawn out by the resistant teenager's ambivalence about leaving high school and leaving home, pressed into action by an insistent, and exhausted, parent who rides herd on production so that the deadlines will be met.

The closer one gets to senior year in high school (with full freedom of independence now in view), the more eager one becomes to engage in older activity—a ferment of adultlike activities, invitations, and opportunities, most of them enthusiastically promoted, hard to turn down, and having a dangerous side. The *social speed of life* accelerates the further along in adolescence one grows. Contrary to what parents often say, the difficulty at this age is not that most adolescents have a problem with thinking. If they have any thought problem at all, it is with taking the time to think at an age when life is moving increasingly fast.

It's hard to slow down and think when accumulated pressures begin to build. There is the *pressure of temptation*—of having fun. There is the *pressure of sensation*—of doing something exciting. There is the *pressure of peers*—of joining in. There is the *pressure of substances*—of daring and not caring. There is the *pressure of impulse*—of focusing on immediate gratification. Add all these pressures up when they converge in one social situation, and you have a potent formula for trouble. *Risk of harm = fun + excitement + joining in + daring + now.* For example, on the spur of the moment (who knows whose idea it was), everybody piles into the car at 10:30 at night for a wild ride to a neighboring city to go to a party, as a designated driver drives a carload of designated drinkers, making it very hard to drive safely when going, and even more difficult driving back when nobody cares if whoever is driving is sober or not.

So how should you advise your late adolescent about what to do when a speed-of-life decision arises? Try suggesting that your son or daughter take the Three Question Test. It doesn't take long, and the minute or so investment of time required can be well worthwhile. What are the questions?

1. "Why would I want to do this?"
2. "How might I get hurt?"
3. "Is it worth the risk?"

And if companions the teenager is with won't allow the time it takes for her to ask herself and answer the three questions before deciding, then whatever they want to do, or want her to do, is probably not a good idea. Most of the serious mishaps that befall young people during the latter stages of adolescence are *speed-of-life crashes* involving teenagers who were so focused on what they wanted to do that they didn't consider if it was wise. It's not that adolescents lack judgment so much as that they don't take the time to consult the judgment they have. The Three Question Test allows judgment to weigh in by accessing past experience, present circumstances, and future possibilities before the adolescent makes a decision that carries some degree of heightened risk.

Among the additional factors that accelerate independence during late adolescence are three specific kinds of freedoms that confer symbolic older standing in the young person's life: *driving a car* (transportation freedom), *dating* (socializing freedom), and *making money* (financial freedom). All three freedoms are important to master, but they must depend on parental permission. Parents need to let the adolescent know that allowing these activities will depend on the young person taking responsible care of business at home, at school, and out in the world. Each freedom is like a rocket that increases the thrust to more independence and the risks that go with it. At the extreme, driving can lead to accidents and death; dating can lead to sexually transmitted diseases, pregnancy, or violence; and making money can lead to spending it on dangerous pursuits. So parents want the adolescent's capacity to assess risk and exercise responsibility to be in good working order. Now let's consider these three major freedoms one by one.

## Driving

When a teen is turned loose to ride with friends who drive or is allowed to drive a family car, these wheels quickly turn into a set of wings. Such mobility creates a sense of liberation from parents. "I don't have to depend on them to get me around anymore! I can take myself!" His coming and going feels more up to him because he can now manage his own transportation arrangements. The impact of having a set of "wheels" for the adolescent is comparable to the thrill of crawling and walking for the infant and toddler. There is this exhilaration of independent mobility and the sense that the adolescent can go to places of his own choosing, when he chooses, that were not possible or allowable before. Back then as now, parents had a real worry: What will their child do with this new freedom to get around? Old boundaries expand, curiosity inspires exploration, new experience pours in, dangerous exposures increase, and risks abound. For parents, when a teenager starts driving, a whole new arena for setting limits and resolving conflict opens up.

Driving a car is a freedom that takes special handling because it comes with potential lethal dangers attached, particularly for young drivers—which automobile accident and fatality statistics, and higher insurance rates, continually show. As the *New York Times* reported, "Car crashes remain the leading cause of death for teenagers, who have a crash rate four times higher than that of older drivers" (Aug. 14, 2012, p. A1). A young person's readiness to take on this responsibility is the parents' responsibility to determine. So you need to start with an assessment:

- Is your late adolescent reliably focused or easily distracted?
- Does he delay gratification for judgment, or is he impulsive?
- Is she socially obedient or into rule breaking?
- Is he reasonably cautious or an inveterate risk-taker?
- Is she organized or forgetful?
- Is he emotionally excitable or reasonably calm?
- Is she abstinent or substance using?
- Is he self-governing or subject to peer pressure?
- Is she conducting the rest of her life responsibly?
- Is he wed to texting while he drives or free to concentrate on the road?

The point is, there are two driving ages required for operating a car. The first is a matter of state law, *the legal age*, sixteen in most states. The second is a matter of maturity, *the readiness age*, decided by parents. A sixteen-year-old who in the opinion of parents is distracted, impulsive, rule breaking, risk-taking, forgetful, excitable, substance using, easily influenced by peers, acting irresponsibly elsewhere, and committed to texting at all times probably lacks the self-control required to safely drive, even if he or she is of legal age. The safety and lives of both the driver and other people are at stake.

This caution aside, however, a good indicator of a young person's responsibility is his or her driving record. If in the first year of driving she has no record of collisions or moving violations or parking tickets, if she has taken care of maintaining the car's basic appearance and functioning, if she has contributed some share of money to cover driving expenses, if she has kept her destination and curfew agreements, if she has driven substance free and kept the car free of substances, then an increased amount of effective self-management has been successfully assumed. Obviously, if the late adolescent has broken speeding laws, driven to endanger, or been guilty of other violations, or if she has been arrested driving under the influence or in possession of illegal drugs, driving privileges need be suspended until some assessment of substance use has been made, legal consequences have been met, and a thorough evaluation of other life responsibilities has been conducted.

### Social Dating

Late adolescence is the time when dating becomes more common. In general, dating at least at first creates some social discomfort, the teenager feeling awkward, anxious, even embarrassed about how to act and what to say. This is why going out with a group is usually more comfortable and less pressured than going out with a single person, when you have only yourself to depend on to be entertaining. In addition, casual dating is less pressured than serious dating. Casual dating tends to focus on fun without loss of freedom from significant involvement. Going together signifies liking and compatibility, the enjoyment of coming to know another person well. When romance blossoms, exclusive dating usually follows, taking young people out of social circulation, the focal relationship starting to be at the expense of social time with same-sex friends.

Should being in love follow (and from what I've seen, only a small minority of high school students fall in love), the serious couple must manage difficult tensions around mixing dependence and independence, togetherness and separation, possessiveness and jealousy. Being in love not only puts the young couple out of social step with most of their peers (who lack that depth of attachment in their dating) but also increases the likelihood of sexual intimacy to affirm the caring connection they feel, in the process making the relationship more emotionally intense and complex to manage. Whatever the level of dating involvement, parents have a lot to talk about with their son or daughter about how to evaluate the rightness of the relationship. They can suggest four basic questions relating to how he or she is treated and how he or she is treating the other person in the relationship:

1. *Am I treating myself well in the relationship?* For example, "Am I taking good care of myself in the relationship and not just taking good care of the other person?"

2. *Am I treating the other person in the relationship well?* For example, "Am I accepting of a different point of view than my own and not always putting it down?"

3. *Am I content with how I am being treated by the other person?* For example, "Am I free to say no without the other person getting angry with me?"

4. *Am I comfortable with the treatment the other person gives himself or herself?* For example, "When I'm feeling unhappy, can I trust that the other person will not automatically blame himself or herself for having done something wrong?"

The young person needs to be able to honestly answer yes to each of the four questions for the relationship to be in good working order. If there are some noes, then there are some fundamental parts that are not functioning well, and there is work to do. In many cases, young people have to experience some bad relationships, or badness in a relationship, before they learn how to conduct one for the good. But learning from sad experience is learning the hard way. In the words of one high school junior: "I never want to have another girlfriend who takes advantage of me like that!"

It's important to remember that young people don't learn how to conduct healthy relationships in class. They learn it from life experience. Thus parents have a role in helping them examine that experience for what it has to teach. *Now = later* is what parents have to realize and point out to their child. How adolescents manage dating and romantic relationships in the present is how they are likely to conduct them in the future. So it is very important that parents help them learn as they grow, identifying the good (such as equity of standing) to carry forward and the bad (such as dominance by coercion) not to experience again.

Then there are the parties. If the challenge of dating is being entertaining company when going out with another person, the challenge of parties is being comfortable in a group gathered to socialize together for the sake of fun. Parties are a more grown-up thing to do. Supposed to be enjoyable, parties for many late adolescents are forced-fun gatherings where one's socializing skills are put to the test. These experiences can be challenging and awkward affairs, particularly if they include a lot of people the teen doesn't know, or doesn't know very well. Parties are not the same as just hanging out with a group of good friends. They are more formally organized by invitation and more likely to include people the teen doesn't know, so it takes more effort to act relaxed and to communicate when he or she is not sure what to say. Nervous energy fills the room as lack of confidence puts many young people on edge.

Because many parents have known what this social discomfort was like for them, or even know what it is like now, they can help their teenager with strategies he or she can use to turn a hard situation into a tolerable or even enjoyable one. For example, parents can suggest to teens that in preparation for the party, they ask and answer four questions:

1. "What can I have to say about myself?" (I can talk about what I find fun to do.)
2. "What can I ask others about?" (I can be curious about what's happening in their lives.)
3. "How can I look friendly?" (I can smile and make eye contact.)
4. "How can I seem interested?" (I can listen and want to hear more.)

One kind of party that parents should avoid enabling is the *empty-house party*, where they leave town for a night or two, entrusting the teenager, who promises he or she is grown up enough for this responsibility, to take care of the place while they are gone. Now what can happen is that unbeknownst to parents, some parallel planning starts taking place between the teenager and a few friends for a small social gathering while the adults are away. Unfortunately, as you surely know from a host of teen movies, friends tell friends who invite more friends, whom your teenager doesn't even know, and now what felt like a good idea is careening out of control. There are two kinds of risks associated with the empty-house party. There are property risks—something is broken, stained, or stolen, or the place is simply trashed. And there are personal risks—someone ends up being injured, molested, or arrested, or your reputation with neighbors is never again quite the same. And parents can be legally liable for what happens to kids on their property. So regardless of how responsible you think your own child is, don't leave your teenager to sit an empty house or home. Better to remember, *when the cat's away, some mice (and friends of the mice) may not be able to resist the temptation to play.*

### Part-Time Employment

Come late adolescence, young people start to learn what their parents already know: that in life most people have to get by on less money than they want, on less than many other people have, and often on less than they actually need. This is a sobering realization at an age when worldly freedom to do, to go, and to have starts to matter and cost so much more. Whereas children are satisfied to live primarily within the provisions of the family circle, adolescents are more discontent to live on those modest financial terms. They want the means to operate in an older, more material world; they want to keep up with their spending friends. That's why adolescents are more expensive than children. And that's why many late adolescents want to get a part-time job.

Entering the workforce feels like an adult thing to do, and it is. Exchanging labor for money is what the teenager will be doing throughout the rest of his or her life. You want your son or daughter to learn the discipline of being able to secure and sustain employment. It takes *initiative* to find a job opening, *assertiveness* to interview for a position, *reliability* to hold a job, *obedience* to work for a boss, *cooperation* to work with coworkers, and *patience* to work with the public (which is what most entry-level employment requires a teenager to do). It also affirms *self-worth* to know that one has skills for which the world of work is willing to pay money. All of this is on the positive side of the ledger. On the negative side can be investing time in the job at the expense of education, because now making money feels more rewarding than making grades. Also negative can be what is learned from workplace associations, such as exposure to more varied substance use. Jobs can grow teenagers up in a hurry as they work alongside older employees. So parents have to see part-time jobs for what they are—an opportunity for growth experience mixed with possibly harmful exposure.

Driving a car, social dating, and making money—separately they each empower independence, and taken together they do even more. I am reminded of the conversation with the father who was bewildered by the dramatic increase in his son's headstrong behavior. "We don't understand it. At the end of sophomore year, he was pretty content to live within our limits, but junior year it's a different story. All he can think about is freedom! What's happened?" So I asked, "Is there anything different going on this year from last?" "No," replied the dad. "Same school, same friends, even dresses mostly the same." Then he made a slight retraction. "Well, of course he's driving this year. He's started to date. And he's got a part-time job to pay his share of the car. But besides that, his life is pretty much the same." "Besides that?" I replied. "You just described firing off three major rockets to independence in close succession, and you're surprised by the change? He's just revolutionized his life. If he can drive, he can take himself where he wants to go. If he's dating, he can act socially older. If he can make his own money, he can make his own spending decisions. Not only that, he's just created a *lifestyle triangle*: he's got a job to support a car, he's got a car so he can date, and he earns money to support both expenses. You'd better let him know that while you want him to step up to managing all three experiences, none of them will be allowed unless he takes good care of business at home, at school, and out in the world. You've given him more independence, so he wants to run more of his life on his terms. Your terms are that he must do so responsibly." What manner of lifestyle an adolescent gets to lead also partly depends on the allowance parents give.

## Managing an Allowance

When parents give a teenager a regular allowance, exactly what are they allowing? The answer: a measure of choice—the monetary freedom to buy something he desires to have or to do at an age when material possessions and entertainment experiences become more socially pressing. Keeping up with the latest fad or fashion and the spending power of peers is more important the further through adolescence one grows. In most cases, whatever allowance you provide is going to be insufficient because your teenager, like others of his kind, is financially deprived. How can this lack be so when you know he is well provided for? The deprivation is a relative one. Your adolescent feels *relatively deprived* when he compares himself to peers who have more and can afford to do more, and when he compares his belongings to new products introduced into the marketplace that make yesterday's purchase seem inferior, out of style, old-fashioned, uncool, and obsolete. For both causes, no matter how much allowance you give, it is never going to be enough to quell material dissatisfaction the teenager is likely to feel. So give what you can financially and emotionally afford to, and think is reasonable, not how much the teenager would ideally wish to have.

An allowance is a powerfully diagnostic gift, and parents should be attentive to what the teenager's response to this discretionary money shows. The allowance question parents need to ask themselves is this: "Is my child by temperament and inclination more of a *spender* or a *saver?*" Psychologically, this distinction can be very telling. If, because of urgent wants and impetuosity, your child keeps feeling driven to spend the money right away on something, anything of momentary interest, to satisfy the need to buy, there may be larger issues for parental concern. You may see matters of impulse control that need attending to. The parent's job is to help the child exercise restraint by delaying and denying immediate gratification. So, in the case of an adolescent who acts like a "born spender," as one parent described it, the management of allowance can help this child learn to spend rationally and not emotionally, to prioritize wants, to slow buying decisions down, and to set money aside for achieving future goals. When a spender learns to save, he gains self-discipline.

Young people who are more inclined to save at least some of their allowance tend to have more self-control and are less likely to give way to impulse in their response to more financial freedom and to other freedoms as well. So saving has both a specific and a psychological value. Come adolescence, it is usually easier to parent a saver than a spender. The first has the foresight to think ahead; the second is ruled by a tyranny of now. And during the last stage of adolescence, trial independence (ages eighteen to twenty-three), when pressure from new freedom and temptation for more spending can be extremely high, the self-discipline from being a saver can indeed be a "saving," stabilizing grace.

The purpose of giving allowance in late adolescence is to teach money management skills that young people will need all their lives as they transact business with the world. With a child, parents teach lower-level money management skills like learning the costs of things, prioritizing wants, saving for something special, and maybe donating some part of this disposable income to charity. With an adolescent, certainly by high school, parents are in the business of using allowance to teach higher-level money management skills like paying for recurring financial needs, budgeting weekly and monthly expenses, managing a checking or debit account, and living within their means. Allowance is increased at this older age to cover regular costs like public transportation, gas, cell phone charges, school lunch, toiletries, recreation, and clothing, for example. These are common expenses that the teenager is now expected to pay. The allowance lesson in late adolescence is that with more financial freedom comes more financial responsibility.

Often parents transition from a weekly to a monthly allowance. Part of the adolescent challenge becomes making their money last, because there are going to be no advances should money run out before the end of the month. This is real-life money management training that the teenager will need in place to successfully negotiate trial independence, when budgeting, banking, and bill paying become essential survival skills for operating out on one's own. Probably the best predictor I have seen for how well a young person adjusts to the demands of trial independence is how responsibly he or she learned to manage money to cover expenses during the high school years.

Is there a time to withhold allowance? Yes. If you have cause to believe that your adolescent is abusing alcohol or other drugs, you may not want to enable this risky behavior by underwriting the cost. It's not that loss of allowance will stop the substance abuse, but it will at least send a message that you do not intend to support it.

### The Parental Agenda

A lot of parents fall down on their job in late adolescence. They are so focused on the risks of grown-up freedoms their son or daughter wants to take, on matters pertaining to school performance, and on what happens after graduation that they neglect the curriculum they should be putting in place over the four high school years. The name of this curriculum is Preparation for Leading an Independent Life, and it is up to parents, not the school, to provide it.

The goal is to equip a young person with the practical knowledge, skills, and responsibility required for successful self-management after leaving home after high school graduation and starting to operate on his or her own. Specifically, the objective is to use those four years, those short forty-eight months, of practical preparation to create *the smallest next step to independence* when that fuller measure of freedom arrives.

A starter list of essential categories of knowledge and do-for-yourself competencies to consider might include the following:

- Housekeeping (laundering, cleaning, fixing)
- Basic household expenses (paying for rent and utilities, shopping for basics)

- Health maintenance (diet, sleep, exercise)
- Medical care (wellness and illness)
- Smart shopping (comparative pricing and discount buying)
- Money management (budgeting, bill paying, banking)
- Employment (searching, application, and holding a job)
- Applicable laws (legal rights and obligations)
- Tax paying (local, state, federal)
- Public transportation (urban navigation and schedules)
- Car maintenance (engine checking and upkeep)
- Credit and loans (agreements and contracts)
- Sexual decision making (contraception, disease assessment, safety)
- Substance use (identification, experimentation, moderation)
- Personal safety (peer pressure, social risk assessment, sobriety)

And then there are such basic life skills as managing change, stress, scheduling, organizing, prioritizing, planning, goal setting, and building adequate self-discipline to responsibly run one's own life.

Most of what parents consider routine parts of living an independent life will now be required of the soon-to-be-departing adolescent. In preparation, when their son or daughter enters high school, parents should list these *exit skills*, specify what operations go with each category of performance, and then decide when and how during the four high school years they are going to address this preparation. They also need to decide when and where they will *transfer support responsibility* by asking themselves the question, "What are we doing for our teenager that she could start doing for herself?" So, for example, parents can stop acting like a morning alarm clock and let the adolescent wake herself. They can stop being a laundry service and let the teenager wash his own clothes. They can stop doling out money on request and provide a monthly allotment to cover basic operating expenses the teenager has to budget. They can stop arranging for medical and dental visits and have the teenager make her own appointments. The information to be conveyed and the skills to develop are too practical to be taught in the school, but they are essential to independent living. So parents must provide this education and training. How adequately they impart this teaching has a significant bearing on how well prepared their older teenager is to successfully cope with the stage of adolescence that is soon to follow.

It's because the late-adolescent high school years are so packed with formal and informal education and preparation that parents get frustrated with their teenagers, often accusing them of not doing enough and being "lazy."

### Lazy Teenagers

The parental complaint I most often hear runs something like this. "I'll tell you what the problem is," griped the dad. "My teenager is lazy! She never wants to do what I want her to do when I want her to do it. She's always putting me off with excuses and delay. All she wants at home is to be left alone, kick back, lie around, network with friends, and do nothing. I mean, how lazy is that, with everything else that needs doing? Her life's so simple. She's only in high school. Wait till she has to function out in the adult world! She has no idea what it's like to be really busy. How do these high school kids spend their time, anyway?" Good question. In response, from conversations with young people over the years, I pieced together what a typical high school day could be like. A student's account might run like this:

"First I have to wake myself up and get myself up after too little sleep because I was up working late getting that history project done while messaging and texting and posting back to all my friends. I don't want them to drop me for not responding and be cut out of the loop. Then I have to fix my appearance for school. I have to look in the mirror to see what my body has been doing, never growing in ways I like. Next, I have to do my face and hair and figure out what to wear. That's the problem with going public: how to show the best and hide the worst. Then I start thinking about school. Which friends are going to act friendly today? What teachers are going to be in a bad mood? When will I have time to straighten out that argument I had last night over the phone? Are we going to break up again? Here comes the hard part: trying to get out of the house without getting into a fight with my parents over things I was told to do but haven't done yet. I know another lecture on the Big R, responsibility, is coming up. I just hope it's not this morning because I have to leave early to make a 7:30 AM practice session at school. So I run out of the house promising over my shoulder to finish folding and putting away my laundry, emptying the dishwasher, and straightening up my room as soon as I get home. And I arrive at school just in time to get called down in front of everyone for being five minutes late. Why is it every teacher and coach thinks their demands of me come first? Now I rush to make first-period class. Major test today. Hope the questions are something I can answer. No matter how much I study, I'm never really prepared. Can't wait to get out of high school, but then what am I going to do? Parents keep asking. How should I know? I haven't even figured out what I'm going to do for senior prom! Rest of the day in and out of classes, rushing to find enough time to catch up with friends and repair last night's argument. Someone passes me in the hall and offers sympathy about our breaking up. Why does everybody know more about my relationship than I do?

"Classes finally over, with assignments stuffed into my note-books, I rush off to my job—a few hours after school each day acting cheerful with impatient customers to make a little money to have something to spend. On paying friends back what I bor-rowed. On paying some of my own expenses because my parents want me to act more grown up. But the more I make, the less I seem to have to get what I want. There's never enough! At last I get home, ready to slow down, settle in, and chill out. But as soon as I turn on the TV, my parents want to talk to me. Responsibility lecture number one zillion and one. I don't have much energy to put up a good fight, so parents feel like their talk went well. To get them off my back I put a few dishes away, fold a few clean clothes, and kick the dirty ones under my bed. Then, to blot out the day, I lay down and relax with some loud music that my parents yell at me to turn down. I'd like to go to sleep—for about a week. But I can't. Not yet. Got to make that phone call and see if we can talk to each other without getting into another fight like last night. Then there's homework to do. More messages to answer. And something else at school I know is coming due, but can't remember what. Then I start worrying and wondering about tomorrow."

So what do high school students do with their time? Well, if parents had as much to do and think about as their teenager, sometimes they might feel like acting "lazy" too. High school can be challenging, all right; but after high school comes the hardest adolescent stage of all.

## Trial Independence (Ages 18–23)

*Trial independence,* the final stage of adolescence, is usually the hardest for the young person and his or her parents. The reason is this: *the only way to learn true independence is to actually try it,* and most last-stage adolescents discover that they have yet to master all the knowledge and skills they need to establish responsible self-reliance. Even in the best of cases, preparation in late adolescence is going to be incomplete. The young person is going to leave parental care for job or further education only partly ready, having to learn many hard lessons about grown-up experience and responsibility from the *Big R*—reality. Now instruction from choice and consequence, from error and recovery, is how the balance of this hard-knocks education must be accomplished.

Trial independence creates a complicated challenge. To deny awareness of the harder side of independence, young people can work hard at believing play is all there is. Cut loose from parental structure and supervision, they are surrounded by peers who are all excited to be "on their own" for the first time, and everyone is up for fun at all hours of the day and night. Loss of parental discipline and lack of self-discipline plus maximum availability of alcohol and other drugs result in much slipping and sliding and breaking of commitments of all kinds. There are broken romantic relationships, broken promises to parents, broken job obligations, broken credit arrangements, broken leases, broken educational programs, and even broken laws.

And then there are parties, the major social vehicle for meeting people and making new friends now that one is living away from home. As in high school, these "grown-up" gatherings still pose a problem for most young people because they lack the confidence and communication skills to mingle and chat with people they may not know that well or know at all. This is where the "get-to-know-you" drug, alcohol, comes into frequent play to provide the liquid courage to loosen up and feel less self-conscious and inhibited about how one looks and what one says. In addition, cigarettes give nervous hands something to do. Obviously, the more the substance use, the more that social and sexual safety is put at risk. If all this sounds chaotic, that's because it is. It's hard to fly free at this giddy time and still stay grounded. It's hard to make steady headway when one has not yet set any clear direction in life. Trial independence demands more knowledge, skill, and self-discipline than most young people can master, at least right away. Consider four aspects of this turbulent time. There are life challenges that come with trial independence, there is a need for parental mentoring at this difficult time, there is the myth of independence, and there is the final lonely battle for independence that must be fought.

## Life Challenges

In counseling, I have seen eleven major challenges that young people commonly face during this last stage of adolescence, each one connected to trying to live independently for the first time. Here is a list of those challenges, and the strength that successfully coping with each challenge can confer.

1. *The challenge of living apart from family.* When adolescents start to live apart from family, they can experience insecurity from separation, loneliness from feeling disconnected, and homesickness from missing loved ones and old friends so far away. Coping with this challenge can teach adolescents the capacity to live at a distance from family while still staying in touch, and to develop an independent social circle of their own.

2. *The challenge of more range of choice.* Living on one's own for the first time can be a chaotic experience. It can be tempting to indulge in one's newfound freedom to excess without considering the consequences and to flout social rules and laws as if they don't apply. Last-stage adolescents can lack the will and know-how to organize and constructively manage all the new decision making. Coping with this challenge can teach adolescents that enjoying increased freedom must be tempered by assuming increased responsibility.

3. *The challenge of finding and keeping employment.* Independent older adolescents can experience a loss of esteem from losing a job, anxiety at how tenuous employment is, and fear of rejection when it comes to applying for a possible opening. Coping with this challenge can teach adolescents that there is no job security and that it can take a lot of work to get hired and to keep the work one finds.

4. *The challenge of further education.* There can be inadequate high school preparation for college, insufficient motivation and commitment to make one attend class and study, and a high likelihood of flunking out. Coping with this challenge can teach adolescents that it is easier to get into college than to complete it, and that self-discipline to show up on time and do the work is required to graduate.

5. *The challenge of living with roommates.* Adolescents can have a lack of competence for managing cooperation, an unwillingness to tolerate incompatibility, and a lack of communication skills for resolving conflict in a shared live-in relationship not experienced before. Coping with this challenge can teach adolescents skills in managing a domestic partnership that can provide valuable preparation for a significant partnership later on.

6. *The challenge of finding and losing love.* Adolescents can be coping with the romantic intensity of first love, there can be significant emotional hurt should a breakup occur, and there can be feelings of distrust and rejection in the wake of love that was lost. Coping with this challenge can teach adolescents that love is risky and is not guaranteed to last forever, and that a broken heart can be mended.

7. *The challenge of living in a drug-filled world.* Adolescents can experience the desire to self-medicate pain or enhance pleasure through substance use, feel the pressure of party socializing that is fueled by drinking or other drugging, and have a substance-induced sense of freedom that momentarily lessens sober caring about what one says or does. Coping with this challenge can teach adolescents how to moderate alcohol and other drug use to avoid harmful effects.

8. *The challenge of indebtedness.* Newly independent adolescents often experience the difficulty of getting by on limited funds, have the temptation to treat credit cards

as free money because payment is deferred, and feel pressure to overspend to keep up with more freely spending friends. Coping with this challenge can teach adolescents about the work it takes to repay what is owed and the importance of living within their means.

9. *The challenge of stress*. Newly independent adolescents often have difficulty adjusting to the increased responsibilities that come with more independence and less parental support, the continual pressure of survival demands, and the costs of inadequate self-care. Coping with this challenge can teach adolescents how to operate efficiently, physically maintain themselves, and not create unnecessary pressure through overcommitment and procrastination.

10. *The challenge of emotional disturbance*. Some adolescents will experience unhappiness from adversity that can take emotional hold, have negative feelings that can overwhelm positive thinking, and feel distraught in ways that can diminish healthy functioning. Coping with this challenge can teach adolescents how to get help if needed, to recover from intense unhappiness, and to develop strategies for maintaining their emotional wellness.

11. *The challenge of future shock*. Newly independent adolescents may fear the future and facing what to do with their lives, feel diminished by the daunting demands of adult responsibility, and experience lowered confidence in their capacity to make their way in the world. Coping with this challenge can create pride in having what it takes to brave the unknown and chart and chance one's course through life.

Trial independence is a "trial" in two ways—"trial" as an *attempt* and "trial" as an *ordeal* because no young person grows through this refiner's fire of challenges entirely unscathed. Not only that, but it may take multiple trials to find a firm footing, and parents need to be patient with the process. When one or more of these eleven challenges come to crisis, it is common for the last-stage adolescent to *boomerang* back home for a temporary stay (in their twenties, maybe 30 to 40 percent of young people do), creating an opportunity for parents to be there to help them recover, reap the lessons of hard experience, and prepare to step off and try independence again.

It's important not to measure the progress of your son or daughter by the greater progress of other people's children the same age. Comparisons can make it hard for parents to be patient with a twenty-some-year-old who is still acting impulsively, immaturely, and irresponsibly. The parent's job is help the young person harness herself to young adulthood by providing her with firmness, faith, and mentoring support. Remember, there is no fixed schedule or one best path to independence. Adolescents need to find their own way at their own pace. To use the adage from Alcoholics Anonymous, what you want to see is "progress, not perfection." For more about coping with last-stage adolescents returning home, see my book *Boomerang Kids*.

### Boomerang Kids

These unexpected returns or "boomerangs" can prove difficult for parents. "Our twenty-three-year-old son finished his master's degree in business and then decided he wants to be a graphic artist instead. Because he was going to school in another city, we didn't know about this change of heart, or mind, until he moved back home. We have tried to treat him like an adult, but he complains about us all the time, about our taking money from his minimum-wage job to cover some of what it costs us to have him back. The job is in a custom printing shop, and he says it will teach him about the commercial art industry. He wants to move to San Francisco, but he says he can't because we take too much of what he earns. He is a bright, attractive, personable, and talented young man who is really scared of growing up. Our patience and our money are running out."

Having a last-stage adolescent move back home after having lived away can present parents with a complicated challenge. How can they house their returning son or daughter, on the one hand, and still encourage growth to independence, on the other? I believe they need to plan a stay that works for them so that they can feel positive about the support they give. This means that they need to be proactive in specifying and ratifying terms of household living for the returning adolescent who boomerangs home. For parents, a few specific talking points to be clarified at the outset include the following:

- Duration of stay
- Objectives to be accomplished while at home
- Household contributions to be made
- Rent (if any) to be paid
- Use of parental belongings and household resources (food, car, computer, TV)
- Allowable social entertaining
- Overnight guests
- Substance use
- Weekly schedule to be followed
- Routine information needs of parents

For the adolescent, among the conditions that need clarification include the following:

- Personal privacy needs of the young person
- Latitude of adult independence expected
- Freedom from parental supervision

- Financial support to be provided (personal expenses to be covered, such as medical and dental care, cell phone, Internet connectivity, car insurance)

Contracting up front so that parents and adolescent are operating on the same page can reduce misunderstanding and tension that get in the way of the mutually helpful relationship that needs to develop. Parents want to be of help to their adolescent, and they also want some evidence of self-help and of household help in return.

### Parental Mentoring

Some parents think that when their son or daughter graduates from high school, adolescence comes to an end, young adulthood begins, and their parenting is mostly over. Wrong! Better to heed Yogi Berra's warning: "It ain't over till it's over." What these parents often don't understand is that now the last and hardest stage of adolescence actually begins. Now young people are set loose to face the daunting task of having to live apart from family, to scramble to catch a responsible hold on life, and to begin to chart a path into the unknown future. Now they must keep a firm footing while they spread their wings; they must watch where they're going while they're not sure where they are headed; and they must act more maturely while they're making more mistakes. There is a lot to learn. To adolescent regret and parental dismay, this final lap around the adolescent track is when more serious missteps often occur.

Simply because the last-stage adolescent is older now doesn't mean he doesn't still need you to be involved in his life. In fact, because of the challenges that come with trial independence, you are needed more than ever before. However, you are needed in a different way—not to tell him what to do, but to help him figure out what to do, not as his boss, but to act more as his brain trust. At this last stage of adolescence, the ground rules for effective parenting significantly change. The age of *managerial parenting* is over, and the time for *mentoring parenting* has arrived. Now parents change their role from being managers (without being asked, imposing supervision and regulation) to becoming mentors (when asked, offering problem-solving consultation and advice). And this is usually a welcome change to their adolescent.

Come their son's or daughter's trial independence, parents have an opening for involvement they didn't have before. While still at home, the high school–age adolescent was mostly not inclined to ask for parental advice because that would mean admitting to ignorance or incapacity at a time when he wanted his parents to think all was firmly under control so that they would leave him alone. But moving out into more independence, young people suddenly encounter challenges of living on their own that they did not expect and for which they were not fully prepared. Suddenly they must confront the impact of their inexperience coping with more complicated demands, and as they do, their perception of parents tends to alter. These adults who were not credited with much knowledge worth offering when the young person was in high school suddenly become people valued for worldly experience they've had and practical advice they have to give. In trial independence, as a young person's confidence starts going down when catching hold proves difficult to do, appreciation of what parents know starts going up. Adolescent openness to parental mentoring is usually created by the separation from home and starting the struggle to lead a life apart from family. Now the old parental complaint comes to mind: "If only youth could hear what age has to tell!" Well, in trial independence, youth can begin to hear. "If only I'd listened to you before!" This opportunity to mentor, however, can be squandered by parents when they violate one or more of three mentoring rules.

**Mentoring Rule Number One:** No parental disapproval or criticism allowed.

Consider what happens when a parent is constantly finding fault. Impatient with the latest mishap in the life of the college-age child, the parent bursts out and says, "What's the matter with you? You're twenty-one years old, you keep making dumb decisions, and you still can't get your life together!" Unhappily, this charge only echoes the painful sense of failure the young person is harboring within herself: "What's the matter with me? I'm twenty-one years old, I keep making dumb decisions, and I can't get my life together!" Now receptiveness to much-needed mentoring is shut down because the young person can't bear additional recrimination when she is already heaping it on herself. So instead of parents berating, "I told you so!" they should say, "Let's think about what your set of choices is now." *Mentoring is based on acceptance, not censure.*

**Mentoring Rule Number Two:** Respect the adolescent's right to make decisions and his or her responsibility to learn from consequences.

Now consider what happens when parents go for control. Here the parents, anxious about the adolescent's free-living and increasingly costly ways, charge in to straighten out their adolescent's life. They may impose a regimen of parental regulation (a takeover), or they may engineer a rescue (a bailout), in both cases interfering with life lessons that could, and maybe should, be learned. Instead of parents ordering, "This is what you're going to do!" they should say, "We believe that how you live your life is up to you." *Mentoring respects autonomy.*

**Mentoring Rule Number Three:** Don't weigh in with opinion and advice without being asked.

Consider what happens when the parents always have something improving or correcting to say. Here the parents, confident that they know better, are continually making unsolicited suggestions about how better the adolescent can lead his life. Thinks the young person, "I want to lead my life without having to hear a constant flow of their opinions about what I could be doing differently for the best. It's my life to live, not theirs to direct!" So instead of parents barging in saying, "Here's what you should do!" they should say, "Let us know if we can help you think things through." *Advice is given by invitation only.*

To become mentors, parents have to shift position in relation to their son or daughter. Parents have to forsake their old managerial *vertical relationship* where authority placed them in a superior or dominant position from which they evaluated conduct, directed behavior, and dictated terms of living. In trial independence, when a son or daughter does not usually tolerate being judged, directed, or having terms of living dictated by parents, parents must reposition the relationship. To maintain a workable connection at this time, when this connection is sorely needed, parents need to establish a mentoring *horizontal relationship* where there is more equity between them, where they are living alongside each other on terms of mutual respect. The mentoring contract is this: *parents will respect the young person's right and responsibility to make independent decisions, and the young person will respect the wisdom of life experience the parents can offer.*

The parents who have the hardest time shifting from a vertical (managerial) to a horizontal (mentoring) relationship tend to be more authoritarian. They want to control, they insist on their rules, they are intolerant of opposition, they know best, they are always right, they insist on taking charge, and they are committed to getting their way. Parents so constituted are often loath to relinquish their managerial role, which they now need to do. To effectively mentor, they must alter their dominant ways. To be an effective mentor means that as parents you are emotionally approachable. You express

- Faith, not doubt ("I believe in you.")
- Patience, not irritation ("Keep after it.")
- Consultation, not criticism ("You might try this.")

- Confidence, not worry ("You have the capacity it takes!")
- Empathy, not disappointment ("It's hard to manage independence.")

Finally, mentoring takes patience because young people can have such mixed feelings about independence. They can become disillusioned about the reality of independence, and so are ambivalent about it. They really want to be responsibly self-sufficient and to operate on their own, yet they really don't. They want to take care of themselves, and they still want to be taken care of. This is why, when respectfully done, parental mentoring can help them move through this period of disillusionment and ambivalence and claim young adult standing at last.

## The Myth of Independence

Life is full of illusions. Beliefs one develops or are taught become sources of great disappointment, even betrayal, when they turn out not to be true. Consider one of the grand illusions of adolescence: "When I reach independence, I can run my life." After all, isn't that the goal of the whole turbulent adolescent process, to be able to operate on one's own grown-up terms? But now, in counseling with young adults in their mid-twenties, what I hear is not a cry of triumph, "Free at last!" but a moan of despair, "Now my life is all up to me!" What happened?

The sad reality is this: when parental authority lets go and steps aside, "the system" takes over. What the young person discovers is that parental protection provided a measure of shelter in which direct exposure to the more complex and arbitrary demands of social authority were kept at bay. This awareness makes for a rude awakening. By comparison to these impersonal forces of social conformity and social compliance, parental attitudes were more caring, parental demands were far fewer, and parental rules were more forgiving.

Now having to pay bills, to hold a job, to make one's way through the world all revise some ideas about basic freedoms that the adolescent was looking forward to, but which the young adult now discovers are really fraudulent ideals. When it comes to freedom of action, the young adult realizes, "I am not free to do whatever I want." When it comes to freedom of individuality, she discovers, "I am not free to be totally myself." When it comes to freedom of speech, he finds out, "I am not free to totally speak my mind." When it comes to freedom of future, she sees, "I am not free to achieve anything I want." When it comes to freedom to get a meaningful job, he thinks, "I am not free to find one that pays a lot of money or is personally fulfilling." To get along, sometimes one has to go along; to fit in, sometimes one has to accommodate; to communicate, sometimes one has to shut up; to make one's way, sometimes one has to take what one can get. As one young man concluded, "About the only real freedom I have now is dealing with any troubles I get into by myself." In so many words, what the young man concluded was this: "I'll never really be as free as an adult as I was as a teenager. Back then, I could rebel, I could question authority, I could ignore some home rules, I could stand out from the crowd, I didn't have to watch what I said, and I didn't have to worry about being on my own. What I wanted, I already had, but I didn't know it at the time—the freedom to have parents who protected me from adult responsibility." And you can also understand his sense of anger. He really felt betrayed by what he was led to believe over the course of his adolescence. Someone had sold him a bill of goods about independence, and that someone turned out to be himself. And now the final battle of adolescence begins.

## The Final Battle for Independence

When it comes to young people navigating the last (and hardest) stage of adolescence, trial independence, I believe Simon and Garfunkel had it right: "The closer your destination, the more you're slip sliding away." Why is that? I believe *ambivalence* and *disillusionment* are the answers. The goal of independence looked so alluring when the journey of adolescence began back in late elementary or early middle school. Come the end of high school, however, independence takes on a much more daunting aspect. Most young people feel unready stepping off into the final stage of adolescence, when they must keep their footing while they try their wings. To their dismay, what they discover in so many painful ways is how "freedom" is not "free."

The primary agent of ambivalence at this age is *procrastination*. Young people put off what they know needs to be done because if it is accomplished in a timely way, it will only bring them closer to the dreaded state of independence that in some ways they want and in other ways they don't. This is the crowning irony of adolescence—it begins and ends with rebellion against authority. The early adolescent resists adult authority, declaring through words or actions, "You can't make me!" And the young person in the last stage of adolescence, trial independence, resists authority as well, but now it is against their own—a lonely, frustrating, self-defeating struggle against their procrastination: "I can't make me!" That old lament immortalized by cartoonist Walt Kelly now rings painfully true: "We have met the enemy, and they are us!" So the last-stage adolescent struggles with *type-one procrastination*—putting work off and so putting themselves under deadline stress in order to get it done at the last minute. And they struggle with *type-two procrastination*—putting work off until inadequate time remains, and failing to get it done at all. Altering either habit requires practicing an earlier start the next time around, but if one must procrastinate, type one is preferable to type two because the consequences of type-two procrastination are usually more severe.

Now the complex demands of independence turn into something unexpectedly hard because the only way to truly claim independence is by assuming self-reliance—making one's own choices and dealing with one's own consequences with no evasion, excuses, or blame. However, this responsibility can be hard to take at a time when to some degree most young people find themselves unprepared, breaking commitments, making mistakes, lacking direction, feeling lonely, falling in and out of love, debt spending, feeling overstressed, fearing the future, indulging in extremes, exhilarated by freedom, escaping from obligations, living in the moment, and having maximum access to alcohol and other drugs.

So the final battle for independence in adolescence is the young person against himself. Now he must come to terms with ambivalence and disillusionment, fighting to defeat the forces of procrastination and accepting the hardships of coping on one's own, until somehow, some way, with a grudging gathering of responsibility, he mostly overcomes these obstacles, and liberating (but costly) independence is claimed at last. And now the reality of young adult independence can recoil back on parents in ways they did not expect.

When their adolescent finally moves off into a self-supporting and self-directed life, parents can face their own ambivalence about independence. Of course this outcome is what they've worked for. They always meant to work themselves out of the child-raising job. However, now that they have, their young adult is so busy building a life apart from them that they hardly get to see her anymore, they communicate far less, and they find they have been moved to the periphery of her social life, when they used to be so central to it. They have been demoted! It's not that they are loved any less, but they have less present standing as preoccupation with her life and other relationships take priority attention. As one mother summed it up, "I worked so hard to help my daughter become independent, and now that she is, she acts more independent of me!" Yes, that's how it works. The reward for successfully helping an adolescent son or daughter reach independence is some degree of parental loss.

A huge amount of growing up occurs during late adolescence and trial independence. During the high school years, parents have a lot of preparation to give to help the adolescent get ready for the next measure of independence ahead. After the young person leaves home, they have a lot of letting go to do and a lot of mentoring to offer should they be asked. For both teenager and for parents, adolescence gets harder the further along in the process one grows. And all the way through, whether one is mothering or fathering a teenage daughter or a teenage son, there is complexity of demands important for parents to understand. These issues are set forth in the next chapter.

## Chapter Four

# Parenting Adolescent Sons and Daughters

"How would you know how to parent a daughter," I told my husband. "It takes a mom to really understand a girl!" "Well, maybe it takes a dad to really understand a son!" was his reply. And we're into again about how we approach the kids so differently since they've become teenagers. And they relate so differently to each of us. What's the problem? Why can't we parent more alike?

Come adolescence, not all parenting is the same. In significant ways, a father is not a mother, and a mother is not a father. In significant ways, fathering a teenage son raises different parenting issues than fathering a teenage daughter; and mothering a teenage son raises different parenting issues than mothering a teenage daughter. Understanding these differences and why they often exist can suggest how each adult can constructively parent a teenage son and a teenage daughter. All the while, keep in mind that the *differences I am describing are tendencies, not certainties*. To start, we'll take a look at some general differences between mothering and fathering.

## How Mothering and Fathering Are Different

At the outset of the infant's life, the mother is the more sacrificial and connected parent. How could it be otherwise? She bears, she births, she even breastfeeds the child—in the process creating a mutual sense of attachment and obligation that is deep and mysterious. Mother and child begin bonded, they are emotionally directed toward sensitivity and knowing, and they share a powerful intimacy. Feelings of familiarity breed a sense of acceptance, often causing *the mother to become the more **relationally** focused parent* in the years ahead, the one who may be more often inclined with adolescents to focus on the concern question, "How are you feeling?"

In contrast, at the outset of the infant's life, the father is the more distant and disconnected parent. A stranger to the infant, he starts unattached as an outsider, before birth supporting the child by supporting the mother, afterwards creating closeness by touching, talking, and tending to build familiarity and trust. He must learn and earn his way into attachment with an infant, who must do the same with him. Hence it is approval that brings them close as they act to please each other, often causing *the father to become the more **performance**-focused parent*, the one who may be more often inclined with adolescents to focus on the evaluative question, "How are you doing?"

Reinforcing this relational-performance distinction can be how the mother and father were socialized in same-sex peer groups growing up. With girl peers, the mother may have relied on personal disclosure and providing empathy to cement friendships. There was a relational focus as communication and confiding created closeness. They talked about themselves a lot together. With boy peers, the father may have relied on sharing interests and adventures to cement friendships. There was a performance focus as companionship and competition created closeness. They did a lot of activities together. Both avenues to closeness—communication and companionship—work, but they are different.

For children, the father's greater distance coupled with his focus on performance can amplify the power of his authority and approval, while the mother's greater closeness coupled with her relational focus can increase her power to nurture and comfort.

In counseling, this difference in parental focus is sometimes rec-ognized by an adolescent who says, "I talk more with my mom about my friendships and problems, and with my dad more about how things are going and what I plan to do."

Again, this doesn't mean that many mothers can't have a strong performance focus or that many fathers can't have a sensitive relational focus, only that this relational-performance distinction often seems to differentiate their parental roles. In addition, women still remain the more involved parents, at least as reflected by the percentages of female and male single-parent heads of household, according to the U.S. Census: about 80 percent are mothers; about 20 percent are fathers. So not only do mothers begin the child's life as the more sacrificial, attached, and connected parent, they usually remain the more committed parent as well.

Because adolescence is a ten- to twelve-year process that begins with the separation from childhood and ends with the departure into young adult independence, your challenge as a parent is to keep the connection with your growing son or daugh-ter while adolescence is causing you and your child to grow apart. For the mother, it can be easier to stay attached and harder to let go. I often hear the teenage complaint about a "controlling" or "overprotective" mother. For the father, it can be easier to pull away and harder to stay connected. The teenager then complains about the "distant" or "unavailable" father. In many cases, at least in the eyes of their adolescent, mothers often hold on too tightly, and fathers often let go too much.

There can also be a significant difference in how mothers and fathers approach and manage that hallmark behavior of parent-ing adolescents—dealing with *conflict*. Between wanting more freedom, experimenting with more individuality, and demanding to live more on their own terms, adolescents usually provoke increased conflict in the family. More often than not, because they are more wed to communication and are relationally trained, mothers tend to be more tolerant of the emotional intensity aroused by conflict. They can be more at ease hanging in there with a hostile or argumentative adolescent than fathers who are more uncomfortable with the emotional intensity and more competitive in disagreement, and who want to prevail, avoid confrontation, or shut it down. Dealing with conflict is a communication and relational skill; engaging in combat is a competition and performance skill. This distinction can characterize how mothers and fathers broker differences in wants and opinions with their stormy adolescent—the mother listening to understand, the father challenged to win. When family conflict is allowed to turn into combat (where victory is all that matters), there is heightened risk that safety will be sacrificed and damage may be done.

Often the mother, taking a relational approach to opposition, treats the *teenager as an informant* and the disagreement between them as a talking point for further discussion, with a goal to open up and better understand the issue between them. She takes a collaborative approach, treating conflict as an opportunity to learn more about her adolescent and to strengthen the relationship by resolving something together. Often the father, taking a performance approach, treats the *teenager as an opponent* and the disagreement between them as a contest over dominance, with the goal to assert parental authority, fighting to stay in charge. He takes a more aggressive approach, treating conflict as an opportunity to show the adolescent who is the boss by settling the disagreement on the man's terms. For the mother, conflict can bring out her connecting side; for the father, conflict can bring out his controlling side.

In general, from what I have seen in family counseling, a more "female" approach to conflict with adolescents seems to work better than the "male." However, mother-daughter conflicts and father-son conflicts often have different core issues at stake. For mother and daughter, the issue is more relational: how can a daughter remain emotionally connected to her mother but emerge as a distinct woman of her own. For father and son, the issue is usually more about performance: how can a son measure up to the father but still follow his independent agenda. In both cases, the adolescent needs the parental blessing. "While we started your life and helped shape your life, whatever you choose to do with your life is up to you. Please know that we will love you as always, as the person you are, no matter what differences in our ways of living there may be, as we hope you will always love us."

Adolescent pain in response to mothers and fathers can also be quite different too. When the mother is the more relationally focused and sacrificial parent, self-blame over failed obligation can inspire guilt in the older adolescent and young adult. "I didn't give back to my mother enough for all she's done for me." "I don't treat my mother all the ways she would like." When the father is the more performance-focused and evaluative parent, self-blame over failed achievement can inspire shame in older adolescents and young adults. "I didn't turn out as well as my father wanted." "I don't measure up to the expectations my father set." With both parents there can be the issue of "not enough"— not enough deserved repayment in the eyes of the mother, not enough earned worth in the eyes of the father.

It's an oversimplification, but adolescents may look for concern primarily from the mother, the relational parent who is often identified as a source of emotional support, and for approval from the father, the performance parent who is often identified as a source of evaluation. It can prove emotionally costly for the young person when neither maternal concern nor paternal approval is forthcoming, when one has a consistently unfeeling mother or a consistently critical father. (Again, the relational-performance distinction is a tendency, not a certainty, as there are many relationally sensitive fathers and many performance-focused mothers.)

Finally, each parent provides the dominant sex-role model in the family, the mother as a prime example of how to define oneself as a woman, wife, and mom, the father as a prime example of how to define oneself as a man, husband, and dad. The challenge for each parent is to express both relational and performance sides—listening and coaching, talking with and doing with, confiding in and enjoying friendly competition with each other. Neither parent has to be limited to one aspect or the other. In fact, by embodying and expressing both, they encourage their adolescents to do the same. However, to the degree that a dad is more performance focused and a mom more relationally focused, how they parent a teenage daughter and a teenage son can raise different fathering and mothering issues, which are described in the sections that follow.

## Fathering an Adolescent Daughter

Fathering a little daughter who adores being "Daddy's girl" is much easier than fathering an adolescent daughter who is now developing into a more independent young woman and wants to be treated that way. "What way?" wonders a father. The answer: when in doubt, he should ask his daughter. She is his best informant and guide about how to navigate the change in their relationship from her childhood into adolescence, particularly after puberty, when gender definition becomes a more focal concern. In general, he needs to stop treating her as a little girl and start treating her as a young woman, and he needs to know how. For example, the silly jokes he told that used to delight her are now irritating, even embarrassing, or are, in her words, "really lame." It now takes longer for her to attend to her appearance before going out, and he needs to be patient with the additional preparation time. Just because he doesn't value constantly talking with his friends to stay in current touch doesn't mean he should discount all the communication she needs with female peers to keep herself well connected socially. In adolescence, her significant world of experience usually becomes more relationally focused than his. And of course he needs to understand that she needs more privacy and more clothes than she did as a little girl.

Because the father has no direct experience with the female way, one challenge in fathering a teenage daughter is to stay connected as her gender differentiation into young womanhood starts growing them apart. Fathers should consider these five possible ways to keep their relationship with their daughters together.

1. The father can confess ignorance about growing up female and express interest in learning what emerging womanhood is like (not in so many words, of course, which would just make her squirm, but instead by asking for help in understanding the importance of female friendships, for example).

2. The father could respond to his daughter as a person with whom he shares certain similar human traits (how both are alike in being stubborn and strong willed and in letting their opinions be known, for example).

3. The father could indicate that he values the gender definition she is developing (how she is sought out for help and is treated as a social leader among her friends, for example).

4. The father could support the advancement of her interests (encouraging and even coaching to strengthen skills she is working to develop or help achieve goals she is striving to reach, for example).

5. The father could welcome disagreement with his daughter and conduct it safely, treating argument as an opportunity to openly discuss some opposition between them (by treating conflict as a talking point to get to know how she sees what happened differently than he does, for example).

What does not work is for the father, out of awkwardness or in willful ignorance, to allow sex-role contrast to become cause for dismissal and estrangement: "Now that she's no longer a little girl, we have no good way to be together anymore." Such a response can cause her to feel discounted in his eyes: "When I became a teenager, my father lost interest in me, maybe because I wasn't into guy things like him and my brothers continued to be." Particularly with adolescent daughters, fathers who have a pronounced performance focus need to broaden their perspective to show an appreciation of the whole person that their daughter is becoming. Otherwise, you get the daughter who confides, "My sports and grades are all my dad ever asks about. He's not interested in the rest of my life, which is most of it."

There are risks when this dismissal and consequent estrangement occur and the dad pretty much leaves the daughter's parenting to the mother. There is the risk that the daughter will experience the father's inability to accept and respect her female path and more relational focus on friends as disapproval. Feeling not worthy of serious attention because she lacks those male performance values and interests that her father holds most important, she can end up feeling treated, as one young woman put it, "like a second-class child." Further risk occurs when, denied this paternal affirmation, she may place herself at a disadvantage trying to compensate for the attention her father did not provide by doing what she can to please other men. Daughters with disinterested, estranged, or absent fathers often end up looking for that missing male affirmation in the wrong places— with immature male peers or older guys who may exploit an unmet need.

The role of the father is to be the *salient male presence* in the life of his adolescent daughter, who learns from him in three formative ways:

1. He provides the primary definition of how men should act and how they should be expected to treat women.
2. How he treats the daughter's mother provides a primary example of how a man conducts himself in a caring relationship with a woman.

3. How he values and respects his daughter teaches the young woman a lot about what to value and respect in herself.

A wonderful example of how a dad provided a salient male presence for his high school–age daughter was once told to me by a woman in her thirties looking back on her early dating years. This is what she described. "I used to hate it! But no matter how much I complained to my dad, he wouldn't stop doing it. Whenever a guy came over to take me out, it didn't matter if he'd taken me out before, my dad would take him into the kitchen. There, my dad would ask about our plans for the evening, and then he would say something like this to the guy: 'Our daughter is very important to us. I am entrusting you with her welfare tonight, and I expect you to respect that trust by returning her by the time agreed, in as good condition as when she left. Any questions?' There never were. 'Fine,' said my dad. 'Go and have a good responsible time.' Like I said, as a teenager I hated it when he took my dates to the kitchen, but looking back I really appreciate it now. All those high school dating years, and not one guy ever gave me a problem because everyone who took me out knew they had to answer to my dad for my safekeeping!"

## Fathering an Adolescent Son

Fathering a little son who wants nothing so much as to be "just like my dad" is much easier than fathering an adolescent son who wants to follow his own agenda and be his own man. "Now that he's a teenager, he doesn't want to do the father-son stuff we used to do with each other anymore," explains the father, saddened by the loss of companionship with his old buddy. "The things I love to do, that I taught him to enjoy, that we shared in common all those years—they're mostly gone. Now he's into activities that don't interest me, so we don't have good ways to be together anymore." This disconnection doesn't have to necessarily be so. The dad is missing the point.

It can be a hard for some fathers to adjust to the reversal of terms that needs to take place after a son turns adolescent (usually starting around ages nine to thirteen) if they are to stay well connected during the remaining teenage years. When he was younger, the little boy wanted to relate on terms that interested his father because being similar to his father created a sense of closeness to the man he wanted to imitate. For example, because the dad loved fishing, the son did too. When that boy became an adolescent, however, it became time to let go childish things and develop older, alternative interests to claim his individuality and independence. Now fishing seems boring compared to skateboarding, which is exciting. Instead of sitting still on a boat in the water waiting for fish to bite with his father, the teenager finds surfing urban streets and ramps and jumping curbs with skater friends more challenging to do. Plus the outlaw image of the urban sport, and how he dresses for it, have a renegade appeal. He carries his own wheels. Or suppose the son who grew up a fan of his father's country music now comes to love hip-hop instead, a more percussive kind of sound not suited to his father's taste.

To stay connected at this transition, it's time for the father to *bridge adolescent differences with interest* and relate on terms that matter to his teenage son. This doesn't mean he has to buy a skateboard too. However, it does mean taking an active interest in his son's new interest, being curious to learn about it by being open to be taught. Now their traditional roles are reversed, as he becomes the student and his son the teacher, the young man feeling respected in this new instructional role. "You know more about skateboarding than I ever will," declares the dad, and the son with some sense of pride agrees. The same holds true for musical differences that develop as the man listens to songs foreign to his ears, has their appeal patiently explained, and the artists described. Again, the teacher-student role is reversed, the father now looking to his son to explain what the young man's emerging world of experience is like. Even in conflict, the more often the father can treat his son as an informant, and the less often as an opponent, the better off their relationship will tend to be. So the man profits from disagreement by learning more about his son from the exchange. As one dad put it, "I've learned to treat any argument as a chance to talk and get to know what my son is thinking and what he wants and why."

An adolescent son growing into young manhood is often in a bind with his father, and it is this. The child son wants to glorify the man, but when he does, come time for adolescence, he has built his dad up into such a hero figure that there is no way the teenager can measure up to the adult exemplar he has worshipfully created. So what is the adolescent to do? Somehow, some way, he must cut his father down to human size; but in doing so he loses his ideal, even growing angry at his father for the loss. Now he finds grounds—frailties and flaws and failings in his father—that help diminish the man. Increased criticism from the adolescent goes to show that his dad is not so perfect after all.

Most fathers are destined to be a disappointment to their sons, who must blame and then forgive their dad for failing to perform up to a standard that was never really meant to be. To further reduce the discrepancy between them, the son can grow himself in ways his father never did, excelling at what his father did not or cannot do. In this process of paternal downsizing, a father can help by admitting mistakes, apologizing for wrongdoing, declaring his limitations and ignorance, and even putting down his own efforts in a humorous way. He can also upsize his son by complimenting the young man, pointing out what the teenager can do that the man cannot, and recognizing his son's expertise by asking for the help of the young man's special strengths and skills. "Since you built your own bike, maybe you can help me fix mine."

Then there is father-son competition—power tests (which can be good) and power struggles (which can be bad).

Adolescent sons usually need to go up against their fathers to measure themselves against them. Power tests of skills provide for safe competition; power struggles for control risk extreme measures that can result in injury. When competition is played out through friendly contests, the boy testing his skill and knowledge against the more experienced and competent man, the outcome can be beneficial to the relationship between boy and man. Encouraging while they play, the father recognizes and praises the young man's growing skills, and takes pleasure when the son honestly prevails. "When you win, we both win!" Two criteria for healthy power tests are that the son gains competence and self-esteem, and the father-son relationship is strengthened from competition that never becomes so serious that it ruins the fun of play. And they compete at what they each are better at—so the father may challenge the son to a game of chess, and the son may challenge the dad to a computer game. In either case, the father must not turn a power test into a power struggle for male dominance.

Power struggles are another matter. When the issue becomes one of control over the son's life, over the choices he makes related to friends or school achievement or future direction, the father may pit his way against his son's way. Now what matters most to the father is asserting his authority, proving that he is in charge, dominating at all costs, and getting his way. At this point, harsh tactics like intimidation, humiliation, and even punishing physical force can be employed by the father to show the son who is boss. It's a contest firmly anchored in the male performance ethic as each refuses to back down. If the father is committed to win at all costs, when he wins, he risks losing on two counts. He may lose love from the son due to the injury that unbridled conflict has caused. And he may lose power through creating an isometric encounter with his son, the young man becoming stronger after each conflict by pushing full strength against his father's greater strength. In this process, the son learns to act like his father, growing equally determined.

The most serious father-son conflicts I see in counseling are those in which the father pushes his agenda of resemblance ("My way is the right way!") so hard that the teenage son feels duty bound to resist ("My life is up to me!"). Now the adolescent son will even rebel against self-interest to oppose his father, failing in high school and hurting his future to spite the educational agenda of his father. Of course the ultimate outcome is always the same. Through active and passive resistance, the son ultimately prevails because in the end, when it comes to adolescent independence, parents never defeat the teenager. The teenager always defeats the parent.

For the adolescent son, his relationship to his father is complicated because it is so conflicted. He wants to measure up to his father, often wanting to follow his father's lead to gain his father's approval through similarity to the man's wishes; yet he also wants to strike out on an independent and individual path and be defined and accepted on his own terms. And it can become further complicated should he want to be better or do better than his father, to fulfill aspirations that his father never could. Hence the young man in counseling explains what motivated his achievement: "I did better than my dad so he could do better through me."

Therefore, just as a father should not discount a teenage daughter for not being similar enough to him, the father should not demand excessive similarity to him on the part of his son. Should the father do so, the young man may pay a high price for independence: "My father treated me as a failure as a son for not succeeding to be a man like him." This is why the son needs the father's blessing: "I love and respect the man you have chosen to become." This reminds me of a father, who had seen no active military service himself, who spent long hours at his returning son's bedside sorrowfully listening to the son painfully recounting his nightmarish experience in a foreign war. The son was grateful. "It was my dad who helped me find my way back home."

## Mothering an Adolescent Son

When he was a small child, the son found spending time with his mother, going places with his mother, talking with his mother, being hugged by his mother all to be pleasurable things to do. The closeness between them felt right—a continuation of the founding attachment to the nurturing parent who bore him and gave him birth. But this enjoyment of special closeness with his mom starts to change with the separation, differentiation, and opposition of adolescence that drive him toward more independence, and particularly with the onset of puberty when he begins the work of defining himself as a young man. Part of this definition requires becoming different from a woman, particularly the primary woman in his life, his mother. He has no such gender distinction to make with his dad.

Growing up requires giving up for both mother and son. Each must let something precious go, but the mother usually feels the sacrifice more because at least her adolescent son has the excitement and satisfaction of growing older to look forward to, while she may mourn the years of easy attachment that have been lost. She will never have her son as little boy again. As for the son, he felt more relaxed with his mother in childhood than he does during adolescence, a much more complicated time. Now the powerful female presence of his mother can feel too close for comfort, threatening to compromise and overwhelm the fragile sense of manhood that starts emerging with puberty. Thus the time to assert gender difference from his mom has arrived. For example, it's hard to feel like a young man when being bossed by his mom. "Don't tell me what to do!" he protests, feeling momentarily diminished by having her "order him around." He accepted her female authority as a little boy, but feels more obliged to resist it as a young man. He can resent having a "controlling" mother as much as he can resent have a "criticizing" dad.

To be manly, he needs to be different from her, and this difference is commonly expressed in three ways. First, he creates more social distance from her, having less contact and communication to show more independence from her than before. Now he may want to spend more time in male company, with his male friends, even with his dad. Second, he creates more contrast to her, developing growing interests that show he has less in common with her than before. Now he may take up more aggressive activities and entertainment that his mother would not pursue. Third, he creates more opposition to her, arguing to show that he is more willing to take on her authority. Now he criticizes her decisions and questions her capacity to understand who and how he is becoming.

In all three cases, he needs to create room from this primal female force to let his manliness develop. Understanding this need to pull away, his mother shouldn't take this as a personal rejection or as a statement that their relationship has ceased to matter. Rather, she should respect his need and at the same time keep up her initiative to stay in active relationship with him, continually inviting him into communication so that he knows she is not pulling away from him. And sometimes he will briefly accept her invitation. Just because he may become less open to physical affection and be less communicative doesn't mean that he has lost any love for his mother or any need for his mother, only comfort in the company of his mother. It can be an awkward time for the adolescent son—to stay close enough to his female parent to feel well connected, but distant enough from her to develop his growing maleness.

For example, he may think that to be a man, he can't be a "mommy's boy," can't be dominated by his mother, can't be too similar to his mother, can't confide as much in his mother, can't spend as much time with his mother. The threat he feels is not of her making, but his own.

Fortunately, there are usually moments, welcome to them both, when feeling more secure of himself or missing the old companionship, the adolescent son will lapse into former openness with his mother before returning to the challenge of developing his sense of manhood in response to her womanhood again. So for many mothers and adolescent sons, the teenage years are a more complicated time for them to get along. Now fighting more with his mom can come to the rescue. For example, a teenage son, sad at distancing from his mother and still missing contact with her, may start an argument. In this case, conflict can feel like a manly and aggressive way for the young man to be with his mother. It allows him to challenge her and feel connected with her at the same time. This dance of closeness and distance brings them together while keeping them opposed and apart over a difference between them, where he asserts himself and stands his ground as they communicate about it and connect.

The rule for the mother on these occasions is this: *no nervous smiles or laughs, no cutting off or cutting down allowed.* She needs to treat these challenges seriously and with respect, because going up against her can be very hard for a young man to do. Of course, having stated her position in the disagreement, she does not have to keep arguing back, only to attend to his arguments and objections so that he is given a full hearing, establishing her standing as a committed listener to whatever he has to say.

How he manages conflict with her, however, does require her supervision. She must not only model behavior she wants him to learn but also monitor his communication both for her sake and for his, taking issue when emotional intensity drives it out of safe and civil bounds. "When you call me mean names because I won't agree to what you want, we have two problems. First, you are wounding me with words, and that is not acceptable. In this family, we don't use language to do each other harm. For the sake of our relationship, you must find a respectful way to express frustration with me. And second, for the sake of your future, hurting me now may hurt you then. If I let you mistreat me and you come to feel that that is okay, you are likely to do the same when in conflict with another woman you care about later on, someone who may end the relationship rather than put up with being mistreated."

When a teenage son is not comfortable just talking with his mother, when conflict has become a tiresome approach to communication, or when distance feels lonely, some mothers (wisely I think) opt for other ways to connect that do not necessitate a lot of conversation. They choose more "doing with" than "talking with" approaches to maintaining the relationship. They understand that companionship is as viable a way for connecting as conversing is. "Let's take a break," she suggests, "and we can do something fun together." And they go out to see a movie of his choosing together.

Sometimes a mother will look at how her adolescent son is growing and feel offended or at least concerned by the "manly" behaviors and beliefs he is learning from male peers—like tough-talking and expressing sexist attitudes. Adolescent boys often engage in "tough-talk" with each other. They do this to learn the push and shove of aggressive speech by which they regulate matters of power and standing in their relationships. When these behaviors are brought home, a mother may have something to say. While respecting his need to hold his own with peers, she may restrict that use of language within the family. "I understand that you and your buddies like to kid and challenge each other with that kind of talk, but I don't want any of us speaking to each other that way at home."

If her son, like many boys, grew up mostly in the company of male peers, entering adolescence without having had meaningful friendships with girls, he may have learned some developmental sexism along the way. He may have learned from other guys what young women stereotypically are like and what things they supposedly like that are not really so. Hearing some of these derogatory or exploitive attitudes expressed, his mother, speaking as the primary woman in his life, may choose to question what is said and offer an alternative perspective that encourages a healthier approach to relating with young women. Of course, the father can and should do the same. This course correction is important because the time for socializing with and dating the other sex will soon arrive. The adolescent's mother is not only the primary role model for being a woman and how a woman should be treated but also a primary female informant about understanding and respecting women in general.

Finally, there is this twist that goes back to a parental role distinction made at the outset of this chapter. There I suggested how the mother often tends to be the relational parent focused more on what needs to be communicated, and the father often tends to be the performance parent focused more on what needs to be accomplished. To the degree that this distinction holds, although the teenage son may complain about his mother talking too much or "always wanting to talk," in fact it is often she who is the parent he will approach when there is a significant concern to discuss. So in counseling, a young man may say, "My mom is easier to talk to about a problem because she's willing to listen. My dad just wants to do something about it right away." So when a painful romantic breakup occurs for her son in high school, it is usually the mom to whom the young man goes for solace and understanding, not the dad.

## Mothering an Adolescent Daughter

Over my years in counseling, I have found that mother–adolescent daughter relationships are often the most deeply conflicted and intense. Why? I think it is because adolescent girls have a more complicated sex-role passage in the family than do sons, and moms are usually more intimately involved in this passage than dads.

Think of it this way. Two major attributes that affect parent-child connections are social attachment and sexual similarity. The more attached and the more similar, often the stronger the bond. By bearing, birthing, and (often) breastfeeding, mothers start with more attachment to children than do fathers. As for sexual similarity, it connects mothers to daughters, and fathers to sons, because each pair shares the same sexual identity.

Over the course of adolescence, issues of attachment versus separation and issues of similarity versus differentiation are contested by the young person to establish independence and individuality. So for independence, the adolescent wants more freedom from family restraint, wants time with friends more than time with family, and wants more privacy and less communication with parents. And for differentiation, the adolescent declares that he or she is now different than he or she was as a child, wants to be treated differently than as a child, is different from how parents are, and is going to be different from how they want that young person to be. So there!

Now consider the complexity of what an adolescent daughter has to do to claim independence and individuality. First, she has a double connection to break with her mother; second, she has a double disconnection with her father to overcome. Her tasks are to stay connected to a dad with whom she was not by birth attached and from whom she is sexually different, and to separate from a mom to whom she was born attached and with whom she is sexually similar. By comparison, the son has a relatively simpler passage, having only a single connection to break with the mother because although by birth attached, he is already sexually different. And he has a single disconnection to overcome with his father, as he was not by birth attached to the man, but does feel connected through the sexual similarity they share.

*The mother-daughter relationship is the only doubly close parent-child relationship in the family—they are by birth attached, and they are sexually similar.* I believe this double closeness is the reason that in the daughter's adolescence it can be so extremely hard to separate for adequate independence and to differentiate for adequate individuality in relation to her mother. It can take a lot of strain on the relationship to break mother and daughter free.

In counseling, a teenage daughter (already attached and sexually similar to her mom) expresses her need for separation and differentiation as an independent woman. "I'm not you, I don't want to be like you, I never will be, just leave me alone!"

But beneath this statement of defiance is an unspoken communication that staying in conflict with her mother conveys. "I need to be independent of you and different from you, but still stay closely connected to you, so don't pull away, don't abandon me!" Witnessing these encounters in counseling is like watching a young woman fighting for her psychological life against the woman who gave it to her.

Sometimes in counseling, a dad who is uncomfortable with conflict will criticize the mom for "always getting into it" with the teenage daughter. "Why can't you just leave each other alone?" he asks, wishing for more peace and quiet. To which the mother replies, "Because the last thing she needs from me right now is to be left alone. She needs to work out the differences between us, and I intend to hang in there with her when she wants to challenge me or disagree." Among other things, engaging in conflict can be an act of intimacy when opposing parties communicate significant feelings and thoughts about some difference between them, coming to know each other and be known more deeply than before. So mother and daughter spend long hours in argument over the young woman's new boyfriend—the daughter wanting the mother to understand his good points, the mother wanting the daughter to understand his possibly harmful side. As they learn more about the boyfriend from each other, they learn more about the different values and perspectives between them. In this way, conflict can also be a process for creating acceptance of significant differences in the relationship. The mom respects the daughter's love; the daughter hears and considers her mom's concerns.

Of course, for the daughter fighting to be different from her mother, there is always this trap: conflict can create resemblance. It's complicated. When opposition leads to imitation, the daughter employing the mother's tactics in conflict against her, unwanted similarity can result. For example, by criticizing the critical mother back, by fighting for control against the controlling mother, by yelling when yelled at, the daughter unwittingly becomes like the mother whose example she has sworn never to follow. That's the dark side of similarity, but there is also positive side. Because it creates commonality, similarity can also strengthen feelings of affiliation and engender closeness. After all, a mom's model can be a positively compelling one to follow. "I'm my mother's daughter. I learned to stand my ground and speak my mind from how she always did with me and how I did with her." By example and interaction, parents (particularly of the same sex) can be indelibly instructive.

All this said, because the ability to engage in conflict is a relational skill, women often tend to be better schooled in it and more willing to endure it than men, who may be better trained in combat, a performance skill, and may be more at risk of resorting to inappropriate and injurious combat skills in family conflict. Of course, how the mother conducts conflict with her daughter is of the utmost importance. The woman must model the kind of constructive dialogue in disagreement that she wants her daughter to use with her and by practice carry forward into their future together, where there will always be differences to bridge.

What you don't want is the situation where a mother won't let go of her daughter and allow independence or won't accept her daughter's lifestyle and respect her individuality. In these unhappy cases, alienation can build, estrangement can follow, and a stubborn rift can grow. "We didn't support her graduate education to have her become a stay-at-home mom!" Of course, accepting individuality and establishing independence are two-way streets. Mother and daughter need both from each other to establish an adult relationship in which, by valuing the differences and respecting the distance between them, the two women can enjoy what they have in common and can lovingly get along. The greatest testimony to mother courage I hear is an older adolescent or young adult daughter saying, "My mom was willing to do as much conflict with me as I wanted. She hung in there with me. Somehow she knew that it was never really about anger, although I was angry a lot of the time. It was about my need to be my own woman and still depend on her loyalty and love."

Parenting adolescent sons and daughters can challenge mothers and fathers in different ways. Just as relationally focused mothers can have a harder time letting go and separating from their teenagers, performance-focused fathers can have a harder time staying involved and connected with their teenagers. The trick for each parent is to use his or her gender preparation to contribute to the adolescent's growth without allowing that sex-role training to limit a fuller range of parenting. A skill that is essential for both mother and father to maintain with their adolescent will be discussed next: spoken communication.

*Chapter Five*

# The Complexities of Spoken Communication

When I want to talk with my teenager, she's in no mood to listen. But when I don't have anything to say, she complains I never talk to her. So last night she was criticizing her appearance compared to other seventh-graders, and she got furious at me for looking at her while she talked. Then this morning at breakfast when she was saying something, I did my best to look away, and she complained I never pay attention to anything she has to say! I can't win for losing!

Spoken communication isn't easy. You have to capture what you mean in words and then convey the voice message so that someone else understands what you intend. Unfortunately, because adolescence is a time when parent and teenager are becoming more separated as independence grows them socially apart, greater demands are placed on communication to bridge the increased distance and difference between them. This chapter covers some basic understandings about managing communication with your adolescent: adolescent shyness, adolescent secrecy, the problem with truth, parental self-disclosure, communicating clearly, and the difficulty of truly listening.

## Adolescent Shyness

At any age, shyness can disable communication by making speaking up very daunting to do. And at the adolescent age, it's hard not to feel shy much of the time. During early adolescence, for example, effects of puberty create a vulnerability to being teased about physical appearance that can make some young people reluctant to interact with peers. Or, simply comparing themselves unfavorably to others, young people can "hate" how they look and keep to themselves in order to be looked at as little as possible. Ill at ease with her or his bodily changes, a sixth-grade girl or boy may truly dread publicly dressing for physical education at school. Shyness often arises from painful self-consciousness. In addition, many adolescents tend to be shyer around adults than they were as children because grown-ups have now become the operating standard for acting more mature. Now it's easy to shy away from adults and feel diminished and inhibited in their company. Whereas confidence can encourage speaking up, shyness can lead to shutting up.

A common exception to adolescent shyness around adults is the only child who has been socialized to act adult by the company of parents, and feels very comfortable talking with grown-ups. She often considers herself her parents' equal and has made friends of their friends throughout childhood. Social confidence in dealing with adults is one common benefit of growing up as an only child. However, this socialization with adults can sometimes create another source of shyness—feeling socially awkward and out of step with age mates. "I fit in better with adults than people my own age. Other kids don't get my sense of humor the way older people do."

Even last-stage adolescents are not immune to shyness. For example, consider college freshmen, not knowing anyone on campus, who must go to parties if they want to meet people. Many self-medicate social discomfort with alcohol so as to subdue painful shyness and become sufficiently uninhibited and outgoing to survive the evening, they hope without harmful incident. Over the course of adolescence, shyness is everywhere.

Then there is temperamental shyness that seems to combine a lack of social confidence, limited conversational skills, and social anxiety, all of which result in the avoidance of social interaction that the young person actually desires. Shyness can create a vicious circle when feeling shy causes the teenager to act shy, which makes feeling shy feel worse. Keeping others at a distance, staying silent, not greeting people, mumbling when spoken to, avoiding eye contact, electing to sit alone—all prevent the teenager from participating in social interactions that he or she fears and misses. Making the problem worse can be others' interpreting a shy person's behavior as unfriendly. One student who decided to break out of her history of shy isolation by making and keeping a "new school resolution" was determined to act more outgoing in high school. Successfully doing so, she described with surprise what her new group of friends told her. "In middle school they thought I was a snob, can you believe it? They thought I was keeping to myself because I felt better than them! They thought I didn't want anything to do with them when being their friend was what I wanted more than anything!" Acting shy can come across as acting disinterested, superior, or even antisocial.

Temperamental shyness can be costly during adolescence when it is the enemy of social growth. Persistently acting bashful in adolescence can limit social functioning in adulthood. So if parents see that their teenager is extremely inhibited—becoming socially avoidant, withdrawn, isolated, or even reclusive—what can they do? One parental responsibility is to think ahead for a teenager who is more preoccupied with what is happening now. So they can say, "We know acting outgoing can be uncomfortable for you, but making an effort to do so is worth your while. Knowing how to approach people, interact with people, speak up to people, and socialize in groups of people are all skills you will need in the years ahead."

In encouraging this growth, parents need to be respectful of four common fears that often contribute to adolescent shyness.

1. *The fear of being known.* "I don't like drawing attention to myself. I'd rather just observe what's going on."

2. *The fear of being embarrassed.* "I don't want to do or say anything that other people might consider stupid. I'd rather not participate."

3. *The fear of being rejected.* "I don't want to reach out and get ignored or be turned away. I'd rather keep to myself."

4. *The fear of being speechless.* "I don't want to start talking and become tongue-tied. I'd rather just say nothing."

Recovering from shyness usually requires overcoming fear. Parents need to make clear that at some points in their lives most people experience shyness. In fact, they can share what times of shyness were like for them, how they felt, and how they gathered the courage to overcome their fears. An important distinction to help the shy adolescent make is between using fear as an informant and using it as an adviser. As an informant, fear tells us we feel endangered, and that can be good to know. But as an adviser, fear can tell us to avoid or run or hide, all of which may make us more afraid. To recover from shyness requires the courage of counterintuitive decision making. Feeling frightened, we must choose to act in bold, confident, and outgoing ways.

Parents need to honor the ambivalence of the adolescent who wants to escape the prison of shyness but fears leaving the protection of that refuge. Then they can give some simple instruction: "Partly wanting to be more socially comfortable is where the power to act less shy begins. Next is courage to practice acting more outgoing. This requires asking and answering the freedom-from-fear question: 'How would I choose to act in social situations if I were not feeling shy?' Now list all the physical, communicative, responsive, assertive, and friendly ways you would behave if you were not feeling afraid. These are some of the behaviors you need to practice. The more you practice them, the less uncomfortable and more familiar they will become, the more social connection you will experience with others as they connect with you, and the less that shyness will get in your way. Courage will build confidence, practice will produce competence, and positive response from others will make your efforts feel worthwhile."

One strategy for helping shy adolescents overcome their fears of speaking up and of engaging in conversation is to tell them that *talking together* is just one way to establish social relationships. *Doing together* is another. Each way creates companionship. For the shy adolescent who doesn't know what to say or doesn't have anything to say, encourage him to join a common-interest group where everyone already shares something in common they like to do, and when they get together the focus is on doing that. Now the shy adolescent is at a social advantage. He likes and knows about what others like and know about. He can immediately begin playing and participating with them. And he discovers he has a lot to talk about with people who want to talk about the same thing. I have seen teenagers start to overcome shyness by joining a variety of common-interest groups—a sport group, fantasy gaming group, moviemaking group, volunteer group, theatre group, or exercise group, among others.

Of course when it comes to shyness, the Internet has been a blessing and a curse. It's been a blessing because a shy person, freed from visual and vocal face-to-face communication, can find relief in conversing invisibly and inaudibly, developing confidence in verbal fluency by typing out what he or she wants to say. This is also partly why texting is so popular—you don't have to be seen or heard, yet the interchange is virtually immediate. The curse is that this practice takes you only so far. There is no substitute for in-person, eye-to-eye, spoken communication where knowing each other is additionally informed by all the nonverbal cues each person is sending and picking up. This is communication with full, not limited, exposure. This is communication that is spontaneous, not carefully scripted. This is communication with no place to hide. A young person who conducts virtually all of his or her relationships over the Internet may shy away from direct, unmediated contacts with people.

By avoiding social discomfort, he or she can increase social incapacity.

A number of years ago, a young man described shyness with a descriptor that really struck me: "When you're shy, you're there but you're really not there."

"Like this, you mean?" and I recited that old childhood rhyme: "Yesterday upon a stair, I met a man who wasn't there. I met him there again today. I wish that man would go away!"

"Yes," he said. "Shyness is the man everyone would like to go away."

Adolescent secrecy is another factor that can shut communication down.

## Adolescent Secrecy

To some degree, all adolescents lead three lives. There is the public life that they are willing to share with parents. There is the private life apart that they want respected by parents. And there is the secret life that they strive to keep concealed from parents. Why concealed? Because growing up occurs partly within and partly outside of what parents approve or will allow. In this sense, adolescence is an outlaw age, teenagers sometimes skirting authority to try forbidden freedoms about which young people believe parents are best kept ignorant and about which parents believe it is their responsibility to know.

It is around this third and secret life that a high-stakes game of hide-and-seek is played, and it is played in several risky ways. First is the case of the teenager who hides his tracks in order to seek illicit freedom. Second is the case of the teenager who hides and the parent who seeks to find her out. Third is the case where one parent wants to hide from (ignore) what the other parent wants to seek (discover). Let's take these variations one at a time.

*When the teenager hides to seek,* he becomes both hider and seeker. The purpose of the game is to conceal the freedom he is pursuing. For example, because he is more expert in the ways of the Internet than his parents, he has developed covert strategies to visit off-limits sites without being found out, unless he slips up. So it appears that he has won this particular game, except that such concealment carries a psychological cost. He can't live partially in hiding from his parents without putting some distance between himself and them. He can't maintain consistent dishonesty without having to be careful all the time, and this attention to detail is stressful. He can't live partially in hiding without some anxiety about being found out. And he knows that if he is caught, his parents will feel betrayed and he will be subject to double punishment—for the violation of family rules and for the lying he has done.

When this happens, parents can use the correctional encounter to explain all the ways illicit freedom is never free. "Your lying is hard on us, but it is harder on you because of all the effort it takes to maintain a lie and live in hiding, and all the ways it shuts honest relationships down."

*When the teenager hides and the parent seeks,* the teenager is hider and the parent is seeker. The purpose of this game is to pit the adolescent effort at concealment against the parental effort at discovery. It is a game nobody wins. For example, the parent suspects something is going on in her daughter's social life because the girl broke up with her old classmate. Now the parent notices that when her daughter goes out with friends, she is careful to dress in a more grown-up way. What she's concealing is her interest in dating a much older guy, something her parents have been set against.

What happens now is that the game of hide-and-seek becomes a game of hide-and-sneak. The teenager pretends, deceives, and denies—nothing's going on. The parent pries, spies, and checks to find out what may be happening. And between texts that were not deleted, communication tucked away in her Facebook account, and a confidential talk with one of the girl's friends, the parent gets the name of this new male interest. Then she confronts the daughter, who is outraged at having her privacy broached, but no angrier than the parent who feels that trust has been broken.

When this happens, parents can use the correctional encounter to explain that when it takes deception to catch deception, everyone feels hurt. "I hate it that you played detective on me!" the daughter complains. "Well, I hate having to act that way to get the truth," is the parental reply. "I was hoping I wouldn't find out what I did! And now we're both angry at each other!"

*When one parent hides and the other seeks,* one parent is more of a hider from knowing all about the adolescent's life, and the other is more of a seeker to make sure everything is okay. The purpose of the parenting game is to decide how much to leave the teenager alone and how much to subject his life to question. For example, although the hiding parent will admit that the son is going through some emotional changes recently, it's probably just normal adolescent moodiness. But the seeking parent isn't sure and wants to investigate in case something more serious is going on, such as early substance use. What happens now is parental disagreement over whether to be laissez-faire and hands off, or interventionist and hands on. The hiding parent says, "If we raise that issue, we'll just stir up trouble and create problems where there's nothing wrong to be found. We need to let him alone." The seeking parent says, "It's better to be mistaken than miss a possible warning sign. We need to check it out."

In this scenario, parents must use the correctional encounter to find a middle way between them so that the question about their son's current state does not become divisive in their marriage. "Maybe we need to seek a third-party consultation to help talk this out. Maybe combine some compromise and concession to agree on what course to take."

Because the communication game of hide-and-seek is endemic to adolescence, parents need to play it carefully and well. What makes the playing hard to do is the problem with truth.

## The Problem with Truth

The truth is that most adolescents are selective about how much truth to tell parents concerning what is really happening in their lives and in their world. "If my parents knew it all, they'd never let me do anything!" There's the rub. The teenager knows that telling the truth will not always set him free. It can often get him in a lot of trouble. So the shocked parent declares, "You did *what?* Your friends are doing *what?* You're staying home until further notice!"

This is why adolescents lead partly open and partly concealed lives—the life about which parents are informed and the life about which parents are not told. There's a fine line between confession and self-incrimination, and most adolescents don't want to cross it because if they do, they'll lose significant freedom. However, when truth is deliberately omitted, denied, covered up, distorted, or fabricated by the teenager, the consequences for parents can be profound. Come adolescence, the young person is the parents' prime informant about what is going on in his or her life. Cut off from valid information, the adults feel out of control. "We can't believe anything you say!" Then there are the emotional costs—anxiety at not knowing what is really going on and anger at having trust in honesty betrayed: "You lied to us!"

At a workshop, a parent once described how she used an object lesson to teach her middle school daughter to stop repeated lying. This object lesson was a risky disciplinary maneuver in which the parent modeled the objectionable behavior in the hopes that, finding it objectionable as well, the child would want to stop it too. The risk was that the young person, rather than learning to cease misconduct, would take the parent's instructional example as a justification for continuing the misbehavior. "Well, you just acted that way with me, so I can keep acting that way with you!"

In this case, the mother told her daughter, an only child, "Sometime in the next two weeks I'm going to tell you a really big lie." The daughter didn't believe the warning. "You wouldn't lie to me. You're my mom!" But then the girl started to get worried. "About being able to spend my savings on what I wanted, is that the lie?" "No," the mother answered, "that's not the lie. You earned the money. You can spend it as agreed." Later in the week, the daughter asked, "Being allowed to go to the overnight this weekend, is that the lie?" "No," the mother answered, "that's not the lie. You can go." Then, deep into the second week, the daughter asked, "Getting the puppy for my birthday, is that the lie?" "No," the mother answered, "that's not the lie. We've already named him."

Finally the two-week wait was over. "So," asked the daughter, by now angry at anxiously not knowing what was true and what was not, "you promised you were going to lie to me!" "That's right," answered the mother, "that was the lie. And that's how it feels to be lied to." And perhaps because the daughter was a mature only child, she took the lesson to heart. It's really hard to live comfortably in a relationship where the other person is telling you deliberate untruths.

Of course, telling the truth is not that simple, because truth is more elusive than we like to think. So, placing people "under oath," we ask them to take a vow no human being is actually empowered to keep: "Do you swear to tell the truth, the whole truth, and nothing but the truth?" Only a liar would swear to that. After all, language only approximates meaning, experience is subject to interpretation, truth is a story that can be told many different ways, accounts of facts are often mixed with bits of fiction, there always are different visions and versions of what happened, perception is biased by personal point of view, truth is a matter of debate and hard to prove, memory is selective, understanding is limited, and recollection is constantly shifting. Like history, the exact "truth" is in a constant state of revision.

So if adolescents live in partial concealment, and the truth is difficult to unequivocally establish, what are parents and adolescent to do? I think what parents can reasonably tell their teenager is this:

"First, understand that nothing destroys relationships so powerfully as deliberate dishonesty—telling lies. There is no trust without truth. There is no intimacy without honesty. There is no security without sincerity. Lies put you in a false position with others and with yourself. Telling lies will get you into far more difficulty than it will ever get you out of. Second, if we don't know where you are, or what is actually happening, we may not be able to help you if you get in serious trouble. Third, if we lose trust because of your repeated lying, we may not be willing to believe you when you need us to know the truth. And fourth, if you keep lying to us, you may put more distance between us because it's really hard to feel close to a liar. That's why lying is such a lonely way to live."

Parents don't need to know everything about their teenager's life, but they need to be told enough to stay adequately involved and available. So it behooves the adolescent to be as honest with parents as he or she possibly can, and it behooves parents to keep holding their adolescent to healthy, honest account.

Dishonesty is one common enemy of forthright communication. Being deliberately frozen out is another. Parents who have a teenager who cuts them off from communication and tells them virtually nothing does so to preserve his privacy and freedom. "He won't tell us anything," the parents complain. "And there's nothing we can do." But I disagree. There are consequences for not talking to parents, and parents need to let their adolescent know what they are. What I suggest is breaking through the barrier of silence by saying something like this:

"Of course, whether you communicate with us is entirely your choice. We are not in the business of pulling information out of you. However, you do need to understand this. Keeping us in ignorance does you no favors. It can have consequences. The first consequence is that in ignorance we may imagine the worst. We may worry that you are in some kind of trouble you don't want to talk to us about. The second consequence is that on the basis of our fearful conclusion, we may decide to limit your freedom for safety's sake, for your protection. Then you may get angry at our false assumption and unfair restrictions because there is really nothing harmful going on. But how could we know that, since you decided to keep us out of the loop about what is happening? Contrary to what you may believe, parents do not keep best in the dark. We don't do well with ignorance, and you won't like how we do. Suspicious and restrictive is how we'll become. Therefore, if you want to educate our understanding and influence our decisions, you may want to keep us adequately informed. But to do so is entirely up to you."

Another contributing factor to how comfortably and openly adolescents communicate at home is adequate self-disclosure by parents.

## Parental Self-Disclosure

Talk to parents about the importance of self-disclosure in general, and they will usually consider it an issue having to do with their adolescent. Yes, they will agree, the teenager should be forthcoming with them about his experience so that they are kept adequately in the know. Most parents want the adolescent to self-disclose to them; however, they are far more reluctant to self-disclose with their teenage son or daughter.

It's a tough question for parents: How well do they want to be known by their adolescent? How much privacy do they want to keep about their present? (The parent may not want it known, for example, that the reason for taking new employment was having been dismissed with cause from the old.) And what secrets do they want kept about their past? (For example, the parent doesn't want it known that she started substance use way back in middle school.) Two common fears stand in the way of self-disclosure. There is the fear of losing their child's respect:

"Will I lose standing in my son's eyes if he knows his dad was fired from a job?" And there is the fear of encouraging imitation. "Will my daughter, having heard about my history, use that as an excuse to act the same?"

*To tell or not to tell, that is the question.* I believe the answer is, if the telling might spare the adolescent from making a similar costly choice, it may be that the painful truth could be profitably told. A parent's bad example can be a source of good instruction. So to her departing high school graduate, the parent says, "Just so you might profit from my mistake, I want to tell you about what happened to me after getting sloppy drunk at my first college party." Because the confession was sincerely told, and because the parent was citing personal life experience, her cautionary tale about the sexual dangers of excessive social drinking was seriously attended to.

It's one of the saddest responses I sometimes hear from older adolescents when I ask, "Tell me about your parents. What have their lives have been like?" and the young person looks at me as though I'm posing some unanswerable question. "How would I know? All we ever talked about was me." What a waste! What a loss! In this case, after eighteen years of living with his parents, he ended up with a sense that he barely knew about their personal history at all. Why a waste and a loss? Because what parents fundamentally have to give their children is who and how they are—the personality they present, the example they model, the interaction they provide, and the present and past life experience they have to share.

How to Live Life is the curriculum parents have to teach. How they have lived and continue to live their lives, for good and ill, makes up much of this instruction and many of the lessons to be taught. So the parent, for example, who believes she should never "bring work home" and discuss it with children deprives them of a wealth of vicarious experience from which older adolescents in particular, who are more interested in the world of employment, could profit. Her teenager, who has an entry-level job serving the public, could learn a lot from his mother about how she's learned to deal with difficult customers over the years.

In counseling, I often try to harness the power of parental self-disclosure by exploring *similarity connections* between parents and adolescents. The opening question I ask is, "In what individual ways is each teenager similar to each of you parents?" Usually they can identify similarities very easily. Says the mother, "My son is just like me. We really like to have a lot going on at one time, being really busy. So it's easy for us to get overcommitted." Says the father, "My daughter is just like me. We're really competitive. We love to win, but we hate to lose! So when we do, it's easy for us to get upset."

This is when I suggest that they use self-disclosure to exploit the similarity connections to educational effect. "Since you've both had years of practice in self-management that your teenagers lack, why not share the strategies you've developed for coping with an ambitious schedule of activities [this to the mom], and why not share the calming strategies you've developed for handling disappointment and frustration when you lose [this to the dad]? Similarity can have so much to teach."

At the end of adolescence, parental self-disclosure can be particularly helpful. During the trial independence stage of adolescence, the older adolescent is trying (and usually failing) to master the many challenges of independent living away from home. Feeling inadequate and incompetent for being yet unable to live up to the expectations of the age, the young person expresses her frustration to parents. "I'm twenty-one years old, and I'm still messing up! What's the matter with me?" This is when parents use self-disclosure to bring some needed perspective to the situation. "You know, when we were your age, just out of college and trying to make it on our own, we didn't find our footing right away. It was mistake-based education, which is the most painful kind, learning the hard way from doing things the wrong way and having to put them right. Let us tell you about some of the false steps we made and some of the responsibilities we really struggled to accept. Then, if you want, we'll give you what advice we can about your current troubles, advice that comes from having lived through many troubles of our own." When parents put themselves on an equal footing with their adolescent, treating themselves just as older human beings with a personal history of struggle, trials, and errors, they open up communication with their teenager, who is relieved to hear that parents have had their failings and failures to contend with too, still do, and always will.

Another opening that is very important is parental receptiveness to adolescent questions. When parents have an *open question policy*, they say and mean, "You can ask us about anything at any time, and we will give you the most informed and honest answer we can. We will not question your question by asking, 'Why do you want to know that?' We will only answer as best we can. Our understanding and opinion are always at your service. We will trust that you have good cause for asking and that you will add what we think and know to what you think and know to make the best choices you can."

In response to a blog post I had written, a young person made this comment: "Being open to questions, any and all of them, is the best thing parents can do for their children. Teenagers aren't just walking hormones with no impulse control. They are human beings with working brains under their skulls that want to know things and understand them. They think things through more than most parents give them credit for, and having an open question policy at home allows teenagers to learn more information that they will incorporate into their decision-making process." I agree, and would add only this. I believe that the open question policy needs to work *two* ways. There needs to be a reciprocity agreement such that the parent asks for something like this: "Anything you ask me about that I openly answer about my life experience, I want to be free to ask you about in your life experience, and get comparable openness in return."

Then parents can do something more. They can practice communicating clearly to their adolescent, who can learn from them how to do it too.

## Communicating Clearly

At best, verbal communication is a clumsy way to keep each other adequately and accurately informed, because words are often poor approximations of meaning we intend to convey. For example, we tell our early adolescent to "clean up" her room, and she assures us that the "cleanup" has been done, yet when we inspect, we find she has only rearranged the mess—shoving the clutter under the covers, into the closet, and beneath the bed. "That's not cleaned up!" we say. "It is too!" she argues. "It looks neat just like you told me!" And that's the problem. We didn't specify what we meant; we only stated a general term. If we had taken the time to objectively define what we meant by "clean up"—dirty clothes in the hamper, clean clothes hung up or folded in drawers, trash put in the wastebasket, for example— we might have gotten something closer to what we wanted.

At a gathering of middle school parents, the question was asked, "What is the best way to communicate with our adolescent?" The answer that immediately came to mind was one that psychologist John Narciso taught me many years ago. "Clearly," I replied. "By 'clearly' I mean making your language more operational and less abstract. That way you can bring a level of definition to your requests, instructions, or corrections that has a higher likelihood of being understood the way you want."

I remember John asking a group of teachers for words that described another person with whom they would value being in relationship. In response, people offered such descriptors as "forthright," "reliable," and "authentic." Yes, he would agree that that kind of person in relationship sounded good to him too. Next he asked for a volunteer to come up and help him out.

"Would you do 'authentic' for me," he would ask.

The teacher couldn't understand.

"Would you act 'authentic,'" he would prompt.

Still the teacher seemed at a loss.

"Is there a problem?" he asked.

"Yes," the teacher replied. "You haven't told me what you mean by 'authentic,' so I don't know what to do or how to act."

"Exactly," said John. "And that's the problem with using abstract language: it communicates, but that meaning is mostly vague. Any two people are going to have a hard time agreeing on what precisely is being said." And so would begin a discussion about the limits of abstract communication—the use of general terms that sound informative but are actually vacant of specific meaning because they come without any marching orders for acting them out. The more abstract the language, the more room for interpretation, misinterpretation, and, most important, misunderstanding.

Now consider parents and a teenager in counseling. I ask the parents to tell their son how they would like him to be in the family. "We just want you to be considerate, responsible, and respectful. That's all." The request sounded reasonable, so I asked the teenager, "What do those three words mean to you?" The young man thinks for a moment and then shakes his head. "I don't know." And he is speaking the truth. In telling the young man what they want, the parents have actually told him close to nothing. So what could these parents do to communicate more clearly? Well, they could follow John's suggestion. They could make their choice of words more *operational*. For example, they could follow up their abstractions with a definition of what they mean, by talking in terms of specific doings, behaviors, happenings, actions, and events.

"By 'considerate' we mean not borrowing our belongings before asking us for permission first. By 'responsible' we mean not discarding your belongings all over the home but picking them up and putting them away in a place they belong. By 'respectful' we mean hearing out what we have to say without interrupting, as we do with you." By making the abstract more operational, they were more readily able to pin down a mutually understood meaning.

One circumstance in which it is particularly difficult to keep speech operational is during times of conflict. The reason is that when one is in conflict, emotional intensity often changes the character of spoken language—not just from positive to negative, but from specific to abstract. So in frustration, the parent says, "You are being rude, and I want it to stop!" The only meaning that has been successfully conveyed by the word "rude" is parental disapproval. Now the parent is engaging in name-calling. Because there is no mention of the specific actions and behaviors the parent wants addressed, the words are more likely to arouse hard feelings than successfully encourage any resolution. Abstracts are good for poetry because they can contain multiple meanings. But if you really want what you say to be understood the way you intend it, a more specific (operational) choice of words often works best. "By 'rude,'" explains the parent, "I mean checking your cell phone for messages when I am trying to talk." So the rule is, when instructing or requesting or correcting with your adolescent, watch your language. If you choose to use an abstract term, take the time to explain operationally what you mean. That way, the meaning you intend is more likely to be the meaning that is received. Of course, receiving any communication depends on listening, and truly listening can be hard to do.

## Listening

After a meeting with some middle school parents, a dad came up to me and shared a wonderful line from the movie *Pulp Fiction*. One character asks another, "Are you listening or just waiting to talk?" The man's point was that this question could be leveled at a lot of parents, self-preoccupied adults so caught up in their own point of view that they don't really attend to what their teenager is trying to say. This made me mindful of how important and difficult listening is to do. Where to begin?

Start by understanding that listening can be very expensive. For example, you have to shift focus off of yourself and onto someone else. You have to invest energy in paying attention to what the other person is saying. You have to process what is being said. You may hear uninteresting or disturbing information you would rather not know. Depending on what you've been told, you may feel obligated to do something in response. Or as the other person emotionally unloads and feels better, you may emotionally load up and feel worse. For example, when another parent unburdens to you about the alarming difficulties she is having with her teenager, one of your child's good friends, you come away glad to have listened and been supportive, but stressed with worry by what you learned. Could your own child be adversely affected by the association?

Then there are the occasions when you have listened at length to your teenager, only to be told you haven't been listening at all. Turns out, the adolescent is leveling four charges against you. How does she know you haven't been listening? "Because you don't understand what I have to say. You don't agree with what I say. You won't change your mind because of what I say. You won't do what I say!" Of course none of these adolescent accusations have anything to do with listening, which is simply taking the time to attend to someone's spoken communication. Thus parents can explain, "When we don't catch your meaning right away, when we see the issue differently, when our decision won't change, when we won't do what you want, we know this can be frustrating for you. But none of this means we haven't listened. We always try our best to hear and pay close attention to what you have to say."

It's when parents actually refuse to listen that they can be silently abusive. They won't take the time. They won't devote the attention. And the message the teenager takes to heart may be, "You're not worth listening to." That's the most important point for parents to remember. *Listening is an act of valuing.* Not listened to, a young person can feel devalued. "But," protests the busy parent, "my teenager picks the most inconvenient times to talk—when I'm really tired or in the middle of a program or have something I have to get done." It's one of the hard realities of parenting adolescents—a good time for them to talk is frequently a bad time for you to listen. However, parents need to understand that the teenager's readiness to talk in a seriously self-disclosing way depends on emotion and mood coming into internal alignment that sets the stage for momentary openness, factors that she doesn't usually control. "I don't feel like talking now," is often not a lame excuse but a psychologically valid reason. So when parents say, "Not now, we'll talk later," later never happens because the momentary opening of readiness has closed. The best time to talk about something that is important for your teenager to share is when she or he feels ready to talk about it.

Among parents who are the best listeners are those who are *accessible listeners*. They are willing to drop whatever they are doing and make themselves available whenever the adolescent has something that feels important to say. Another group of parents who listen well are *empathetic listeners* who attend to feelings that underlie the teenager's words. By responding with this sensitivity, these parents express a deeper level of concern, and a deeper, more intimate connection is often made. So the parent used her emotions to sense what was going on in her son's experience: "When you were describing your difficult day, it sounded like you're feeling frustrated and disappointed. Would you like to talk about that?"

Mitigating against parents and teens fully attending to what they are saying to each other is the huge problem of electronic distraction that interferes with everyone's capacity to purely listen to anyone in this increasingly technological age. So you want to talk to your teenager, but she is networking on the computer or texting, or he is deep into a video or computer game; or your teenager wants to talk to you, but you are watching a movie or the TV news. In either case, the speaker is given partial attention, talking to the side of somebody's head. The age of multitasking, and competing communication devices has created the chronic condition of *divided attention*. What is the solution? If you really want to listen or be listened to face-to-face, go for *clear-channel communication*—attending to what each other is saying with all electronic devices turned off.

Always, of course, assert your right (and responsibility) to limit your listening in the cases of emotional overload and unacceptable communication. Supportive listening can lead to emotional overload for the listener, so there may be times when you need to say, "That's all I can listen to right now. I'm feeling worn down and need to take a break. In [specify a time] I want to hear what else you have to say." Listening to deliberately hurtful communication is unacceptable. You need to say, "I am willing to hear what you have to say so long as you say it appropriately. Name-calling, yelling, threats, or verbal insults are not appropriate. They are not kinds of communication I will agree to hear. I don't talk that way with you, and I don't want you to talk that way with me." Then you can explain to your adolescent that the issue goes far beyond how he is talking with you. "If I let you communicate with me this way, it will only encourage you to communicate with others this way later on. Then people who are not your parent, people you value, may break off their relationship with you to stop the mistreatment, and you will have lost a good friend, a love interest, or even a significant partner. So stopping this deliberately hurtful communication is not just for my sake, but for your own."

Perhaps the hardest time for parents to listen to a teenager is when there is active disagreement. Now the temptation is to listen with one's mind made up, preoccupied with one's defense, preparing one's rejoinder, focusing on what one is going to say next, not on what the adolescent is saying now. At this point, if you find yourself missing much of what your teenager is trying to communicate, ask yourself the *Pulp Fiction* question: Am I really listening or just waiting to talk?

The complexities of spoken communication between parents and adolescent are with us to stay. Shyness can make speaking up scary, secrecy can be tempting, truth can be elusive, self-disclosure can be uncomfortable, clarity can be difficult to achieve, and listening can be truly hard to do. Yet with all these complexities, accurate and adequate spoken communication is what parents and adolescent must rely on to stay informed and connected. Hardest of all times to communicate can be when they are in conflict, when opposition and emotional intensity make the sharing and receiving of significant information more challenging to do. Dealing with conflict is the topic of the next chapter.

## Chapter Six

# The Use and Abuse of Conflict

How did two parents who grew up in families with
so little taste and tolerance for conflict end up with
two adolescents who love to fight? Our son delights
in turning any discussion into a disagreement, and
when our daughter's had a bad day, she likes to get
into it with us to get her anger out. Then after each
argument with our son or blowout with our daughter, we're exhausted, but they're not even winded.
Why does conflict work so much better for them
than it does for us?

Conflict is a wonderful growing medium for adolescents, particularly when conducted with their parents. The young person
takes on these primary authorities in her life to assert her
growing power of independence. Speaking up for herself and
standing up for herself are self-respecting acts. The process of
conflict matters both because it affects the parent-adolescent
relationship and because how the teenager engages in conflict
with parents will have formative impact on how she learns
to conduct conflict with significant others later on. So this
chapter outlines aspects of conflict with your teenager for you
to consider: the nature of parent-adolescent conflict, arguing
with your adolescent, the problem of emotional extortion,
managing parental disagreement, and bridging differences with
interest.

## The Nature of Parent-Adolescent Conflict

Parent-child conflict increases during adolescence as the healthy teenager pushes for more independence to grow and healthy parents restrain that push in the interests of safety and responsibility. There are five psychological "engines" that drive growth to independence—*separation, expansion, differentiation, opposition,* and *responsibility*—and each carries its own emotional cost and creates a different source of conflict.

- The engine of *separation* pushes for more association with peers and distance from family than was true in childhood, creating a competing life apart that enables the adolescent to socially grow. For the teenager, the emotional cost at home can be loneliness and estrangement. The resulting conflicts with parents are disagreements over *time with peers versus time with family*.

- The engine of *expansion* pushes for a larger and older field of life activity than that of childhood, creating more varied life experience from which to grow. For the teenager, the emotional cost can be more uncertainty and anxiety about how much more exposure there is to manage. The resulting conflicts with parents are disagreements over *what one is old enough for versus what one is not old enough for*.

- The engine of *differentiation* pushes for more experimentation with alternative interests, images, and associations, creating the context within which a new identity can grow. For the teenager, the emotional cost can be the risk of social intolerance and rejection. The resulting conflicts with parents are disagreements over *what expression of individuality is okay versus what expression of individuality is not okay*.

- The engine of *opposition* pushes for more active and passive resistance against established authority, creating the opportunity for more self-determination to grow. For the teenager, the emotional cost can be disapproval and reprisal. The resulting conflicts with parents are disagreements over *living on the adolescent's terms versus living on the parents' terms*.

- The engine of *responsibility* pushes for more willingness to own choices made and consequences that follow, creating more answerability for one's actions as one grows. For the teenager, the emotional cost can be regret and sorrow from making poor decisions. The resulting conflicts with parents are disagreements over *which decisions one is held accountable for versus which decisions one is not held accountable for*.

Given this inevitability of more friction in the relationship once adolescence gets under way, here are ten notions to consider about conducting conflict with your adolescent. (For more information about managing family conflict, see my book *Stop the Screaming*, 2009.):

1. *Parents are trained in conflict, and they need to know what their training model is.* In their family of origin, they witnessed and participated in conflict in formative ways. If it was a safe and constructive model (calm discussion leading to reasonable resolution), they might want to continue it with their adolescent; if it was an unsafe and destructive model (loud attacks leading to hurt or injury), they might want to change it with their adolescent.
   If they grew up avoiding conflict with parents or older siblings out of fear of getting harmed, they are likely to back off when their adolescent threatens conflict, as the old fear keeps them from speaking up or taking a stand. However, parents are not trapped by history unless they choose to be. If they want to, they can modify the model of managing disagreement that they learned growing up. They can learn to do a different dance of conflict with their adolescent than their parents did with them.

2. *Conflict is cooperative.* Conflict can occur only when opposing parties agree to actively contest some significant

point of difference between them. Conflict requires joint effort. It takes two to start a conflict, and only one (by disengaging) to stop it. As the well-posted bumper sticker points out, "Suppose they gave a war and nobody came?" Or only one side came? In either case, no matter how powerful the disagreement, no conflict would result. Anytime parents find themselves fighting with their teenager, they need to ask themselves, "Why did I agree to cooperate in this argument, and do I want to discontinue my involvement?" To stop an argument, just stop arguing back. Just as bickering siblings are jointly accountable for their ongoing rivalry, parent and adolescent are jointly responsible for any conflict between them. Parents must take their share of responsibility for any conflict with their teenager. They must treat engagement in conflict as a matter of personal choice.

3. *Conflict can create resemblance.* The influential conduct of one party can often provoke imitation by the other. Thus, if the teenager starts interrupting, raising his voice, and making general accusations when in conflict with the parent, it can be tempting for the parent to respond in kind. However, the adult must resist this temptation and model the kind of mature behavior she wants the adolescent to learn instead—hearing the other person out, speaking calmly, and sticking to specifics. When conducting conflict with their teenager, parents want resemblance to come their way.

4. *Conflict can be instructive.* The adolescent can learn from the exchange of opposing ideas because conflict is just two different ways of looking at the same issue. So, arguing to be able to do something fun with her friends, the teenager gets to consider the dangerous side of fun by hearing the basis of her parent's opposition. In addition, conflict is not something parents have with their teenager; it is

something they *do* with their teenager. It is a performance act. Every time they have conflict with their adolescent, by their example and interaction they are training that young person in how to approach and conduct conflict. For example, for some parents the primary purpose of any conflict with the adolescent is not to win but to communicate about and better understand the nature of the difference between them. It is this approach that the young person will take out into other significant relationships, like partnering and parenting, later on.

5. *Resemblance can create conflict.* When parent and adolescent share similar antagonistic traits, it is easy for them to get entangled. Perhaps they are equally stubborn. Perhaps each one has to have the last word. Perhaps they are both very strong willed. Perhaps they are highly competitive. When parents recognize such a similarity connection, they need to bring it out in the open for discussion. They do this with the adolescent in order to find strategies for managing future disagreements without getting trapped in the old familiar, similar way. So the parent might say, "Since we both are prone to lose our tempers and start yelling when an argument between us drags on, maybe we can stop arguing before the yelling point, take a time-out, and then resume the disagreement again after we've had a chance to cool down." The problem with conflicts of resemblance between parent and teenager is that they intensify very quickly and resolve very slowly, if at all, unless alternative strategies can be found.

6. *Cooperation can create conflict.* The problem with cooperation is that it requires that two parties manage to *share something in common.* So telling teenage siblings to share the computer creates all kinds of cooperation questions that can lead to conflicts. Who goes first? Who's

in charge? Who gets most? What is fair? What is a fair share? Who decides? Who knows best? Whose is the right way? When is it whose turn? If parents want to reduce cooperation conflicts between siblings, then they can declare how cooperation is to be managed by specifying the answers to these sharing questions in advance. Making cooperation work takes a lot of communication, coordination, concession, and compromise, skills that will serve the adolescent well in relationships ahead.

7. *Conflict is how siblings get along.* Conflict doesn't mean siblings are not getting along; it is how they often get along when a disagreement arises between them, as it increasingly does when they are of the same sex and close in age. Conflict confers many benefits on teenagers. It allows siblings to create something to do, provoke interaction, compete against each other, practice arguing, take up for themselves, test their power, assert dominance, work out differences, and vent emotions, among other things. So long as parents monitor the conflict to make sure no verbal, emotional, or physical harm is being done (in which case they need to intervene, stop the proceedings, and confront the violator), and so long as siblings also have harmonious times together, the push and shove of sibling conflict can teach them how to accept conflict as a normal part of close relationships (something an only child doesn't usually get to learn growing up).

8. *Conflict can change the quality of communication.* Choice of language tends to alter with rising tension. So, for example, as impatience builds, the words parent or teenager choose to use can change from objective, declarative, and moderate ("You didn't do what you promised") to evaluative, accusatory, and extreme ("You're completely untrustworthy!"). It's up to the parent to

monitor the level of discourse so that it does not become inflammatory. When harsh words intensify conflict, parents to need to stop the action, temporarily set aside the issue at difference, and take time to discuss constructive language that needs to be used. "Before we carry our disagreement any further, I need to talk about changing the kind of words you are using with me. They are deliberately insulting and meant to be hurtful. I don't use those kinds of words with you, and I don't want you using them with me."

9. *Conflict can lead to violence.* When frustration with opposition leads to anger and when anger is allowed to escalate, then rage can lead to verbal or physical abuse. This is why the number-one priority in family conflict is the management of emotional arousal. The issue at disagreement is always of secondary importance. What matters is that each person takes responsibility for monitoring and managing his or her own state of feeling. If anyone, parent or teenager, feels in danger of emotionally "losing it," that person needs to declare a time-out to cool down, and commit to resuming the dispute at a specific and more emotionally sober time. In any family conflict, the rule of safety must prevail, and it is simply this: *conflict is never to be used as an excuse to do anyone in the family harm.* "Well, I only said that because I was angry," explains the adolescent or parent. No. That person needs to find a safer way to manage anger. Between parent and adolescent, disagreements are normal and conflict is to be expected, but violence is neither.

10. *Tolerance for conflict can vary between parent and adolescent.* The teenager is more often up for an argument than the adult. Why is that? Conflict is one way the adolescent takes on the adult to fight for social freedom, older standing, and ultimately independence, against the most

powerful person in her world. Even if she loses the argument, the teenager comes out stronger for having tried. Argument takes assertiveness, something teenagers need to develop to cope with the more aggressive push and shove of adolescent peers. Parents are like sparring partners in this way. A good argument with parents sharpens your skills, increases your conditioning, and keeps you in training. So after a few rounds of intense debate with weary parents, the young person is feeling fit, talking on the phone with a friend as though nothing had happened while the parent is collapsed on the couch needing time to recover. Adolescents simply have far more energy for conflict with parents than their parents have. This is why adolescence is the age of argument.

## Arguing with Your Adolescent

Arguments and adolescence go hand in hand. What can teens argue about with parents? For the adolescent, often any issue will do, because the point of the dispute can often be argument itself. The young person is testing his or her power of disagreement with parents by contesting their power of authority. Stop and think about it. A healthy adolescent is supposed to push for more freedom to grow, just as healthy parents are supposed to restrain that push within the limits of safety and responsibility. It is this conflict of interests, most commonly expressed by arguing, that unfolds over the course of adolescence, winding down (one hopes) after the young person, somewhere in the mid-twenties, achieves functional independence and retires Mom and Dad from the parental supervision business.

In frustration, particularly during their child's early and mid-adolescence, parents will often hold the teenager responsible for this increase in argument, but such blame is misplaced. As previously mentioned, argument, like all conflict, is a cooperative activity. It takes two to start one. If parents want to stop the argument with their teenager, the solution is not to get him to stop acting argumentative. The solution is simply to stop arguing back. "But he's so insistent and provocative," they complain. Even so, he can't provoke an argument with them without their permission and collaboration. If they believe he can, then they are giving him control over their behavior, and they should never do that.

If parents choose to cooperate in an argument with their adolescent, then there are two provisos worth observing. First, *treat the argument seriously.* I say this because some parents who are uncomfortable in conflict will display that discomfort with a nervous smile or laugh. This is a mistake, because when a young adolescent has gathered the courage and resolve to confront the most powerful adults in his world and now feels as though he is being ridiculed, humiliation and resentment will follow. So if you have decided to cooperate in an argument with your teenager, treat it seriously and show him or her proper respect. Second, *if the matter at disagreement is one about which you are already resolved, do not argue.* Simply state your position again, explain it if you haven't already, and declare that your decision is not subject to change by further discussion. To agree to argue about what you have already decided is to encourage the teenager with the false hope that he can change your thinking. Then, when he finds out you had no flexibility from the outset, he will get very angry about being led on. Anytime you agree to argue, you open up the expectation in your teenager that he or she might persuade you to change your mind.

Here again, remember how conflict creates resemblance. That is, in a conflict, each party tends to imitate the other's influential tactics. So the child explains the exchange of blows with a sibling, "I hit him back because he hit me." Or the parent says, "I yelled at my teenager to stop her from yelling at me." Imitating counterproductive conduct in conflict only causes misconduct to continue and makes the conflict worse. Now two people are behaving badly instead of one. So when in argument with your teenager, model constructive behavior so that she has a chance to learn good conflict habits from imitating you.

How you refuse to argue with your teenager can also be inflammatory when you choose to offer no rational defense for your decision. This is when the teenager accuses parents of being "unreasonable," of taking a stand without having adequate (or even any) logic to back it up. And the young person is often correct, because many demands and limits parents make have very little to do with reason, which is only one basis for parental decision making. There are others. There is *authority*: "Because I say so, that's why!" There is *fatigue*: "Because I'm tired, that's why!" There are *values*: "Because I believe it's right, that's why!" There is *experience*: "Because I know what I'm talking about, that's why!" There are *tolerances*: "Because I can't stand it, that's why!" There is *self-interest*: "Because I want it this way, that's why!" Teenagers partly argue with their parents out of the belief that all parental rules, requests, and restraints should be governed by reason, and in many cases they simply aren't. When parents don't have a good reason, they can still have a solid basis, and they can say what this is.

One of the problems in arguments between parents and teenager is the inequity of benefit. In general, the adolescent derives more benefit from arguing with parents than parents do from arguing with the teenager. For this reason, parents need to have adequate *conflict avoidance skills* so that they can keep the frequency of argument within their tolerances, and only engage in conflicts of sufficient importance to them. If they cannot, they will suffer stress from more conflict than they have the energy to afford. There are many ways to stay out of arguments when your teenager is up for one and you are not. You can declare what you want without having to justify it. "This is what I need to have you do." You can explain your stand or request without having to defend it. "I need the cleanup done before our friends arrive." You can discuss to understand a difference without arguing over who is right. "I'm not trying to change your mind, just giving you my point of view." You can listen to disagreement without having to rebut it. "I hear what you say, and I am glad to know what you think." You can respectfully refuse an invitation into argument. "This isn't something I have the inclination or energy to debate."

There are two times not to avoid an argument with your adolescent. The first instance is when you are doing so out of anxiety over having an unpleasant or intense confrontation. To avoid argument out of fear is to give the adolescent emotionally extortionate power over your freedom to speak up and your responsibility to take a stand. The second instance is when avoiding the issue creates a delay that allows it to get worse. An unhappy example of both instances arises when parents avoid raising concerns about their teenager's substance use because they know he will vigorously deny what is going on, and while this confrontation is delayed, the substance use or abuse may get worse.

One rule for conducting conflict on both sides of the parent-adolescent divide is to keep the communication declarative and not allow it to become manipulative. This means that no one employs emotional extortion or allows this manipulation to let the other person get his or her way.

## Emotional Extortion

What is emotional extortion, and where is it learned? Little children do it all the time. Powerless when refused what they want by a parent, they may signify displeasure by communicating disappointment (sulking), hurt (crying), or outrage (tantrum). What happens next is formatively important, and in most parent-child relationships this response occurs some of the time. Faced with the child's sulking, crying, or tantrum, the parent feels regret or remorse for saying no, or simply seeks relief from the emotional intensity and so relents. "All right, just this once, you can have it [or do it], since it matters so much to you. Just stop making such a fuss!"

Now the child brightens up—and learns that there is power in the strong expression of emotion, particularly unhappiness. It can be used to get his way. In fact, one psychologist, John Narciso (see his book *Declare Yourself*, 1975) called this category of behaviors "get my way techniques." Another psychologist, Susan Forward, wrote a book about this emotional manipulation (*Emotional Blackmail*, 1997). In one of my early books, *Keys to Single Parenting* (1996), I called it "emotional extortion." During adolescence, when gaining freedom from parents becomes increasingly important, manipulation of parental authority through lying, pretense, and pressuring becomes more common. Emotional extortion can combine all three. Thus, when pleading and argument fail to win a parent over or get a parent to back down, the tactics of emotional extortion can come into play. The particular emotions employed vary according to the emotional susceptibility of the parents, but the objective is always the same: to persuade parents to give in, give way, back down, or change their mind. Consider a few of the forms emotional extortion can take.

- Parents who are *uncomfortable with emotional intensity* may tiptoe around a potentially explosive teenager and avoid confrontation to avoid upsetting him, thereby letting an important issue go. *They don't want to face an unpleasant outburst.*

- Parents who are *susceptible to flattery* may become easily led when a teenager gives them her loving appreciation and admiration in order to get what she wants. *They are hungry for praise.*

- Parents who *can't stand disappointing* others may relent when told by a teenager how they have let him down. *They hate failing to please.*

- Parents who are *prone to guilt* may give in to assuage the teenager's expression of hurt and suffering for which she holds them responsible, and they agree. *They are easily stricken with self-blame.*

- Parents who are *fearful of harm* may act intimidated when a teenager acts aggressively, allowing him to bully and get his way. *They are scared by anger.*

- Parents who *feel lonely without a close connection* may capitulate to a teenager who acts apathetic, as though she no longer cares and is ready to dismiss the value of the relationship. *They don't want to be abandoned.*

In each case, strong emotional expression by the teenager can exploit an emotional vulnerability in the parent to extortionate effect.

Parents need to identify what feelings make it emotionally hard for them to hold their ground, because their adolescent will know what these feelings are, and may play on them to get his way. To discourage these manipulations, parents must refuse to play along with the extortion. They must resist their own susceptibilities to emotional discomfort, flattery, rejection, guilt, intimidation, apathy, and the like and refuse to let these emotional vulnerabilities influence their decisions. Give in to these tactics, and they will feel bad about themselves, their teenager, and their relationship; more important, they may reluctantly allow what they know is unwise and potentially harmful to the adolescent. "I know I shouldn't have let her go. I didn't want to. But she was so unhappy with me for refusing, I just couldn't say no, and now look at what has happened!"

Parents must not only hold firm in the face of this emotional manipulation but also hold the teenager to declarative account. Thus when the teenager uses intense anger or suffering to overcome a parental refusal, the parent needs to be able to say (and mean), "Acting outraged or hurt is not going to change my mind. However, if you want to tell me specifically about why you are feeling so upset about what you want to have happen or not happen, I certainly want to listen to what you have to say."

Declaration creates understanding, but emotional manipulation creates distrust. For example, the tired parent comes home at the end of the day, and the teenager, genuinely wanting to express her love through an act of consideration, has the evening meal all prepared. But the parent, having been softened up by such acts of apparent caring before, is unwilling to act appreciative. Instead, he responds by asking a cynical question: "What do you want this time?" That's one consequence of emotional extortion; it can discredit the expression of honest feeling.

Of course, just as the adolescent first learned the power of emotional extortion in childhood, so did you. Therefore, do not resort to this manipulation with your teenagers. For example, don't use sorrow or pity for yourself, sulking or brooding, sadness or suffering, to elicit guilt in your teenager. It's a bad bargain: she gets to stop feeling responsible for your unhappiness in exchange for you getting your way and cheering up after she capitulates to what you want. When in conflict, declare what you want or do not want to have happen in specific terms, then discuss and negotiate the disagreement. If you use the strong expression of emotion to get your way, through your own bad example you will encourage extortionate behavior by your teenager. And do not use emotional extortion when in disagreement with your partner either. There will be enough disagreements about your adolescent without making them harder to resolve than they already are.

## Managing Parental Disagreement

It's easy for parents to get crossways about their adolescent when they perceive teenage conduct or wants in contrasting ways and differ about what the best response should be. So one parent thinks they should let the young teenager go to the concert, and the other parent thinks they should just say no. The first parent has always been a risk-taker, the second parent more inclined to consider safety first. Because parents are different people, they will naturally approach parenting differently, and those differences are in constant play between them, and disagreement is one expression of this play.

The problem of parental disagreement dates from the child's birth, when diverging ideas about child rearing unexpectedly arise. For example, when the infant is whimpering in the other room, they can have opposing beliefs about how to react. Says one, "We need to pick her up and provide comfort right away." Says the other, "Do that and you'll spoil her; she needs to get herself back to sleep." What's going on? In this case, there is a value difference they didn't know they had until now. One parent believes that providing security is a priority; the other parent believes that training in self-reliance should start early. Who's right? They both are, because each possesses a significant piece of the parenting puzzle they bring to child raising. Security and self-reliance are both important to encourage in a growing child.

Every marriage is like this, a union between two people from different family backgrounds, with different values, practices, and traditions. In addition, sex-role development and gender training also set them apart (as described in Chapter Four). This natural diversity between them needs to be treated as a source of richness and not divisiveness, as a source of wisdom and not a cause for argument. Value differences in parenting are not to be quarreled about; they are to be respected. Parents should not be in the business of questioning or criticizing each other's child-raising values. Rather, they need to translate their value position into what each wants to have happen and then negotiate those wants to create a decision both can support, leaving the value difference between them intact. So, in the case of the fussing infant, for example, parents reach a compromise: delay but not denial. They decide to wait five minutes, and if the child doesn't stop whimpering, they will pick her up then.

What is the right parenting decision? That is hard to determine, because short-term benefits (protection in the present, for example) can have long-term costs (risk aversion in the future, for example). There is rarely the luxury of knowing what decision is best because parenting is not a science based on verifiable principles of child raising. It is a well-intentioned process of decision making, problem solving one issue to the next being what most parents try to do. Consulting "parenting experts" only provides more food for thought, not certainty about how best to proceed.

Parenthood is full of surprises. Parents probably didn't know they would have child-raising differences when they were a childless couple. Relatively speaking, sharing individual lives as partners was simple. But roles change and complicate relationships. When partners transition into becoming parents together, wife becomes mother and husband becomes father. Neither has inhabited or known the other in that role before. In addition, they haven't had any experience or given much thought to how they want to define and operate a family of their own. So during the years when they are raising young children (up to about age nine), they are defining their respective parental roles and developing the practices of family. As for the kids, for the most part they accept the parental roles and family structure they are given, roles and structure on which parents mostly agree.

Come the onset of adolescence (beginning around ages nine to thirteen), however, when the five developmental engines that drive young people toward more individuality and independence—separation, expansion, differentiation, opposition, and responsibility—begin to fire off, their parenting is challenged in ways it was not before. In this process, managing their teenager's freedom-loving conduct usually creates more disagreement between parents. For example, just consider a few of the either-or decisions parents must make:

Should they notice or ignore?

Should they confront or let go?

Should they accept or question?

Should they permit or forbid?

Should they talk to or punish?

Should they believe or distrust?

Should they help or stay hands off?

Should they say something or nothing?

Should they treat it seriously or lightly?

Should they stick to their word or change their mind?

These questions have the power to provoke disagreement between parents.

As the adolescent pushes for more risky behavior, the seriousness of parenting decisions increases. Parents have to be able to reach agreement. If they can't, their indecision will rule, their disagreement will send a double message, and the teenager may be left to have the deciding vote. In either case, the teenager is likely to exploit parental uncertainty or disunity for freedom's sake. This is not to say that parents must operate exactly the same. In fact, there is an important distinction to be made between differences in parental styles that are to be expected, and differences in parental decision making that are counterproductive.

Because of the individuality of each parent, each will have his or her own way of communicating and relating to their adolescent, and that needs to be accepted by them both. So, for example, one parent may be more inclined to jump in uninvited with an opinion, while the other parent is more inclined to withhold advice unless requested. About the first parent, the teenager says, "I always know where my mom stands and what she thinks." About the second parent, the teenager says, "I can always get a good listen from my dad and some suggestions if I ask." Both parents are valued and valuable, but each in a different way.

Each parent's view of the adolescent and relationship to the adolescent is going to be somewhat different, and that is okay as long as both parents communicate the same message when it comes to family rules and limits. There, parents need to arrive at the same place. A shared front both unifies parents and creates stability for the teenager. For example: homework and household chores will be done, curfew and parental needs for information will be respected, and significant family functions will be attended.

As for parental disagreement about what response or decision to make, parents need to appreciate several benefits that this discord can bring.

- *Parental disagreement can be expansive.* Having access to two different ways of looking at the same issue or problem can broaden and deepen parental understanding. The perspectives of two can be "smarter" (more adequate) than the bias of one. So one parent says, "I know you think her lack of motivation at school comes from being mad at the move, and that we have to be firm about her accepting what she doesn't like. But I think what may also be going on is that she is sad and misses her old friends. Maybe we need to do something to help her with that."

- *Parental disagreement can be corrective.* Both parents can be a helpful observer of each other's parenting, offering suggestions when the other gets stuck in an unproductive interaction. So a mother suggests to a father, "Maybe you're too hard on him. Constant criticism isn't going to motivate him to do better. He'll only feel hurt and angry and act worse. Give him some positive recognition for all that he is doing well." Or a father suggests to a mother, "Maybe you should stop fighting to control her all the time. The more you try to micromanage her, the more she's going to fight you back. Give her some room to make her own choices."

- *Parental disagreement can be strengthening.* By sharing and understanding divergent points of view and by reaching a mutually acceptable decision, parents enhance the intimacy in the relationship. Each parent comes to better know and be better known by the other when they forge agreement out of disagreement and further unify the marriage. So one parent testifies, "I didn't fully appreciate how we believed so differently about this, and I feel closer now having reached a choice we both can support."

Children, particularly adolescents, give parents a lot to disagree about. How parents manage this disagreement is only secondarily about the welfare of the child. Primarily it is about their partnership and how by marrying their views on a difficult parenting decision they can further strengthen the marriage they have made. A healthy parental partnership needs dialogue over disagreement because adequate parental separation contributes to the support of a strong marriage. Or, as it has been more wisely put by poet Kahlil Gibran, "The pillars of the temple stand apart." To stand apart and stay together, whether as partner with partner or as parent with adolescent, requires the capacity to bridge with interest the differences that are causing the separation.

## Bridging Differences with Interest

It's a practice of parenting that's worth considering when your children enter adolescence: *bridging differences with interest.* Think of it this way. Two kinds of differences in the relationship between parent and child increase when adolescence begins—differences in individuality and differences of disagreement. *Differences in individuality* increase as the young person begins to explore and experiment with new expressions of personal definition and identity. This is done in order to discover the unique individuals they will become, in contrast to the children they were and the way parents are. *Differences from disagreement* increase as the young person engages in more opposition and conflict with parents in order to live on more independent terms within the family.

A parent who is intolerant of unfamiliar differences ("Turn off that noise you call music!") and who allows no differences of opinion ("Don't you talk back to me!") asserts authority to his or her cost. Now significant human differences, instead of becoming a bridge to more understanding, become a barrier to communication and an obstruction in the relationship. So consider this parenting question: Are you going to treat normal differences between you and your teenager as a source of divisiveness that sets you further apart or as a source of richness that can draw you more closely together? For example, suppose the parents I just quoted had responded differently to their respective teenagers. Suppose instead of objecting to the music, the disapproving parent had said, "Your music is really different from what I'm used to; could you tell me what you like about it and help me appreciate it too?" Suppose instead of forbidding disagreement, one of the offended parents had said, "We really see things differently; could you help me better understand your point of view?" Now, instead of closing down communication, these parents are opening it up.

At issue is whether a parent treats the adolescent, whose tastes are changing, as an offender or as an instructor. At issue is whether a parent treats an adolescent, who engages in more family conflict, as an opponent or an informant. A parent doesn't have to like an adolescent's changing tastes (in dress or entertainment, for example) to be interested in learning what they express for the teenager and what appeal they hold. A parent doesn't have to agree with the adolescent's point of view in their more frequent conflict (over schoolwork or social freedom, for example) to be interested in understanding what and why it is. The skill lies in turning differences into talking points.

Frequently parents will complain about how argumentative their adolescent has become, and I always ask, "Why are you complaining?" After all, argument is interaction, information is being offered, and communication is going on. Would they rather live with an unknowable, silent, withdrawn, mysterious teenager who refuses to talk at all? Or parents will complain about the worthless activities and tasteless fads and wasted time the adolescent spends his or her life on. Would they rather live with a teenager who never outgrew childhood preoccupations or had no older activities of interest or was totally out of step with the changing adolescent world?

Perhaps most important, there is a huge life lesson that parents can teach their adolescent regarding the management of differences in relationships—whether arising from contrasting individuality or from contentious opposition. It has to do with learning the art of intimacy, an education that will serve young people well in the conduct of their caring relationships later on. There are two paths to intimacy—the easy and the hard. The easy path is sharing similarities, what the couple has in common, what they do and share together. Having a lot in common is definitely important in their enjoyment of each other's company. The hard path is supporting the union by mutually working through and around normal human differences, with both parties respecting and resolving issues of diversity between them. Partners in a relationship who say with pride that they never disagree actually only have half an intimacy because they suppress or avoid confronting the reality of human differences between them. So if a parent can teach the adolescent how to bridge differences between them with interest, how to turn differences in individuality and in disagreement into informative talking points, this will well prepare the young person for healthy adult intimacy to come.

Typically, parents have less in common and more in contention with the adolescent than with the child, and that is to be expected. Given this reality, I believe it is best to heed the view a seasoned parent once offered at a workshop a number of years ago: "For me, the changes of the teenage years have been a chance to get to know my kids all over again."

Recognizing the use and abuse of conflict with adolescents requires appreciating the healthy function it serves and how that use can be subverted—when resolution is reached in a manipulative and not a declarative manner, for example. Keeping conflict constructive is key to keeping parent and teenager connected as more differences arise between them. Also key is understanding what forms of parental discipline tend to work well and what forms do not, to be discussed in the next chapter.

## Chapter Seven

# Discipline That Does and Doesn't Work

> I tell you I've done all I know to control my teen-
> ager. I've tried every kind of discipline short of
> something physical that I could think of, but I'm
> up against a wall. The harder I push, the more
> determined she gets. I'm military, used to com-
> manding, and never thought I'd meet a recruit who
> could out-stubborn me. She's only fourteen years
> old and refuses to do what she's told! You're a child
> psychologist. You tell me some punishment that
> will work!

Discipline is about much more than what parents do or say to
right a child or adolescent who's been acting wrong. Discipline
is the ongoing combination of instruction, approval, and correction through which a son or daughter is influenced to live within
family rules and according to family values. The power of instruction is that it gives direction to behavior. The power of approval
is that it encourages continuation of desirable behavior. The
power of correction is that discourages continuation of undesir-
able behavior.

The goal of parental discipline is to teach teenagers to
responsibly manage themselves independently. In this sense,
the function of parental discipline is to teach the adolescent
self-discipline. To examine discipline with an adolescent takes
exploring the problems of balance, authority, punishment, anger,

criticism, yelling, and effective practices. Start with keeping an appropriate balance.

## Balance

During the child's adolescence, as the teenager becomes more oppositional and pushes for more freedom, parents tend to feel less in charge, less in control, and more anxious. And as they do, they often start thinking of discipline in more punitive terms, relying more on the powers of correction to get the adolescent to do what they say, relying less on instruction and approval—to their cost, because when punishment becomes the only disciplinary influence they have, they aren't left with very much.

In my opinion, to maintain effective discipline, there needs to be about 90 percent instruction and approval, and at most only 10 percent correction. Reverse that proportionality, as some frustrated, frightened, or angry parents do, and the adolescent's behavior is likely to get worse, not better, because the more consistently negative parents become, the more resistant and negative the adolescent acts in response. As one defiant teenager put it, "Who wants to do what parents want when all they want to do is punish you?" Instruction and approval make positive contributions to the relationship and build the *collateral of cooperation*—the teenager is motivated to work with parents. When parents make no positive deposit, they are less likely to get a positive return.

When parents think of adolescence itself, they often focus on that poster characteristic of the age—*teenage rebellion*. Two common types of rebellion are against socially fitting in (rebellion of nonconformity) and against adult authority (rebellion of noncompliance). In both types, rebellion attracts adult attention by offending it. The young person proudly asserts individuality from what parents like or independence of what parents want and in each case succeeds in provoking their disapproval, wearing it like a badge of honor. This is why rebellion, which is simply behavior that deliberately opposes the ruling norms or powers that be, has been given a good name by adolescents and a bad one by parents. Now begins a running contest over who will live on whose terms. And as the relationship becomes more frequently embattled, parental discipline is faced by a host of new matters of concern. For example, in early adolescence there commonly are more issues over completing homework, in mid-adolescence more issues over doing chores, in late adolescence more issues over setting a nightly curfew, and in trial independence more issues over who pays for what. All along the way, parents are struggling to maintain authority as they lose more control.

## Authority

Why is parental authority important? Parents need authority in order to support the enormous responsibility they have assumed for a child's daily care and healthy growth. Parental authority is easier to establish during your son's or daughter's childhood (up to about eight or nine) than it is to maintain during the young person's adolescence (beginning nine to thirteen). At this time, when their child is in late elementary or early middle school, parents start hearing more statements of opposition like "Why should I?" "I don't have to!" "You can't make me!" And there are more complaints like "It's my life, not yours!" "All you do is order me around!" "You're not the boss of the world!" In addition, there are the unending arguments: "Give me a good reason!" And there is the persistent play for delay: "I'll do it later!" So what happened to the cooperative child?

Adolescents contest adult rules and restraints because they want to establish more independence. Determined to operate more on their own terms, they protest the imposition of demands and limits on their freedom. Where *the child lived in the age of command* ("I do what my parents say because I have to"), *adolescents have entered the age of consent* ("My parents can't make me or stop me unless I agree"). The formula for adolescent obedience to parental authority is simply this: *command + consent = compliance*. Parental authority is not automatic or absolute. It is not a matter of parents being able to control adolescent choices; it's a matter of controlling their own choices in ways that allow them to assert influence on the choices the teenager makes. And it takes work, this working for *consent*.

Consent can be secured by a variety of parental approaches. For example, you can declare your need for cooperation, make a serious and firm request, attach motivational consequences to compliance or noncompliance, repeat insistence to show you mean business, explain reasons that are persuasive, or negotiate a deal to get what you want that the teenager agrees to keep.

Sometimes I will hear parents complain about their adolescent's change of attitude.

"The problem is, my teenager no longer respects my authority!" The dad was angry.

"How can you tell?" I asked.

"Because she argues with anything I tell her to do!" was his reply.

"And after the argument?" I continued asking.

"Well, then she finally does what I wanted, on her own good time. It's exhausting! See what I mean? No respect!"

But I disagreed. "If she paid attention to what you said by taking issue with it and then ended up doing what you asked, this means she still respects your authority. She just likes it less and resists it more."

During adolescence, obedience to authority often comes with a couple of unwelcome compromises. First, the father's daughter needs to have her say (to have her protest be given a full and fair hearing) before the father gets his way (and then she consents to do what he wants). And second, although he gets to state what he wants, delay before it is accomplished is up to her. After getting enough "say" and enough "when," she does what he asks—or at least partly. So she finally washes the dishes, but she doesn't use soap, and now the dad feels as though he's back to square one. But he keeps insisting to wear down her resistance; and to get him to stop what she calls his "nagging," she finally does what he asks. Both protest and delayed compliance with parental authority show respect, just respect of a more resistant and grudging kind. It is ignoring and refusal that show disrespect. Come adolescence, parents often won't get exactly what they want, exactly how they want it done, exactly when they want it done, and this is to be expected. The older the adolescent grows, the more she pushes back against parental authority. And this opposition is functional because it ultimately yields independence—parent and adolescent willing to let each other go, the young person finally shouldering responsibility to direct her own life.

In childhood, the benefit of parental authority—parents declaring what to do, what not to do, what is right, what is wrong, what works, what doesn't work—is that it gives structure and direction to a child's life. It gives the child a reference for making decisions that he can internalize and follow without having to figure out how to believe and behave entirely on his own. The child depends on this foundation for safe and healthy functioning. Although adolescents still need the preparation and protection of parental authority, they also need more experience of becoming their own authority if they are ever to become functionally independent. Turning over increased amounts of responsibility to the teenager is how this education in becoming one's own authority is done.

"How am I going to control what I spend if you stop giving my allowance to me on a weekly basis and start giving it to me a month at a time?" asks the high school sophomore. "You are going to have to be your own boss about how to make your money last," reply the parents. "You are going to have to tell yourself what to do and then make yourself do it. You have to learn to make yourself make your money last because if you run out before the end of the month, there will be no advances."

What the teenager discovers is that although he has fought their authority on many fronts, in many ways accepting their authority has made his life easier to manage. Giving up reliance on parental authority and establishing independent (responsible) authority is not as easy as it looks, as many adolescents in trial independence (eighteen to twenty-three) will testify: "When I was in middle school I fought my parents all the time. 'You can't make me!' I would say. But since I'm in college and they're not around to push me or stop me, my complaint is different. 'I can't make me!' is the problem now. Getting myself to do what I know I should is a battle I lose more often than I win."

Parents who seem to have the most difficulty when adolescent resistance begins are those who link their authority to self-esteem—they need to be right, unquestioned, obeyed, and in charge. Any loss of authority can feel like a loss of face and so is intolerable. This is when power struggles can ensue, a parent determined to go to any lengths and employ any means to prevail, so as to prove who is boss. This is when parental punishment can get out of hand, doing more harm than good.

## Punishment

Punishing their adolescent is one of the more unrewarding parts of parental discipline. Not only does it add negativity to a temporarily strained relationship; it can provoke the adolescent to punish parents in return. This payback is commonly administered by acting mad, complaining about mistreatment, or refusing to talk to them for some period of time. This is a kind of "You showed me"–"I'll show you" exchange of disfavor. Punishment is *not* for minor infractions like leaving the refrigerator door open again or not turning out the lights. It is not for continuing aggravations like playing music too loudly or not picking up or cleaning up after themselves. It is not for resisting responsibilities like "forgetting homework" or delaying chores. These last two are supervisory matters.

*Supervision = checking up on + keeping after about.* Supervision is the relentless application of parental persistence to overcome adolescent resistance to taking care of normal household business. Threaten punishment for not doing homework or chores, and you make it sound as though the adolescent has a choice as far as you're concerned. Choose not to do them and face a punishment instead. No. These are no-choice activities. They *will* be done. Parental supervision stays informed and uses exhausting repetition to wear adolescent opposition down so that chores and homework are completed. The teenager is correct to label supervision "nagging," but nagging is honorable work. It is drudgery to do, but it needs to be done because it shows that parents are serious and will follow through with insistence to get what they requested.

The purpose of punishment is to discourage recurrence of a major rule violation by applying a consequence of sufficient impact to discourage the young person from that particular misbehavior again. The magnitude of the offenses that punishment is meant to address are such serious transgressions as sneaking out after hours for a night of adventure on the town, taking an underage joyride in the family car, stealing from a family member, and the like. These are all infractions that either risk or actually commit harm. Of course, punishment is not the primary or only way to deal with serious violations. First, try to use communication to hear out, talk out, and work out an agreement with the teenager so that any damages are dealt with, amends are made, a lesson has been learned, and repetition of the offense is not likely to occur again. Assuming there is no likelihood that the violation will be repeated, then communication is enough, and there is no need for additional punishment. The power of punishment to reform is vastly overrated. It often fails to motivate positive behavior because it only enforces what not to do, but it doesn't prescribe and instruct and reinforce what to do differently instead. A punitive consequence has far less corrective power than thorough communication.

Reflecting back on her mothering, a grandmother who had effectively raised four children of her own once testified to the power of pure talk. "When any one of them stepped out of line, they all knew what was coming: a good old fashioned *talking to*, only they called it a lecture, and there was nothing they hated worse. I think they would have preferred something quick like a spanking to get it over with, but I've never been the spanking kind. For however long it took, and it could take a while, I'd get me a cup of coffee and we'd sit down to talk the trouble out, me talking enough to them and they talking enough to me, until I was satisfied we both fully understood what happened, why it happened, and how it wasn't going to ever happen again. And it never did."

It's when communication is insufficient to teach an adequate lesson that punishment is called into play. Now, to get their message across about the seriousness of the violation, parents use punitive actions to teach what mere words will not convey. At this point punishment is employed to make a corrective point by catching the young person's attention, causing her to rethink her actions and, the parents hope, encourage her back into compliance. So parents have their middle school child pay for her part in papering all the trees at a nearby elementary school by first hearing what the offended principal has to say, then spending the next weekend hosing all the paper down and picking it up, and the two following Saturdays donating free service to work on the school's grounds. It's pretty unlikely that the young woman will participate in this kind of vandalism again. And sometimes the natural consequences of the violation provide sufficient deterrence. Thus when the twelve-year-old, against home rules, plays with fire that starts getting out of hand, the young person—burning himself in the process of frantically patting it out, frightened lest the conflagration spread—may be cured of doing it again. In this case, just talking with him about the scary experience and ministering to the hurt may be all parents have to do. The violation itself has proved punishing enough.

In the same way, parents don't have to double punish for what has already been punished by outside authorities. If a school violation has occurred, with several days of in-school suspension ordered to pay for the infraction, then parents simply have to help their son or daughter connect the misbehavior with the consequence. "It sounds like school is really serious about not permitting that kind of behavior. So now you know." Because outside authorities are willing to play the heavy, "the bad guy," parents don't have to double punish by adding one of their own at home. They have the luxury of empathizing with their adolescent. "School must feel lonely when you're unable to see your friends." But silently they support the consequence that was justly given, and encourage learning positive lessons from a negative experience.

When it comes to punishing their adolescent, most parents understand that even if they resorted to spanking (or other acts of physical hurt) when he or she was a child, now with a teenager this corrective response does more harm than good, as it may have done back then. From what I have heard in counseling with young people, physical punishment creates enormous humiliation and anger in the teenager and deeply alienates the relationship. Physical punishment that teenagers accepted as children, even though they didn't like it, they object to as adolescents because they feel they should have outgrown that kind of parental discipline by now. Not only does it seem inappropriate; it feels demeaning. At worst, in those cases where the young person decides not to take it, and stands up and physically fights back, it risks power struggles in which one or both parties can get seriously hurt. Besides all this, spanking causes the adolescent to lose respect for parental authority as it teaches a formative lesson. If you are bigger or stronger or adult, are angry or want to get your way or need to be in control, using physical force to inflict pain is okay. *Spanking teaches hitting.* And the lesson can stick. Getting hit at home by a parent can encourage more use of hitting with siblings. How someone was treated as a child can also influence how he treats children of his own later on. And this aggressive inclination can even activate physical mistreatment when in dispute with a romantic or marriage partner.

As for the parent with teenagers who fear crossing him lest more physical reprisal comes their way, he may think that they respect his authority, but he is mistaken. In reality he has become a bully in their eyes, an object of their resentment and contempt. Unhappily, his future relationship with his adult children can be marked for evermore. Even if the treatment is forgiven, the "angry whippings" are not forgotten. Punishment needs to be free of parental anger. Otherwise parents can be emotionally encouraged to use punishment to get back at or to get even with the young person, hurting him or her to retaliate for being crossed. At worst, coupled with punishment, anger can impel parents to release frustration through harsh words or extreme actions that they may have later cause to regret, and the young person long remembers. "When I got caught, my mom and dad made sure I'd never forget how angry they were. And I never have."

If they are going to penalize bad behavior, and punishment is the most extreme penalty they can impose, parents must also be sure to recognize and reward the incidence of good. Otherwise, the teenager may be left with the impression one young man shared: "My parents think all I'm good at is messing up. I guess they're right." Then accepting their discouraging verdict, he continued his errant ways. In this case, it would have helped if parents had not fixated on the misconduct but had acknowledged his record and capacity for constructive behavior as well. After all, a young person, no matter the difficulties he is creating, is far greater than the sum of his misdeeds, and parents must communicate their vision of this larger definition, particularly when they are in punishment mode. "Bad choices like this are not the only ones you make; they are the exception to the rule. Good choices are most of what you do." They need to acknowledge his history of positive performance and his positive potentialities, so that, seeing them in himself, he can feel encouraged to choose a more constructive way.

When it comes to punishing their adolescent, parents' number-one choice seems to be *deprivation*—temporarily removing something of value in the young person's life in consequence of his or her committing some serious misdeed. The "game of takeaway," as one teenager called it, is played by parents when their teenager doesn't play by basic family rules. Resources that seem to be most commonly denied in this electronic age are cell phones, messaging devices, and the computer. Without them the young person is handicapped in his communication with peers at a time when being in constant touch with them feels all-important.

Of course, the most common deprivation that parents use to punish major infractions is the loss of social freedom—*grounding*. For most adolescents, freedom is the breath of life, so denying social freedom by imposing home confinement can really hurt. Social circulation is cut off while the social interaction among friends keeps going on. On the plus side for parents, their power of permission is amplified by their power to restrict. On the downside, however, they lose some freedom as well because now the jailers are forced to keep uneasy company with the unhappy person being jailed. Because deprivation has considerable effect, parents need to use it judiciously. Here are four guidelines to consider:

1. *Do not strip your teenager of every freedom, as parents who punish in anger can be prone to do.* When you take every resource and freedom away, you have just liberated your adolescent because he or she has nothing left to lose. "Now you've got nothing else to take away!"

2. *Do not take away a pillar of self-esteem.* For example, do not prohibit participation in some activity like sports or a special interest through which the young person nourishes her development and good feelings about herself. To do so

is destructive, not just corrective. Find some valued resource or freedom to temporarily deny that is not at the expense of the teenager's growth.

3. *When grounding, do not cut off all social contact for your adolescent.* Your purpose is to temporarily reduce full freedom of contact with friends, but not to cut that contact off entirely. So if you are keeping her in this weekend, don't disallow cell phone and computer communication. This way, she can be out of the social flow but still be in touch with what is going on.

4. *Keep grounding short term—a matter of days, not a matter of weeks or months.* The longer you take your young person out of social action, the more you put her at risk of losing social position, the lower her social standing among friends when she returns, and the more subject to peer pressure she may be as she struggles to reestablish herself.

An alternative to *grounding in*, exercised less frequently, is *grounding out*. This is usually invoked with late adolescents, maybe seventeen years old or so, who want to live at home but now feel entitled to throw off all the traces of parental restraints. A common example is rejecting any parental curfew. "I'm old enough to stay out as late as I like, overnight if I want to, and you can't stop me!" To which statement of defiance, parents wisely agree. "That's right. We're running a home, not a prison; but a home still has rules. You are free to ignore our curfew; that is up to you. But we are obliged to enforce it; that is our responsibility." And then they explain how "grounding out" will work. Different from grounding in (and limiting social freedom), grounding out (and limiting residency) is explained to an older adolescent like this:

"Should you decide to miss your curfew, when you return the home will be locked against you for twelve hours from the time we start our day. Leaving is up to you; but when you are allowed back in is up to us. Now you must make your own arrangements to stay elsewhere, unable to come back and use anything or get anything you need until the day away is over. Then you can call us, and at our convenience we will agree to meet with you at a neutral place where we will explain the hours you need to keep in order to live with us, and you can choose to commit to meeting our curfew or not. Should you decide to come home and then break curfew again, the waiting period before return will be twenty-four hours, a third time forty-eight hours, and so on. Of course we'll miss you and wish you were at home with the family, but as you said, how late you stay out is ultimately up to you."

I've seen only a few parents do this with older adolescents over the years, but it has mostly proved effective.

In general, deprivation has a major drawback as a corrective. It is passive punishment because all that parents are asking the young person to do is to do nothing or to do without. It makes no demands on the young person's energy or time. This is why a more effective punishment than deprivation is *reparation*. Reparation is active punishment because it prescribes tasks to be done to work off the offense. Thus the parent says something like this: "In consequence of what you did that you know you shouldn't do, there's going to be some additional work to do around our home [or service to provide in the community] that will need to be completed before I set you free to do anything else you want to do. And that work must be performed to my satisfaction." Not only do parents or the community get some benefit from the young person's sentence; while engaged in this labor, the teenager keeps in mind the rule violation he or she is working off. Some parents even keep a list of household projects that need doing around the place tacked on the refrigerator in anticipation of the next infraction. "For starters, see these windows? Well, they all need washing—inside and out."

Deprivation and reparation can both be effective punishments, with this proviso. After the terms of punishment have been duly accomplished, then parents need to consider the violation paid for "in full," which means they do not refer to it again.

A parent who holds on to past violations, who will not let them go, "keeping books against me" as one teenager called it, builds up a history of complaints that no young person can ever overcome. "My parents remember everything bad I've ever done. And the next time I get in trouble, which sooner or later is bound to happen, they bring it all up against me. Nothing I do wrong is ever over with. It's just added to the list of all the wrong I've done."

When a young person's serious rule breaking causes hurt or injury to someone else, reparation takes on the added dimension of *restitution*. This involves meeting with the victim (if the victim is willing); getting to hear from the victim about all the material, physical, and emotional damage that was done; and then working out some actual amends to the person to compensate for the hurt. So the high school junior offers to wash his older sister's car each weekend for the next two months as amends for "borrowing" it without permission and returning it trashed from a night's ill use.

It's easy for a parent to get angry at a major teenage infraction because the parent feels violated. "You wore my favorite shirt to the beach and lost it?" "You led me on by lying about what really happened?" "You used my credit card?" This is where anger normally comes into play, to identify violations to one's well-being and energize an expressive, protective, or corrective response to what feels wrong, unfair, or unjust.

## Anger

*Never punish in anger.* First because you are likely to overpunish by letting emotion do your thinking for you. Second because, having overpunished ("You are grounded for a year!"), you will have to modify or retract your decision, thereby showing that you didn't mean what you said. Or having given verbal or physical injury, you feel you have to apologize for what cannot be undone. And third, your anger will get in the way of the lesson you are trying to teach when the teenager believes you are only punishing because of being angry, not in response to what she has done. Always take time to think before you punish, making it a rational and not emotional decision. Besides, waiting for you to calm down and collect your thoughts before you decide and he is told what needs to happen becomes part of the punishment your teenager has to endure.

But what if you are an *anger-prone parent*, easily triggered into temper outbursts by normal adolescent aggravations? If so, it helps to know how you can be primed to emotionally overreact when such minor challenges occur. Although anger, like all emotions, is a very good informant, it can be a very bad adviser when it encourages "thinking" with one's feelings instead of consulting better judgment. So, confronted by a defiant adolescent, the anger-prone parent explodes and says some hurtful things both she and her daughter have painful cause to regret.

So how do you tell if you are an anger-prone parent? Consider five characteristics:

1. You have a *high need for control* and get angry when dominance is challenged or lost, or use anger to get your way. So the parent exclaims, "I will be in charge; you will do what I say!"

2. You are *highly judgmental,* feeling easily offended when others don't meet your standards or don't do things as you like, which you believe is the best and proper approach. So the parent exclaims, "I am correct; my way is the right way!"

3. You *take personally what is not personally meant,* assuming that accidental slights or offenses were deliberate when that was not the case. So the parent exclaims, "You did that on purpose; you were out to get me!"

4. You *use anger as an outlet* to express built-up irritation and stress. So the parent exclaims, "I've had enough; this is too much to take!"

5. You *hold on to past grievances*, storing up resentments that can be easily inflamed when a similar affront or injury occurs. So the parent exclaims, "This is just like before; I'm being mistreated again!"

These characteristics are not immutable. With practice they can be modified. If needed, counseling and therapy can help parents learn to step back from the precipice of explosive anger and stop overreacting by recalibrating their emotional set points. For example, they can practice being less controlling, less judgmental, and less ready to take affronts and irritations as intentional insults. They can process injuries and frustrations as they arise, and can become more willing to let go of old injuries and grievances.

Now consider two kinds of discipline that generally don't work, at least for the good—criticism and yelling.

## Criticism

It's tempting for parents to criticize their adolescent. As the compliant and endearing child becomes the more resistant and abrasive adolescent, parents miss the old communication, companionship, cooperation, and closeness that have been lost. Now the adolescent suffers by comparison to the child. From this contrast, parental criticism can grow. They can resort to *name-calling*, using abstract descriptors to negatively characterize the adolescent. Criticizing the adolescent's disorganization, parents may call the young person "messy." Criticizing the adolescent's reluctance to do chores, parents may call the young person "lazy." Criticizing the adolescent's forgetting about homework, parents may call the young person "irresponsible." Criticizing the adolescent's self-preoccupation, parents may call the young person "inconsiderate." Criticizing the adolescent's impulsiveness, parents may call the young person "thoughtless." Criticizing the adolescent's argumentative ways, parents may call the young person "disrespectful."

Parents essentially blame the young person for growing up. Better for them to accept normal changes that come as part of the adolescent process and then hold the young person accountable for how he or she chooses to manage that change. Do this in a nonevaluative manner. Instead of attacking character, take issue with decisions the young person has made. "We know that with so much growth going on, it is easy for you to become more disorganized, but we still need to have you keep your room cleaned up on a regular basis." "We know that you dislike doing chores more now that you are older, but we still need to have them done." "We know that you will want to argue with us more about freedom, but how you argue must be done in a civil way."

What most parents fail to understand is that adolescence is a very self-critical age. Comparisons and insecurities plague young people through every stage of growing up, so parental criticism catches the young person at an extremely vulnerable time. Why? The answer is that she is a work in progress and is painfully aware of this. Knowing she is no longer child and not yet adult, she is often at a loss as to exactly how to be, or is dissatisfied with her current state of definition. She compares herself to popular friends and media models, and comes up lacking in her own eyes. She accuses herself of deficiency—in appearance, in social skills, in competition, and in performance, for example. "I'm never going to look attractive!" "I'm no good at meeting people!" "I'm not keeping up with my friends!" "I can't do anything well!"

Because she is extremely self-critical and thus extremely sensitive to criticism from others, she definitely doesn't need more criticism from the most powerful people in her world, her parents, particularly in the form of any kind of *teasing*. This is the most destructive form of criticism there is. It is the kind that insecure young people now use more frequently with each other as the age of social cruelty begins—when more teasing, exclusion, bullying, rumoring, and ganging up come into play (see Chapter Nine). This is the age when young people put each other down to keep themselves up, when they cause others to feel worse to feel better about themselves, when virtually no one feels as though she can afford to give compliments to anyone else for fear of empowering the competition. Developmental insecurity from adolescent change can make potential enemies of them all as each tends to become more self-critical, receives more criticism, and acts more critical of others.

Of course, when parents do criticize the adolescent, he takes pride in not letting the injury show, expressing that standard statement of bravado, "I don't care what you think!" This is a lie. Pretending he doesn't care, he actually takes their criticism to heart, using their perception as a trusted mirror to reflect how he is becoming. "Maybe they're right, and I never will be successful at anything!" Now he gets more down on himself in response. "I don't care" really means, "I care too much to let my caring directly show." Indirectly, however, he will let them know. Nothing that I have seen fuels adolescent rebellion like unrelenting parental criticism. So he takes the hurt received personally, turns it into resentment, and uses resentment to become more resistant to the powers that be. At which point an angry parent compounds the problem by saying, "And I'm going to keep criticizing you until your attitude improves!" Not likely.

I believe that the best approach to correction—and being faulted is often a key component—is a nonjudgmental one. It recognizes that correction is criticism enough. The teenager already knows that parents are sufficiently concerned and displeased to take serious issue with his behavior, so they shouldn't couple correction with attacks on the young person's capacity or character. Better to simply disagree with the choice he has made. Thus, rather than talk about "what a stupid and irresponsible thing that was for you to do," they make a nonevaluative corrective response instead. The corrective message they give is specific, explanatory, and compensatory. "We disagree with the choice you made. This is why. In consequence, this is what we need to have happen now. And this is what we hope you learn from what you did."

Finally, criticism is an enormous disincentive for compliance. When parental criticism rules, consent from the adolescent becomes harder to get. Criticism is nothing but negative, and for the adolescent it just reduces the positive value of the relationship. Why comply with a parent when feeling bad is all you get for your efforts, when there's nothing good to work for? To recover this relationship, parents must replace criticism of the young person with expressions of concern, affirmation of constructive behavior, and a willingness to talk about whatever is going on. As for coupling parental criticism with yelling, that only reduces corrective power. Misguided parents think that yelling will strengthen what they have to say by turning up the volume, when the opposite is usually true.

## Yelling

No question, the adolescent tests parental patience more than the child used to. So it can be hard for parents to keep their cool with their teenager. "How many times do I have to ask you?" "You did *what?*" "When will you ever learn?" "What did I just tell you to do?" "What is so hard to understand?" "Can't you remember anything?" Now parents are more often frustrated, which is where parental yelling comes in. Why do parents yell at adolescents? Probably for the same reasons children yell at parents. Both people are throwing tantrums to achieve the same objectives: to release emotion, to command attention, and to force agreement. So if parents want their child to outgrow throwing tantrums, they have to outgrow the temptation to yell themselves.

Of course, parental yelling can work. More noise lets out more frustration and anger. More noise is harder to ignore. More noise can intimidate the object of the yelling into compliance.

The problem is that parental yelling comes with a number of costs. Most parents injure self-esteem by yelling, allowing themselves to tantrum like a child to get their way, and they lose respect from their son or daughter in the bargain. The yelling parent loses the capacity to listen in disagreement, so constructive dialogue is diminished as strong emotion replaces reason to broker conflict. The emotional battering from being yelled at can hurt the adolescent's feelings, threaten the young person's safety, and alienate the relationship. Fear and resentment from being yelled at can cause the adolescent to become more manipulative and dishonest in communication with the parent. Yelling can encourage yelling back as conflict creates resemblance: the adolescent imitates the parental tactic, creating yelling matches between them. Yelling can cause the yelling parent to choose and use intemperate words as weapons to deliberately injure the opposition, wounding words that no apologizing afterwards can amend.

Whereas parents think they are showing they are serious about what they are saying, they are really just showing helpless desperation at not getting their way. When parents lose control and yell to gain control, the young person ends up in control, having been given the power to provoke their parent to act out of control. And when parents say, "You make me so angry," "You get me so upset," "You leave me no choice but to scream at you," they have just placed the adolescent in charge of their emotions, something they should never do. Sometimes it's helpful to remember, as mentioned back in Chapter One, that how parents treat their adolescent is how they treat themselves. For example, threaten their adolescent, and they treat themselves as a bully. Tiptoe around their adolescent, and they treat themselves as a coward. Scream at their adolescent, and they treat themselves as a screamer. So treat your adolescent in ways that cause you to feel good about yourself and in ways you want your adolescent to treat you. For most parents, yelling accomplishes neither objective.

If you find yourself trapped in a pattern of yelling, break the habit by catching yourself before the yelling point, taking a time-out to cool down and restore emotional sobriety, and then reengaging on more rational terms. When you do this, you are showing your adolescent how to control emotions without letting emotions control him. And consider expressing a different cue than yelling to show that you are serious about the issue at hand. Instead of using clamor, use calmness. Lower your voice. Speak slowly and softly. So the teenager says, "When my mom's voice slows down and she gets real quiet, I know we have some serious talking to do." Now is the time to act effectively, not emotionally. Now is the time to practice effective discipline.

## Practices of Effective Discipline

Over my years of counseling with parents, I've seen a number of disciplinary practices that when conscientiously applied seem to make a positive difference in how adolescents grow. Ten of these are briefly described here.

1. *Clear rules are consistently supported.* Parents specifically describe what is and what is not allowed, and what must and must not happen, and they do not break faith with these fundamental ground rules by sometimes sticking by them and sometimes not, making exceptions when administration is inconvenient. These are the indisputable and unwavering "facts" of family life. There is no confusion or inconsistency that sends a double message— "Sometimes we mean what we say, and sometimes we don't" (encouraging the adolescent to bet on "don't"). The teenager knows where parents stand because they keep standing in the same place. For example, parents have made clear, "There is no using someone else's belongings without receiving permission first, and

everyone will contribute unpaid labor (chores) to support the needs of the family."

2. *Patient insistence is relentlessly applied.* When parents ask for something to be done, they will calmly and repeatedly keep after the teenager until their request is met. There is no getting upset to get their way. There is no forgetting about what was asked for, or giving up. The teenager knows that if it's important enough for parents to ask for, it's important enough to parents to steadfastly see that it gets done. Their nagging insistence wears down resistance. For example, the parent persists, "The household help I requested an hour ago, I am asking you for again."

3. *Correction is nonevaluatively given.* When parents act to correct misbehavior, that correction is free of criticism or blame, focusing only on choices the adolescent has made and needs to make differently. The teenager knows that being held accountable does not bring personal censure as well. Correction is criticism enough. As mentioned earlier, and worth repeating here, in response to an infraction, parents say, "We disagree with the choice you made. This is why. In consequence, this is what we need to have happen now. And this is what we hope you learn from what you did."

4. *Constructive conduct receives positive recognition.* When parents oversee adolescent behavior, they not only supervise what needs improvement and correction but also approve what merits appreciation as well. The teenager knows that parents always place any mistakes and misconduct within the larger context of everything she is doing well (and everything that she could be doing badly that she is not). For example, parents maintain a positive perspective: "Any trouble you get into or problems you cause are the exception to the rule, small parts of a large person who we believe generally manages very well."

5. *Speaking up is expected.* When parents confront the adolescent about some mistake or misdeed, they stand ready to listen to his explanation of what occurred and why. They value understanding his version of events, even though attending to it may not change their minds. The teenager knows that whenever parental discipline of the corrective kind is called for, he will get a full and fair hearing so that his side of things gets to be told. For example, they listen as he explains, "I got caught up in what everyone else was doing and just followed along."

6. *There is reciprocal giving.* When parents make contributions to the adolescent's life, they also expect the adolescent to make contributions in return. In this sense, the parent-adolescent relationship is a contractual one, the parent making clear how it needs to work two ways, not one. The teenager knows she lives in a family system where to get, one also has to give. For example, parents keep reiterating, "We do for you when you do for us."

7. *Concern is expressed before consequences are given.* When parents encounter the adolescent's misbehavior, their first response is not corrective but empathetic. They want to know if the teenager is all right, if she is feeling okay, if there is anything the matter that the teenager needs to talk to them about. Wrong or mistaken behavior can signify that there is something else going on in the adolescent's life that may be amiss. The teenager knows that even in response to misbehavior, parental concern for his well-being comes before deciding what is due for what he did. For example, after a teenager took the car without permission and then got in an accident, the parents' first question was "Are you okay?" not "What did you do to our car?"

8. *Individual choice is respected.* When parents have a child who enters adolescence, they know that the age of

command (believing "I have to do what I am told") is over and the age of consent has arrived. "You can't stop me, and you can't make me!" exclaims the defiant teenager. "That's right," parents agree. "You are in charge of your own choices (and facing the consequences of those choices), and we do not dispute that freedom." For example, parents explain: "How you choose to behave is your business, but you need to know that your choices affect how we choose to behave in response."

9. *Guidance is faithfully given.* When parents undertake child-raising responsibility, they commit to providing ongoing guidance that explains the world, instructs about conduct, instills values, and gives ongoing feedback about how the adolescent is experiencing and managing life. Because this communication is delivered directly and with sensitivity, the teenager knows that any counsel given is with her welfare in mind, and so is taken to heart. For example, after she's given her version of what happened when she got into trouble in company with her friends, parents make this offer: "We have a different way to think about what went on that we'd like to you to consider."

10. *The first consequence is always communication.* When parents are deliberating how to respond to the latest minor or major infraction, the first consequence they should choose is communication. "Whenever something serious like this happens," they explain, "before we decide on any penalty, we need to talk out what happened. We need to hear what you have to say to your and our satisfaction, and you need to hear all that we have to say. Then we'll have to take time to consider what, if any, further consequence will occur." For example, from repeated experience, the teenager has learned this much: "Any time I mess up, I know the first thing that's going

to happen will be me and my parents just talking about it."

Parental discipline is a responsibility and an art—creating influences that keep your adolescent on a constructive passage, restoring a healthy direction when he or she has momentarily fallen away. Instruction and approval are most of what it takes. Correction needs to play a lesser role. It's when parents, in the extremity of their concern and frustration, invest most of their influence in correction and ignore providing instruction and giving approval that hard times with the adolescent tend to get worse and not better. In these strained situations, as punishment becomes the disciplinary choice of first resort, parents are often left with very little influence at all, and much to regret down the line.

A young reader of my blog wrote to describe the cost of having parents who got into a pattern of being purely negative and were never able to get themselves out. "My parents being harsh gave my rebellion a longer life than it needed. I did not feel loved as a teen and it just got worse over the years. But my parents' continued harsh bashing drove me into the arms of the people they wanted me to stay away from. If you don't show your teen appreciation, they will find someone who does, and that won't always be the best person for them."

Distinguishing between discipline that works and discipline that doesn't work is a discrimination parents of adolescents need to make, because when it does work, it helps make their teenager's conduct better, and when it doesn't work, it makes conduct worse. What is effective with a compliant, eager-to-please child often proves counterproductive with a contrary, oppositional adolescent. Therefore, to encourage change in their teenager's behavior, parents often have to modify their own. Throughout their child's adolescence, parents are not only providing much direct instruction but also helping the adolescent learn lessons from the ups and downs of his life experience as well, the subject of the next chapter: formal and informal education.

## Chapter Eight

# Informal and Formal Education

In elementary school, our son did fine. He worked hard, was really conscientious, and was very high achieving. But now in sixth grade, the bottom's fallen out! He's lost concentration or motivation or something. He's so disorganized he can't find anything. He forgets or even lies about having homework, claiming he doesn't have any when he does. Then when we make sure he does complete what he brings home, sometimes he doesn't turn it in. What kind of sense does that make? From having a kid who wanted to do well we've got one who's content with merely getting by!

Adolescent education comes from informal experience and formal instruction. In both cases, much as parents wish otherwise, trial, error, and recovery mark the learning curve of growing up. It's a halting process. There are two steps forward and one step back, there is progress and regress, there is staying on course and falling away. A mixed performance is the best most adolescents can accomplish as they stumble their way to independence. Consider five enemies of education with which parents must contend during the child's adolescence: escaping responsibility, the early adolescent achievement drop, cheating in mid-adolescence, procrastinating in late adolescence, and lacking self-discipline in college (trial independence). This chapter discusses the challenges of each and how parents can be of help.

## Escaping Responsibility

Some types of learning depend on *before-the-fact education*, when parents provide preparation. For example, they give their teenager practice driving before he is licensed to operate a car independently. Other types of learning occur after the act. In *after-the-fact education*, parents insist on responsibility. So when the teenager's unwise choice to shoplift leads to being caught, they allow unwelcome consequences to occur so a painful lesson can be learned. Sometimes the consequences can be severe. Consider this parental and legal injunction to the teenager: "Don't drink and drive." When preparation fails to convey this sober caution to the adolescent, then recovery from a drunken choice may be required to convince. After-the-fact education is more costly than instruction provided before, but it often has deeper impact. A young person charged with a DWI (driving while intoxicated), for example, faces a mandated court appearance, license suspension, attorney's fees, a legal fine, community service, a substance use education course, and whatever else the presiding judge decides. In childhood, the age of dependence, listening to the advice of a conscientious parent is often a sufficient education. In adolescence, the age of independence, confronting hard consequences of unwise choices often teaches more.

Unhappily, sometimes parents who wish to protect their teenager from outcomes that might cause discomfort in the present or complicate the future will intervene to prevent this invaluable instruction. To get him or her out of trouble, they will excuse the behavior or quash the charges, so that the teen escapes responsibility. "He didn't mean to." "She promised never to do it again." "He just wasn't thinking." "She's really a good kid; give her a break." "I don't want him to have a juvenile record." In the long run, this kind of parental help can really hurt. When consequences are avoided and responsibility not taken, an important life lesson goes unlearned.

Better to support *mistake-based education* and let the young person encounter and learn from the errors of his or her ways. For example, consider some "reasons not to rescue"—common examples of good lessons that consequences of bad choices can often teach.

| **Suppose that from confronting natural consequences of . . .** | **The adolescent learns to . . .** |
| --- | --- |
| Doing wrong | Act right |
| Forgetting a promise | Remember commitments |
| Breaking the law | Be law abiding |
| Escaping work and failing | Bear down and succeed |
| Yielding to peer pressure | Behave independently |
| Indulge immediate gratification | Resist temptation |
| Getting drunk | Remain sober |
| Lying | Be honest |

Perhaps the hardest informal education that parents have to give during adolescence is *closing the loop of responsibility*. It works like this. Consider three common social limit–breaking activities that can occur during early adolescence (ages nine to thirteen)— pranking, vandalizing, and shoplifting. They are all usually done in the company of peers in the spirit of shared adventure to see what rules are real and what can actually be gotten away with. What none of these young people would dare to do alone, all will agree to do together. So the seventh-grader, for example, has two friends over for the night, and at about 2:00 AM, long after parents are asleep, one of them gets this fun idea. They decide to make a threatening prank call to the old guy down at the end of block, and the result is very satisfying. He gets really upset. Thinking they have pulled it off, they are congratulating themselves when the phone rings and one of the parents picks it up. Turns out the man had caller ID, and he is not happy. What do parents do? They close the loop of responsibility. They march the three young miscreants down the street to confront the victim of their prank, to hear from him what it felt like to get a call like that, and then to arrange some reparation to be made. Pranking that began as something funny turned out to be not so funny after all, particularly when they are told the man has a heart condition that could easily have been aggravated by emotional upset. It scares them to think that they could have provoked a medical emergency. Who's frightened now?

Or to show a guy they all agree to dislike how much they dislike him, a group of middle school girls sneak out and egg and Oreo his parents' car. Next day, on condition of secrecy, they boast about it to a friend, who tells the boy anyway, who tells his parents, who call the parents of the girls. So what do the parents do? They close the loop of responsibility. They have the girls confront the victims of their vandalizing, hearing what it felt like to be attacked in this way, cleaning off the car, and coming up with some reparation to make up to the boy and his parents for the physical and emotional damage done. Vandalizing that began as girls' paying mean attention to the boy ended up bringing unwanted consequences to themselves. Who's sorry now?

Or a group of friends, not to get anything particular they wanted but to see what they could get away with, created a diversion while one shoplifted CDs from a store. Once outside, the one in possession is picked up while the others escape. The police are called, and they take him to a detention center, where he calls home. So what do the parents do? They listen to the teary voice, promise to come down right away, wait a couple hours, then, after signing out the unhappy adolescent, drive away—but not, as the youngster observes, the familiar way back home. "This isn't the way home; where are we going?" he asks. "We are going back to the store," reply the parents. They are closing the loop of responsibility. "I don't want to go back to the store," protests the young person. "I know you don't," they explain, "but that is what we are going to do. And when we get there, you're going to confess to the manager. You're going to hear what it felt like to be stolen from, and then work out some way to pay that person back for what you've done." Shoplifting that began as an adventurous idea with peers ended up as a costly experience for the adolescent. Who regrets his decision now?

When parents fail to close the loop of responsibility and dismiss early adolescent social limit breaking as innocent mischief or simply deal with the issue discretely by punishing the infraction at home, they are likely to encourage more significant limit breaking later on. They avoid their role in the young person's informal education—holding him or her to responsible account. Then there is holding the adolescent to account for formal education at school.

## The Early Adolescent Achievement Drop

Early adolescence (around age nine to thirteen) can be the enemy of school achievement. Separating from childhood and rebelling against being defined and treated any longer as a child, some middle school students resist the educational system at their own expense. Asserting their newfound sense of independence against instructional authority, they can refuse to make academic effort, this failure resulting in falling grades. What parents may first notice is a more disaffected attitude toward academic achievement. Common expressions of this disaffected "independent" attitude include "It's dumb to ask questions," "It's smart to act stupid," "It's stupid to work hard," "It's pointless to try," "It's cool not to care," "It's good to act bad," "It's right to buck the system," and "It's good enough to just get by."

This change in motivation can catch parents off guard when the conscientious child who took pride in doing well becomes the apathetic adolescent who seems not to care about doing poorly. The old academic priority of working hard to achieve gives way to a more urgent priority, to socially connect with friends. For example, energy that used to be invested in doing homework is now diverted to texting, messaging on the computer, and social networking on the Internet. Now the social priority trumps the educational objective as inclination to do schoolwork falls away.

In most cases, this performance drop doesn't really mean that the adolescent no longer values doing well academically; it just means that he or she doesn't want to do the work it takes to do well—class assignments, homework, reports, projects, papers, and studying for tests. So it is at this juncture that parents find themselves confronted by a number of antiachievement behaviors. The most common ones are

1. Not delivering or intercepting deficiency notices sent home to parents
2. "Forgetting" or lying about homework assignments
3. Not turning in completed homework
4. Not finishing class work
5. Being inattentive or socially disruptive in class

All these behaviors contribute to the *early adolescent achievement drop*, and they are all easily remedied. What is needed are parents who are willing to take a stand for the adolescent's best interests against what he or she wants, pushing for more academic effort at a time when the young person is inclined to favor less. Two stands *not* to take to address these behaviors are becoming emotionally upset or resorting to rewards or punishments to encourage different choices. Although both stands can work with a young child who wants to please and values material incentives, they tend to be counterproductive with the adolescent who often courts parental disapproval. When parents express significant upset (disappointment, worry, or anger) with his falling grades, they just turn a performance issue into an emotional one. Now they have given the rebellious adolescent another tribute to his independence by showing him that he is in charge of something they feel very strongly about. As for offering a material incentive, parents believe that such a payoff for good grades will be seen as a reward, when it is not. In fact, most adolescents will see it as a threat that they resent. "If you say you're going to give me five dollars for an A, that just means that if I don't get an A, I don't get the five dollars." As for punishment, if certain grades are not maintained, taking away some resource or freedom "until grades improve" is an approach that usually engenders more resistance than cooperation. So the obstinate seventh-grader defiantly declares, "I don't care what you take away; you can't make me do my work!" And the adolescent will go down in flames to prove to parents that such power tactics are doomed to fail. When parents reward or punish grades, they only turn a performance issue into a power struggle with their adolescent.

So what then are parents supposed to do? Just stand by and watch their early adolescent fail by failing to work? Sometimes that's the advice middle school teachers give to parents. "Don't be overprotective. Let your child fail and learn responsibility from the consequences." This is usually bad advice because unless the early adolescent manages to self-correct in consequence of failing, deciding to bear down to bring grades up, he or she will only learn to adjust to failure, treating failure as okay when it is not.

After all, a report card is meant to act like a mirror, the adolescent seeing in that evaluation an adequate reflection of his or her academic capacities when a reasonable effort is made. How to determine what level of performance to hold the young person to? Find an *academic benchmark*—your adolescent's grades for one marking period when all class work, homework, and projects are turned in and all tests are studied for. Then hold him or her to that specific operating account. Don't say, "Just do your best, try your hardest, and live up to your potential." (Nobody can do that.) Instead say, "Given your record when you've made a full-faith effort, you have shown you are capable of A's and B's, and we expect you to work hard enough to continue at that level. Should you fall below that, we will give you the support of our supervision to bring your grades back up." Often, before the achievement drop sets in, a middle school student will unwittingly give parents such an academic benchmark—like the first six weeks of sixth grade, for example—as she strives to catch hold in this more challenging world of secondary education and succeeds. So hold her to that account.

For parents to say to an unmotivated adolescent who is capable of A's and B's, "All we want you to do is pass," is tantamount to giving up on their child, abandoning their responsibility to help the young person keep operating capacity in line with ability. But if emotional upset and rewards and punishments tend to be ineffective with the early adolescent achievement drop, then what are parents to do? The answer is *supervision*. Remember that the early adolescent, unlike the child, is now feeling too socially independent to welcome parents showing up in his or her world at school. This is one of the more reliable tests for determining that adolescence has begun. The first-grade child is excited by a surprise classroom visit by parents: "Mom! Dad! Look who's here!" The sixth-grader adolescent is mortified: "Mom! Dad! What are you doing here?"

The desire for more social independence that early adolescence brings causes most young people to keep parents out of his or her society of peers, particularly at school. Now the company of parents at school feels like a public embarrassment because he or she should be able to handle school without their interference. To which parents reply, "We have no desire to interfere at school so long as you are taking care of business. However, if you do not do schoolwork and if you are acting inappropriately, we will extend our supervision into your school to help you make better choices. This is not what we are wanting to do, but is what we are willing to do."

The operating term for supervision of this kind is "together." So if deficiency notices are not brought home or the mail was intercepted, parents may want to say something like this: "Since information for us that the school entrusted to you was not delivered, we and you will meet with the teacher *together*, and you will have the opportunity to explain why the notice failed to reach us, and what you are going to do differently next time so it does." If parents are told there is no homework when it turns out there was, they may want to say something like this: "Since you said you had no homework, but you did, we and you will meet *together* with the teacher. At that time, you will have the opportunity to explain why you said there was no homework when there was, and what you will do differently the next time so we will be told the truth. And this weekend, before you get to do anything you want to do, you will have to complete the missed assignments, turning them in for zero credit because they are now late." If the adolescent still fails to bring assignments home, parents may want to say something like this: "Since you can't manage to bring homework home, we will meet you after your last class and *together* we will walk the halls and make the rounds of all your teachers to pick up your assignments." And if the adolescent does the homework but chooses not to turn it in, parents may want to say something like this: "Since you can't manage to turn your work in, we will go up to school with you and *together* walk the halls and make the rounds of all your teachers to make sure they receive your assignments." Why would an adolescent do the work and not submit it? It makes perfect resistant sense: "You can't say I didn't do it, but you can't make me turn it in!" Middle school backpacks and lockers are stuffed with completed homework that never made it to the teacher's desk.

If the adolescent is talking or acting out disruptively in class and not completing teacher assignments, parents may want to say something like this: "Although this is not something we want to do, we are willing to take time off from work and sit *together* with you in class to help you behave appropriately as the teacher asks." For most early adolescents, this is way over the line: "You can't do that! You'll embarrass me!" To which parents reply, "We have no desire to embarrass you. If you don't want us there, simply take care of business at school. Otherwise we will provide you with this support."

Usually, an early adolescent will not welcome any of these options, considering them outrageously invasive, preferring to correct self-defeating conduct instead. What parents are saying in each case, however, is that so long as self-correction does not occur, they are committed to steadfast supervision because they know improved school performance will ultimately cause the adolescent to feel better about himself or herself (grades are, after all, one pillar of self-esteem) as well as keep educational options open for later on.

But now another pernicious anti-educational behavior enters the picture: *cheating* as a shortcut to get out of work and to artificially improve performance, usually beginning in mid-adolescence as a rebellious way to outsmart the powers that be.

## Cheating in Mid-Adolescence

Cheating usually starts in mid-adolescence as an antiestablishment game many young teenagers want to try, but in high school it becomes more academically motivated, adopted as a serious strategy to academically survive, succeed, and get ahead. The psychological formula for cheating at school is simply this: *cheating = sneaking + lying + stealing*. You sneak to conceal what you are up to. You lie about what you have done. And you steal credit for performance you did not earn. So there are three ethical violations in one when you cheat by plagiarizing papers, copying homework, using secret cheat sheets on tests, procuring questions and answers in advance, or altering grading records.

Many mid-adolescents will tell you there is nothing "wrong" with cheating. Because adolescence is a countercultural period of growth, young people can see the adult-run "system" as the enemy to oppose and also to manipulate. This is why "beating the system" is one common goal in adolescence. It shows how a young person is smarter than the ruling authorities and can get away with ignoring, getting around, or breaking rules that they impose. Cheating in school—on homework, on papers, on tests, on records—symbolically represents this subversive power. Over the years, I have heard a variety of adolescent rationales for cheating in addition to "beating the system."

- The "majority rule" rationale: "Everybody does it sometimes."
- The "intelligence" rationale: "It's stupid to play by the rules when others don't."
- The "efficiency" rationale: "With so much to do, I do what works."
- The "success" rationale: "Sometimes you have to cut corners to get ahead."

From what I have seen, students with low motivation tend to cheat the least because cheating takes more effort than simply not doing the work at all. Moderate-achieving students tend to cheat to get out of doing their own work. High-achieving students tend to cheat for competitive advantage as they strive to get ahead. Teachers sometimes let possible cheating go because it takes special surveillance to detect. And they may want to avoid confronting or sanctioning a cheater because that can entail a conference with defensive and angry parents. Policing cheating can take and stir up a lot of trouble. So if a teacher says that your adolescent has been caught cheating, you need to appreciate the conscientiousness and courage such a communication can take.

So how should the school deal with cheating? Maintain surveillance, confront the offender, and give a failing grade. Most schools give a double message: accept that it will go on, but take an official position against it. Accept that with all the rationales adolescent students have, many young people will perceive it as an acceptable way to cope with school. Meanwhile, set school policies and procedures that prohibit cheating, which students are expected to live up to. School staff must set an adult cultural norm that opposes cheating to compete with the adolescent norm that endorses it. As for encouraging students to uphold a school honor code by reporting other students who are cheating, it's hard to create a positive incentive for students to do so. The cultural rationales for cheating are in place; more important, informing on another student is not likely to win friends and may result in some social reprisal. Even with an honor code in place, there is no glory from turning in a peer. Whistleblowers don't earn a lot of popularity.

The problem is, however, that the experience of growing up is a formative one. As earlier noted, now = later. The adolescent of today is the adult of tomorrow. Therefore, cheating one's way through school can encourage cheating one's way through life. Thus parents and teachers do have a responsibility to encourage ethical behavior in adolescence that encourages ethical behavior in adulthood. If policing to monitor for cheating students is one option for the school, there is also another: teach students to police their own cheating behavior. Why would they want to do that? Because of the psychological costs that accompany cheating. The interesting thing about the student rationales that justify cheating is that they are necessary at all. Because they are self-justifying, these defenses are often evidence of how most adolescents, on some level, experience cheating as doing something "wrong." *Cheating creates an internal ethical conflict.*

Then there are other costs. *Cheating lowers self-esteem.* Although you may be clever enough to beat the system, it is an admission that you don't have the will or capacity it takes to meet a performance demand or challenge by dealing with it honestly and directly through your own efforts. *Cheating creates ignorance.* You get the answers without ever learning to work on the questions. Of course, *cheating creates jeopardy.* Cheaters have to live with worry about being found out, caught, and punished. Finally, *cheating puts you in a false position.* The appearance or reputation of competence and knowledge you create is very different from the secret reality only you know. This is why a cheater can feel like a fraud.

A high school counselor once told me an example of this cost. She said that a student who had graduated five years before came back to her because his history had finally caught up with him. "I started practicing cheating in middle school, cheated my way through high school," he confessed, "then college, and now I'm accepted into medical school, and I haven't learned all that I'm supposed to know. What should I do?" The counselor's advice: "Delay your admission for one or two years to actually study what you missed, and never cheat on yourself again." Her final phrase has always stuck with me. *Cheating is ultimately an offense against oneself.* So if your teenager decides to cheat at school, at least tell the young person this: "Cheating is powerfully instructive and personally harmful. Cheating to get out of doing schoolwork or to get ahead teaches you to treat yourself like a sneak, a liar, and a thief. Anything you gain isn't worth the personal penalty that you pay."

Another personally penalizing behavior that is heavily practiced in the late adolescent years of high school is *procrastination*—putting off schoolwork to a later time. A problem in high school, it turns out to be even more problematic in college because away from home the young person no longer has the checking and reminding support of parental supervision.

## Procrastination in Late Adolescence

As I discussed in Chapter Three, I think of two types of procrastination. Type one involves putting off a task until the last minute, but it finally gets accomplished under duress. With type two, a task is delayed to the point that there is no time left, and the work never gets done. Type one is what most young people struggle with, and it is expensive. Procrastination proves very costly because as delay shortens the time available, deadline pressure induces stress to meet the demand or get the project done, or to give up on doing the project entirely.

The habit of procrastination is naturally come by, as most young people first fall into it as a strategy of resistance in early adolescence, delaying their response to parental requests for help, chores, homework, and the like. What parents typically experience with their young person during this time is not only more arguments (active resistance) but more delay (passive resistance) in response to what they want. The young person routinely puts parents off: "Not right now," "Can't it wait?" "I will as soon as the TV show is over." "I'll do it in a minute!" This is why a ten-minute task can take a teenager several hours, the young person doing all he can to escape the immediate necessity of meeting a request, demand, or obligation. Procrastination is often installed as part of the *early adolescent work ethic*: "Work as hard as you can, as long as you can, to get out of doing as much work as you can." (Work = any undertaking adults demand that you don't want to do.)

With continued practice, adolescents mature procrastination into a self-defeating strategy in the high school years that follow. After graduating from high school, many young people take this delay habit with them to college, making that demanding experience more stressful too. For example, stoked with stimulants to stay awake, they pull an all-nighter to get a paper done, stagger to class to turn it in. Quickly fleeing to go and get a good day's sleep, they miss lecture content they will be tested on next week, falling further behind.

I believe that procrastination is a key contributor to the high rate of flunking out or quitting in college. Sometimes I think there should be a self-help, 12-step recovery program—call it Procrastinators Anonymous—available on college campuses for young people who are struggling to break this bad study habit. The further along in his formal education the adolescent goes, the more costly this habit tends to become.

The twin traps of procrastination that are encountered in the late-adolescent high school years are buying present freedom at the expense of increased future demand, and making those demands more stressful by reducing the time available to get them done. Procrastination usually turns out to be a bad bargain. First, putting off work in the present just results in adding more work to be done later. Second, with less allowable or available time, there is more pressure to get it done. Of course, procrastination is employed not only to put off work but to forestall dealing with the unpleasant. When one puts off what one dreads, worrying about it only makes delay feel worse. So the anxious high school senior wonders, "How can I go to class and explain to my teacher that I didn't use the extension she gave me for my medical excuse and that I still need more time to get the paper done?" Procrastination can create more torment than relief.

The relationship between procrastination and stress is a complicated one. It creates stress by increasing time pressure to get work done. The ultimate time stress is the "deadline"—a line in time somebody draws, after which the project is supposedly "dead," you are "dead," or you're both "dead." The closer you get to the deadline with work unaccomplished, the more stress you are supposed to feel. *Deadlines are urgency motivators*, but in many cases, they are not as absolute as they pretend to be, because work submitted after deadline, even with a penalty, is still alive and okay (as are you). When procrastinating students discover the flexible nature of some deadlines in high school, the lesson that may be learned is, "Deadlines are made to be broken." They are mostly effective because they are extortionate, not because they are absolute. In a way, procrastination can also be productive when a person uses the stressful sense of crisis created by delay to generate urgency motivation.

In the words of one dedicated student procrastinator: "The problem with doing work early is that it takes longer when there's no pressure to get it done. But wait until the last minute, and I rush right through it because I have to."

"How do you feel after the crisis?" I asked.

"Blown out," he replied. "But that's just the price I pay. I work best under pressure." (By which he meant that without pressure from stress he couldn't get work done.) The "price" he pays, however, if this becomes his constant operating style, can be constant stress from running behind, feeling in crisis, and worrying about all that needs to be done.

Then there are the two major "games" of procrastination that serious young practitioners seem to enjoy playing. There is the exciting "put it off–pull it off" game in which the player tests how long he can wait before getting the task done just "under the wire." And there is the productive "put it off–do instead" game in which the player tests how much other work she can get done during the delay before having to address the task she is avoiding. In this game, procrastination can cause people to get a lot of "other stuff" accomplished. "I got all my CDs reorganized by not sitting down to study right away!"

As a confirmed habit by the end of high school, procrastination not only undermines the capacity to succeed in higher education, contributing to the low student retention rates reported by many colleges, but also can lay the foundation for adult lifestyle stress. Some people seem to become dependent on stress to function. In the process, stress can satisfy a variety of needs: to get motivated, get started, keep going, get things done, feel challenged, feel excited, feel busy, feel important, find meaning, make excuses, and feel validated by being in constant overdemand. In most cases of adult lifestyle stress that I have seen, procrastination has an essential role to play.

How to help your late adolescent stop procrastinating, if that is something he or she wants to do? The answer is, don't recommend cutting it off abruptly or out entirely. Instead, suggest a gradual approach. Advise your adolescent to consider trying this: on each occasion that he is inclined to procrastinate in the face of some unwanted demand, he just starts addressing it a little earlier than he otherwise might. Don't fight the habit. *Respect the habit to reverse it.* Still procrastinate, but try doing it a little less by slightly moving up the starting time. Bit by bit, as the old practice is worn away, the young person is able to make a more timely response to demands. Just as procrastination is habit forming, so is timeliness. And as the adolescent's response to work becomes less delayed and more immediate, ask her to reflect on all the stress that she is missing.

Should the adolescent be fortunate enough to attend college, it's definitely for the best if he or she will not pack along an entrenched high school habit of procrastination. At this fragile next step into trial independence (ages eighteen to twenty-three), the inability to accomplish work in a timely fashion can undermine the self-discipline required to meet the demands of undergraduate study.

## Lacking Self-Discipline in College

The figures are pretty dramatic. According to the *Journal of College Retention*, in the United States "only about 66% of high school graduates attend college and about 50% of those who attend college earn a bachelor degree." If a student drops out of high school, encourage her in two ways—first to gather more power of responsibility by getting employment to pay more of her own expenses, and second to keep in mind that graduating high school is always an option should she want to pursue a GED (General Equivalency Diploma).

Of course, as just noted, student retention rates demonstrate that entrance into college is no guarantee of graduation from college. Because college retention rates vary around the 50 percent average, you might want to request the student retention rate, and how it is calculated, for any college to which your son or daughter applies. Your child's chance at higher education, his or her ability to afford a student loan obligation, and your own investment are at stake.

The retention figures are enough to make parents wonder: What's the matter with these colleges and students anyway? Is higher education failing to adequately engage the students, or are students failing to make an adequate effort? The answer is probably a mix of both. Colleges would like to think that last-stage adolescent students are ready to assume this more grown-up educational responsibility, while students are assuming that high school study habits are adequate for college. Both are wrong, and they need to get on the same page. Expectations on both sides need to be clarified: a college student is still an adolescent, and college is not the same as high school.

As described more fully earlier (see Chapter Three), this fourth and last stage of adolescence can be the hardest. Why is this final stage so hard? To briefly recapitulate: for many young people, to be away from home at college creates too much freedom and too much stress to competently manage. *Adequate self-discipline is often lacking.* They are not ready to assume the additional personal responsibility that this next step of independence demands, at least not right away, and they are not up to mastering all the trials of life they face. On both counts, that's why I call this last stage of adolescence "trial independence." They are "trying" to manage more independence than they have ever attempted before.

Although there are multiple reasons why last-stage adolescents flunk out of college (including inadequate academic preparation, financial pressures, homesickness, or substance abuse), lack of adequate self-discipline is high on the list. Consider three challenges of independence that self-discipline must manage. There is enormous *latitude for choice* because now what you do with so much freedom is entirely up to you. There is enormous *responsibility* because how well you manage all depends on you. And there is enormous *distraction* because so many of your friends are out for having a good time, day and night. It takes self-discipline to get up to attend a roster of classes, to do the assignments and turn them in on schedule, to study for exams, and to do all of this when there is no one to make you except yourself.

To some degree, most young people abuse the increased freedom that comes with trial independence. In consequence, they incur the cost of many early failures. There are failed relationships, failed jobs, broken promises, broken commitments, broken laws, broken leases, and poor or failing grades. Freedom at this age is also made more difficult to manage by the company one keeps—peers who are losing their footing, slipping and sliding, breaking agreements, and floundering just like you. And now the period of maximum use of alcohol and other drugs begins, harder drugs becoming more common than before. Although not usually chemically dependent, these students do bear unmistakable signs of *psychological dependency*, which is not exactly the same.

They have a hard time getting traction because they lack the self-discipline to catch hold. They make intermittent effort and brave resolutions, but they end up spinning their wheels. They can't, in their own words, "seem to get anywhere." Three signs of psychological dependency have to do with the inability to achieve completion, commitment, and consistency. When it comes to *completion*, they can start a lot, but they can't finish much. When it comes to *commitment*, they can make all kinds of promises and resolutions to themselves and others, but they can't keep many of them. And when it comes to *consistency*, they can work in spurts, but they can't maintain continuity of effort over the long haul. People who are psychologically independent demonstrate the self-discipline in which completion, commitment, and consistency skills are in working order.

Add to all this complexity the many sources of stress that now beleaguer their lives. Last-stage adolescents often experience sleep deprivation from continually staying up late, last-minute pressures from procrastination, indebtedness from

overspending, and loneliness away from home. They also may
have social insecurity in new situations, poor nutrition and
health maintenance, and no clear future direction in life to
follow. They are likely to fall into more substance use for
recreation and escape, failure to keep all obligations, and low
self-esteem from feeling incompetent at this older age. Despondency, anxiety, and exhaustion are common problems at this
time. The hardest stage of adolescence comes last because
now the young person is up against the toughest challenge of
all: how to finally learn to act *independently* grown up.

This population of last-stage adolescents makes up the student
body that higher education is challenged to teach. And a challenge it is, as frustrated teachers ponder the *fatal four questions*.
"Why don't students speak up to teachers?" "Why don't students
turn work in on time?" "Why don't students show up regularly
to class?" and "Why don't students stay enrolled?"

The answer is that these young people have difficulty with
taking four kinds of academic responsibilities that support true
independence:

1. It's hard to take responsibility for speaking up to a teacher
   when you have not yet assumed sufficient adult
   independence to assert equal worth and standing in the
   conversation. *So you avoid talking with your professor.*
2. It's hard to take responsibility for turning your work in on
   time independently when you still bridle at meeting an
   outside agenda, and use delay to insist on your own
   schedule of terms. *So you turn assignments in late.*
3. It's hard to take responsibility for independently showing
   up regularly in class when you have no one to wake you up
   or make you go. *So you let yourself sleep in and skip.*
4. It's hard to take responsibility for meeting independent
   commitments in your life, such as getting through college,
   when the dependent part of you rebels against your own

authority and says, "Don't work that hard; it's easier to quit." *So you drop out rather than hang in there and tough it out.*

College is where the final battle for adolescent independence is often waged. Now last-stage adolescents are fighting within themselves for and against what they have elected but don't want to do. And they are acting out that resistance against their teachers. It's like early adolescent rebellion all over again, except that this time the authority they are opposing is their own.

As for parents, if they respond as a corrective or critical authority, they encourage the beleaguered young person to escape the necessary self-encounter about who is really in charge of (and responsible for) the conduct of her life. Now she can act as though her parents are the problem. However, if parents respond nonjudgmentally, respecting her right and responsibility for making independent choices and for dealing with consequences, then the struggle remains back where it belongs—within herself. For many young people, college becomes the gateway passage from the end of adolescence into young adulthood. This passage can be a struggle, not because college work is so difficult (although some students are not sufficiently academically prepared), but because assuming full responsibility and asserting self-discipline are so hard to do—as they are for us all.

What can a parent helpfully do? Maintain adult demands and expect young people to meet them. Accept no excuses, make no exceptions, and attempt no rescues. Listen respectfully and empathetically and do not criticize the young person for not measuring up to what you or college expected. Encourage learning more responsibility from facing the consequences of how one chose to act. Support the courage to keep growing forward in life. And explain, "If you want to use college to keep growing yourself up, *show up, speak up, do your work (on time), and don't give up.*"

And parents can do one thing more. They can expect the young person to earn part of his way, because the self-discipline it takes to regularly do a part-time job can help support the self-discipline it takes to study and can boost psychological independence. Plus, the fifteen to twenty hours a week that a job demands will provide a real-world structure that is costly to ignore. Skip a class, and you miss a lecture; skip a shift at work, and you will lose a job. It's very hard for many last-stage adolescents to grow up in college when they are treated by authorities as dependent in two ways. When totally defined by the student role, they are treated as a dependent person in preparation for adulthood. When totally financed by their parents (often also with loans), they are treated as a dependent person to be supported until adulthood. On both counts, growing up to more responsibility and independence can be delayed. What a part-time job can offer is a more adult definition in the workplace, some sense of financial independence through generating one's own income, a measure of practical responsibility, and on-the-job training in self-discipline. In addition, students who work part-time to help pay their way through college tend to be more invested in pursuing and completing that education. At a minimum, they develop the self-discipline to meet an employment schedule. A part-time job in college is not a magic bullet or a guarantee of graduation, but from what I've seen, it often can provide some help.

Informal and formal education can both be hard for adolescents—the first because it involves learning the hard way from the consequences of unwise choices, the second because it requires self-discipline to do. As for social learning, most of that comes from the influence of peers, to be discussed in the next chapter.

## Chapter Nine

# Problems with Peers

Of course we want our teenager to have a group of friends; but what we don't want are the kinds of trouble that can come from hanging out at this age—the risk-taking, the getting hurt and hurting each other, going along with the crowd, doing crazy things, breaking the law, substance use, sexual relationships. We want good companions for our child, but not bad influences. Is that asking too much?

Pressure from peers does have a lot to answer for during adolescence, for the swaying influence it can have on your child, and for the swaying influence your child can exert on others, because peer pressure goes both ways. Parents often censure peer pressure as some unalloyed evil: "Peer pressure is nothing but trouble!" Whether the pressure is from a significant friend or from a group, they fear their teenager caving in to a bad decision to her cost, experimenting with risk and getting hurt. This rush to parental judgment is partly mistaken. In reality, peer pressure isn't only for the ill. In fact, it is often for the good.

Separating from family in search of social independence, a teenager wants the company of friends to rely on and a peer group to belong to, all of whom become like a second family in which members often *look out for* and *take care of* each other. They look out for each other, for example, when they encourage an angry friend to walk away from a fight, when they tell a friend she can't drive drunk, when they shut up a friend who wants to mouth off to the police officer. And they take care of each other, for example, when providing consolation to a friend over a parental divorce, when cheering up a friend who failed the cut to make the team, when problem solving what to do about a friend's boyfriend or girlfriend. Most young people know that adolescence is no time to go it alone. Just as "it takes a village to raise a child," it takes a community of peers to support an adolescent's growing up.

All this said, there are significant problems that can arise from peer relationships during adolescence, problems with which parents should be prepared to assist. During early and mid-adolescence, there are issues related to social intolerance, adolescent discomfort with puberty, and the rising incidence of social cruelty. During late adolescence and trial independence, there are matters of substance use, managing caring relationships, dealing safely with romantic breakups, and managing sexual experience. Let's take these issues one at a time.

## Social Intolerance

Early adolescence is an age of more intolerance—of self and of others. Now that they are separating from childhood and parents, feeling lonely and disconnected on that account and fitting in less well at home, young people find themselves more in need of a family of friends with whom to socially belong. Coupled with this need for affiliation is the fear of appearing different from the dominant social norms valued by their peers. To be socially labeled as "different" risks being out of step, not fitting in, getting put down, being rejected, and being left socially alone. A lot of the appreciation and acceptance of human variation that experience was slowly broadening in childhood can begin to narrow come ages nine to thirteen when developmental changes of early adolescence, and the social insecurity they bring, provoke more intolerance of diversity.

*Developmental intolerance* begins toward himself as the young person starts rejecting and casting off his childish ways. Differentiating from how he used to be, the early adolescent may decide he is now too old for "kid stuff" that he previously did and still enjoys, but now feels impelled to give up, thereby creating loss. For example, he may feel too old to accept physical affection from parents, too old for former companionship activities with grandparents, too old to play younger games or with beloved toys, and too old to participate in family traditions. Now he doesn't want friends putting him down for acting like a child. The power of the peer group is amplified at this age because the more one separates and distances from family, the more one needs social closeness and affiliation with friends. When the young adolescent says, "My friends are everything!" that is a true statement of how detached from family she feels and how much the companionship of peers now matters.

However, the problem with joining a peer group, particularly close social circles like in-groups, cliques, and gangs, is that membership is not free. What holds these groups together is not only intolerance of diversity but also extreme demands for conformity. In these small social worlds, the informal but strict rules for belonging insist that to be a member in good standing, one must "be like us, believe like us, behave like us, appear like us, hang out with us, like us best, take sides with us, not do better than us, and not go against us." When it comes to freedom for individuality and independence, peer groups can be oppressive. In consequence, these tight-knit groups provide very poor social preparation for making one's way in a larger and more diverse world.

To counter these limiting influences, parents can increase social exposure for their adolescent by involving him in community volunteering, by taking him traveling, and by encouraging him to join multiple social groups so that no one group counts for too much. Parents should also pay close attention to the young person's reports about how human differences are being perceived and treated in his social world, particularly at school. This includes treatment seen, treatment received, and treatment given. "He's from another country and talks funny; that's why we pick on him," explains the seventh-grader to his parent, who makes this reply: "If you were going to school in that country, were just learning the language and 'talking funny,' we would hope resident students wouldn't pick on you. Adjusting to life in another country takes a lot of effort and courage to do." This is not a critical comment; it just provides another perspective.

At school, it really helps if the classroom teacher keeps socially mixing students up—changing seating and work-group assignments on a regular basis, for example—so that diverse association is part of what students learn from each other. In the words of one teacher, "Part of my job is to continually stir the pot." In most cases, intolerance of diversity will cause adolescents to exclusively congregate based on perceived similarity, unless responsible adults keep moving them around to experience new exposures.

The onset of adolescence and the need for social belonging create intolerance for human differences. On the basis of dress, focal interest, or other cultural identification, young people may elect not to associate with peers who don't fit in to their group. Students who exit middle school with little acceptance of diversity (perhaps still only hanging out with old elementary school friends) may find that intolerance has a limiting and even harmful effect as they socialize in their high school years. When intolerance causes young people to cling to social similarity, in-group allegiance can dictate, "Find your own kind," "Hang out with your own kind," "Favor your own kind," "Include your own kind," "Advance your own kind," "Defend your own kind." As for relating to other groups who are perceived as "different," another set of dictates can apply: "Ignore their kind," "Avoid their kind," "Distrust their kind," "Exclude their kind," "Put down their kind," "Rule their kind." When social intolerance in older adolescence is allowed to take root, unchecked and at worst it can breed intergroup antagonism and conflict.

The exception is the "universal student." Every year or so in counseling, I will run across one of these high school–age people, and they never cease to move and amaze me. I always wonder how the young person has been able to grow this way. A member of no particular social group, he or she seems welcomed in every group. It's as though social differences have never been a barrier for this young person, only a bridge. Just as he or she has this wide range of social acceptance, he or she is widely socially accepted too—as a citizen of the world. I wish I knew how to prepare more of their kind. I think they must have escaped the harsh intolerance that comes with puberty.

## Response to Puberty

Psychologically, the onset of adolescence creates intolerance for being defined and treated as just a child anymore, and the adolescent begins to act more grown up. Affirming this determination to be older are the hormonal changes of puberty (the one-and-a-half to three years of growth to sexual maturity) that usually begin during early adolescence. Puberty now creates two problems in one. First, it creates a process problem: how to manage the physical changes that are besetting their bodies. This is the problem of self-consciousness. And second, it creates an identity problem: how to act young manly or young womanly. This is the problem of sex-role definition. *Puberty is a peer-group issue because it can have profound social consequences on both accounts.*

The physical changes of puberty make growing older more apparent. Among other alterations wrought by puberty, there are growth spurts that create bigger bodies to manage. For girls, hips broaden, breasts swell, and menstruation begins, and they can produce eggs. For boys, muscles enlarge, voices drop, and ejaculation begins, and they can produce sperm. For both male and female, there is more hair around sex organs, more body odor, and more active skin glands that can create blemishing. Now intense bodily self-consciousness begins. For most young people, puberty is the enemy of self-esteem. It changes how they look, at a time when physical appearance becomes more important for social acceptance and social standing. As body shape and characteristics alter, they feel more vulnerable on that account, whether they are physically maturing too fast or not fast enough. This is the period when self-examination is microscopic, when any new blemish can be a source of misery, when it takes much longer to "get ready" to go out into the world, when what to wear and how to groom absorb protracted attention. Waking up in the morning, they have to gather the courage to look in the mirror and behold the latest physical change that has afflicted their body overnight that they must take to school for all their world of peers to see.

At home, parents must remember that the changes of puberty are no laughing matter. The rule for parents is that there must be no teasing, no joking, and no making fun of the young person's self-preoccupation, physical appearance, bodily changes, or choice of dress. There is enough of this torment from peers, who are all suffering from similar insecurities themselves. And this is no time for a young person to be uninformed about what is going on in their bodies, because in ignorance they will believe they are unique and wonder what is wrong with them, when nothing is. This is a time for parents to explain the process of puberty that unfolds for everyone and what changes to expect. An easy way to do this is for parents to search online for sites or a book explaining puberty, find one that they like, and then read the information with their son or daughter, inviting any questions the young person may have. Normalize the process so that the young person doesn't "abnormalize" himself or herself and believe that "there's something the matter with me!"

Adolescence does not depend on puberty to start. In fact, in most cases adolescence begins first. Parents first notice the personal disorganization (more forgetting and messiness), negative mind-set (more criticism and resistance), and early experimentation (more testing limits and seeing what can be gotten away with) that are the hallmarks of early adolescent change. But when puberty does begin, the adolescent transformation from child to young adult becomes emotionally intensified and more complex. In addition to the physical changes that accompany puberty, as a young person becomes capable of sexual reproduction, a powerful sex-role change starts to occur—the daunting sex-role journey to young manhood and young womanhood begins. Now how to look and act manly and how to look and act womanly become pressing and problematic questions to answer.

At least at first, puberty causes young people to feel bad about their bodies more often than good, to feel insecure about their emerging sex-role definition more often than confident, to feel unmanly more than manly or to feel unwomanly more than womanly. These role changes are revolutionary. A lot is at stake when puberty arrives, because it forecasts how one's manly or womanly appearance is likely to turn out. At this juncture, popular media become very influential. They parade models of youthful perfection before young people, who compare their own bodies to these ideals and come up wanting. Boys can feel that they do not look big and strong enough, and so start bodybuilding. Girls can feel that they do not look thin and pretty enough, and so start dieting. Imitate one's idols if you can or somehow compensate if you cannot—these are the marching orders of the age. Few early adolescents can see their reflection in the mirror and come away feeling positive about their appearance. "What's wrong with me?" "I hate how I look!" "I'll never look good!" are common cries of discontent. At this self-conscious and self-critical age, it is easy to believe that physical appearance determines most of one's social and self-worth. This is why parents need to encourage a broad base for self-definition during early adolescence that includes a host of affirming qualities, interests, activities, and relationships, so that when it comes to self-esteem, the single attribute of appearance does not count for all.

It is the cultural ideals for being a man and being a woman that young people find most alluring, ideals portrayed in the images and messages and icons that media advertising and enter-tainment constantly communicate. To approximate these young manly and young womanly attributes means incorporating some of them into one's desired appearance. So come puberty, the social and sexual stereotypes kick in as young women worry about weight and thinning down their bodies by dieting, and young men worry about muscle size and strengthening their bodies by lifting weights. According to stereotype, the male is encouraged to be sexual aggressor, and the female is encouraged to be sexual attractor. You can see these images played out at middle and high school football games, for example, where young men bulk up to play a collision sport in front of young women who trim down to dress and dance in form-fitting clothing to cheer them on. These are very incomplete, but very influential, sex-role definitions.

To make matters worse, girls who are not deemed womanly or attractive enough by their peers, and boys who are not deemed manly or aggressive enough by their peers, can get punished for not measuring up—girls picked on for being too fat, for example, and boys picked on for being too physically weak. And now the changes of puberty become fodder for a lot of the social cruelty that can occur, particularly in middle school, so parents needs to be informed and stay on the alert.

## Social Cruelty

By the term "social cruelty" I refer to five kinds of mistreatment young people can inflict on each other; these peak in middle school, when virtually all the students have entered early ado-lescence and most are undergoing the awkward physical changes of puberty. Feeling developmentally insecure on both counts, early adolescents can rely on these mean behaviors to compete for social belonging, assert social dominance, and defend social position in order to gain and maintain membership with their group of peers.

The five kinds of mean behavior that comprise social cruelty are *teasing, exclusion, bullying, rumoring,* and *ganging up.* These behaviors do not begin in adolescence; they also occur in childhood. However, they become much more damaging during the early adolescent years because young people are now so unsure of themselves and thus more easily and deeply hurt. Social cruelty achieves critical mass in middle school as opposed to late elementary school because now virtually all students are fundamentally redefining on two fronts: they are coping with early adolescent change, and most of them are additionally destabilized by the onset of puberty. As secondary school begins, they feel more cut off from childhood and family; more self-conscious about how hormonal changes are altering their body; more uncertain about how to define themselves in young manly and young womanly terms; more urgent in their need to socially belong with peers; more anxious about the scary world of older experience opening up before them; and more challenged by the larger, more complex, more impersonal, and more rough-and-tumble student life in middle school. No wonder young people feel so developmentally insecure and vulnerable at this time of life.

*Most acts of social cruelty are not committed by "bad" kids, but by good kids acting badly in order to socially survive,* as I describe in my book *Why Good Kids Act Cruel.* In addition to the emotional costs students pay as victims and witnesses of this mistreatment, there is a serious educational cost. The academic focus of targeted and onlooking students is diminished because they have now become primarily concerned about their own physical and social safety. It is much more difficult for students to attend to instructional tasks and perform up to potential when their school experience is one in which they daily feel afraid and feel the need to protect themselves. The safer the school, the better that students are likely to learn. The scarier the school, the more that subject concentration in the classroom suffers.

Consider one example of social cruelty that began in sixth grade and continued unabated through high school, a combination of teasing, rumoring, and exclusion, about as bad as such mistreatment gets. This was how a young woman, now out of college and gainfully employed, described what her secondary education was like:

"I don't remember now who started the name-calling, only when. In the first week of middle school, I was walking down the hall and someone called out, 'Watch out, here comes the It Girl!' Then a friend of hers took up the call, 'The It Girl, watch out for the It Girl!' That's when people began looking at me funny, sometimes whispering, sometimes laughing, repeating the charge until everyone knew. The deal was nobody wanted anything to do with me because I had 'it,' whatever 'it' was. Something bad, something shameful, something contagious was how I felt. Like some kind of physical or sexual disease nobody wanted to get close to me and risk catching. With just one word and lots of repetition, my reputation was made. To keep their own reputations, and to keep from being contaminated, everyone kept away from me. So except for the teasing and the stories people told about me, I was left alone. Being too stubborn and proud to defend myself, even to tell my parents, I let the label stick, though it wasn't me who put it on or could take it off. I just ignored the teasing and rumors, kept to myself, and all through high school I was my only friend. But it was pride and stubbornness that got me though, getting good grades to spite them all, no thanks to any teachers who must have known what was happening to me but never tried to interfere. In all those years, not a single teacher or counselor ever stepped into stop what was happening to me. Thank goodness when I got to college, life was different at last, but I've never forgotten how mean other kids can act and how uncaring adults can be."

That she never told her parents was typical. Most parents understand the adolescent's push for *social independence from family*. What they usually *don't* understand is the adolescent's determination to preserve *social independence with peers*. To protect their social world from adult interference, early adolescents often strive to keep parents uninformed to keep them uninvolved. The teenager believes that he should handle any social difficulties by himself, and further there is the code of the schoolyard: "Don't tell on peers" (or face peer reprisal). There is the adolescent belief that parents (and teachers) are best kept in the dark. Supporting this belief are several others that enable acts of social cruelty to go undetected by the grown-up world: "Adults don't know what's going on." "Adults don't care about what goes on." "Adults can't do anything about what is going on." If parents play along with these beliefs, an *abandoned youth* group is created, over which no adult oversight is allowed. At worst, social cruelty can lead to a *Lord of the Flies* scenario, where young people brutalize themselves and each other because no adult influence is present to educate them about healthy social treatment. I believe that parents and teachers must prove early adolescents wrong. During the middle school years, there is a window of adult influence to teach young people how to treat each other; that window closes by high school, when patterns of social conduct are pretty much set.

When middle school begins, parents must let their son or daughter understand that they are in the social know. Thus parents can say, "At this age, we are aware that there is more social meanness as people compete to join groups and fight for position. Teasing, exclusion, bullying, rumoring, and ganging up all become much more common. Should any of these forms of social cruelty come your way in person, on your cell phone, or over the Internet, please tell us so that we can support and coach you in how to respond and, with your permission, intervene if you can't get it to stop. And of course, please do not get involved in committing or going along with this social meanness because that just makes the problem worse."

As for teachers, they can set rules of communication and treatment in the classroom community for which they are responsible:

About teasing: "Only call people by the names they want to be called," and "Don't use names or labels that hurt people's feelings."

About exclusion: "If you see someone sitting alone, invite them to join you," and "Don't shun people or try to keep them out."

About bullying: "Don't push anyone around to get your way," and "Don't make threats to scare anyone."

About rumoring: "If mean gossip comes your way, don't automatically believe it or pass it on," and "Don't make up stories about people you know can be hurtful if believed."

About ganging up: "Don't join a group to pick on anyone," and "Don't go along when others are mistreating someone."

It also helps if parent or teacher describes the specific power to harm attached to each social cruelty tactic, to help young people understand the psychological forces in play.

- The purpose of *teasing* is to humiliate with insults. It plays on the *fear of being inferior*, expressed by the statement "There's something wrong with me!"

- The purpose of *exclusion* is to shun with rejection. It plays on the *fear of isolation*, expressed by the statement "I have no friends!"

- The purpose of *bullying* is to intimidate with threatened or actual harm. It plays on the *fear of weakness*, expressed by the statement "I can't stand up for myself!"

- The purpose of *rumoring* is to slander with lies. It plays on the *fear of defamation*, expressed by the statement "I can't control my reputation!"
- The purpose of *ganging up* is to pit the group against the individual. It plays on the *fear of persecution*, expressed by the statement "Everyone is against me!"

Does every student this age receive this mistreatment? No, but they all witness it. Thus a single act of social cruelty poisons the well for all. Everyone knows that what happened to someone else could happen to them, so they better watch out, be careful, and be on guard. Does every student participate in this mistreatment? No, but they all see it, and when they choose not to intervene, they only enable its continuation. And severe social cruelty can be formative. For example, the bullied student can grow up to become submissive, and the bully can grow up to become coercive. Habits of social behavior learned in middle school and unquestioned in high school can carry forward into adulthood.

How to tell when your child might be the target of unrelenting social cruelty when he or she will not tell you directly? Here are six signs to look for:

1. An observable drop in self-esteem, expressed by talking badly about herself: "I'm a loser just like everybody says I am!" This can be a sign of taking social cruelty personally, believing mean treatment is deserved.
2. Unexplained anxiety about attending school, more difficulty getting ready, or making up excuses not to go ("I feel sick today") even though nothing physically the matter can be found.
3. Observable changes in normal behaviors—acting sad, anxious, socially withdrawn, less communicative, or angry—before and after school.

4. Secretive and dispirited response to electronic communication (phones messages, texting, or online postings).

5. Evidence of being physically harassed or hurt—unexplained bruises on body, torn clothes, or possessions damaged or missing ("lost").

6. Drop in grades as fears for social safety cause a loss of academic focus.

So what can parents do when they detect or their child reports receiving some of this mistreatment at school? Because they have already communicated an understanding that this kind of thing can happen, they can then move into helping mode: listening to the child's account, empathizing with her feelings (particularly fear), offering their emotional support, specifying exactly what is happening, strategizing ways to deal with the aggression, and coaching behaviors to combat it. For example, in response to dealing with mean teasing, they might offer these kinds of coaching advice:

- "Don't take mean teasing personally. It's not about anything wrong with you; it's about them wanting to act mean."

- "Don't credit the insults you are told. Insults from mean teasing can't hurt without your agreement, so don't believe in whatever you are called."

- "Understand what mean teasing reveals. Mean teasers tease about what they fear being teased about themselves."

- "Don't give mean teasers satisfaction. Ask yourself how they predict you will react, and then don't give them the response they expect or want."

- "Don't keep friends who keep teasing you in mean ways. Good friends don't treat each other badly, so if yours won't stop the meanness, maybe it's time to find other companions."

The main support parents can provide when their adolescent is repeatedly targeted for social cruelty is this commitment: "It's not just you against them now; it's *us* against them, and together we will find a way to bring this to a stop."

Usually because young people are feeling more secure with themselves, and because of the larger size and breakdown of former cliques, high school offers some relief. However, some social cruelty can continue and even become more serious, as when verbal gay-baiting in middle school, for example, becomes physical gay-bashing in high school. If your adolescent was mistreated by social cruelty in eighth grade, you need to keep a weather eye out for his or her social experience in ninth grade.

And now, coinciding with the high school years, another set of risks among peers increases at this time, those associated with social substance use.

## Substance Use

*Substance use is a peer-group issue because most adolescent consumption of alcohol and other drugs occurs in a social context,* in the company of friends, thus providing the rationale that "everybody does it" and that it is thus normal and okay. Whether parents like it or not, their children grow up in an increasingly drug-filled world. We live in a society that encourages the use of chemical substances, not only for treating sickness but also for health and wellness, pleasure, performance, relief, and escape. There are more varieties of legal and illegal psychoactive (mood- and mind-altering) drugs available to people today than at any other time in human history. Huge legal and illegal profits mean that mass availability of these drugs is never going to go away as supply encourages more demand, and demand encourages more supply. No wonder so many adolescents fall prey to the temptations of substance use. By the end of high school, most students have at least experimented with one or more of the big three drugs—nicotine, alcohol, or marijuana. And as they enter the final stage of adolescence, trial independence (eighteen to twenty-three), when they are living away from home and are an open market, the most intense and varied period of substance use begins.

Adolescence encourages experimentation with all kinds of risks, "just trying it" the motivation that begins most substance use. The risks of substance use include the impairment of judgment, the loss of sober caring, the reliance on impulse, and the making of dangerous choices. *Substance use can affect decision making for the worse.* For example, significant substance use is associated with higher rates of social violence, sexual misadventure, fatal car accidents, dangerous physical risk-taking, lawbreaking, and dropping out of school.

But how are parents to know if their adolescent is engaged in some level of substance use? In most cases, it will not be because the teenager has told them about it. It will be because he has gotten caught. Then they will receive the standard lie: "This is first time I tried anything, and I'll never do it again!" No. The first time caught is rarely the first occasion of use. And once he has started, he is more likely to use again. He has announced that he has become an active user. Hereafter, he will be more careful to conceal what is going on.

For parents, there is no good news when it comes to adolescent substance use. When we assess five progressively serious levels of use—experimental (out of curiosity), recreational (for social enjoyment), excessive (accidental or intentional overuse), abusive (acting harmfully), and addictive (driven by compulsion)—the bad news is that by the end of high school, most students have had experimental, recreational, and excessive experience with substances, alcohol being drug number one. Although no degree of use is safe from risk, the first two-and-a-half levels (up through accidental excess) have less potential for long-lasting harm than do the final two-and-a-half. This means that repeated episodes of intentional excess (drinking to get drunk, for example), abusive use (getting into fights when under the influence, for example), and addiction (inability to stop using when resolved to do so, for example) all warrant parents' seeking outside help to intervene.

When adolescents start substance use, they usually do not confess it to a parent in words; they betray it by their actions. Typically conducted in the company of friends, substance use is commonly concealed from parents, so parents need to know what to look for to discover when significant substance use is going on. There are three kinds of telltale signs: uncharacteristic behavior change, signs that overlap with common adolescent changes, and nonoverlapping signs that bear directly on substance use.

To begin, parents should pay attention to *uncharacteristic changes* in their son or daughter's behavior, like some of the general warning signs on the list that follows. Parents should take notice when

Smart kids make stupid decisions

Good kids act badly

Truthful kids lie

Mindful kids can't remember

Conscientious kids become indifferent

Even-tempered kids develop mood swings

Kids with little money have more to spend

Academically achieving kids fail

Dedicated kids lose interest

Communicative kids shut up

Open kids become secretive

Nice kids act mean

Responsible kids act irresponsibly

Reliable kids default on their agreements

Motivated kids start not to care

Careful kids act careless

Obedient kids break rules or laws

Focused kids have accidents

Healthy kids become run down

None of these changes individually is a guarantee of substance use; however, over time, a pattern comprising a number of these alterations should be cause for possible concern.

What makes detection of teenage substance use particularly difficult is the similarity that many signs of substance use have to normal changes that are often part of adolescence. Therefore, it is helpful for parents to discriminate between overlapping and nonoverlapping signs of use.

*Overlapping signs* (typical both for adolescence and substance use) include

Unpredictable mood swings

Less willingness to communicate

More insistence on privacy

More volatility in conflict

Distraction, daydreaming, inattentiveness

Disorganization and lack of focus

Attraction to drug-themed entertainment

Less willingness to cooperate at home

More countercultural interests and dress

More manipulation to get needs met

Disinterest in what traditionally mattered

Disengagement from old friends you know to new ones you don't

Increase in forgetfulness

Increase in rebelliousness and argumentativeness

Urgent focus on the present and unconcern for the future

Avoidance and evasion of issues parents want to discuss

Lack of caring about doing schoolwork

Steady decline in school performance marked by tardiness to class, skipping school, homework and class work not completed

All of these changes can accompany normal adolescence; however, they can also be markers for substance use.

*Nonoverlapping signs* (those more directly related only to substance use) include the following:

Money or valuables that can be pawned are missing from other family members.

There are unexplained charges on parental credit cards.

The adolescent is regularly caught smoking cigarettes or using spit tobacco.

Drug paraphernalia, such as rolling papers, pipes, clips, tubes, foil, and butane lighters, are found among belongings.

Full or empty bottles, cans, seeds, pills, or substances in powdered form are found in the adolescent's bedroom, pockets, backpack, or car.

Bottles of alcohol disappear from parents' liquor supply or are diluted.

Pills are missing from psychoactive prescriptions in the medicine chest.

There is a dramatic change in eating or sleeping habits, either much more or much less.

The adolescent has new friends who avoid introduction, who are not named, who are older, or who are always met away from home.

Major house rules like curfew and car use are continually broken despite promises to the contrary.

There is a medical emergency precipitated by excess chemical use.

The adolescent receives mysterious phone calls, particularly late at night, and when parents answer, the caller hangs up or declines to give a name.

The teenager lies about inconsequential events and insists on lying about having lied when caught in a lie.

There are drug or alcohol violations of the law (in possession, selling, acting under the influence).

There are conflicts with school or other authorities.

Teenager's physical condition declines; for example, he is constantly fatigued.

There are incidents of acting uncoordinated, unclear speech, confused thinking.

The teen has bloodshot eyes, run-down appearance, coughing or runny nose with no sign of being sick, unexplained bruises, or what could be injection marks on the body.

The adolescent is in possession of or in need of unexplained amounts of money.

The adolescent has a reputation for drug use among peers or for running with a using or partying crowd.

The teen's dress and person frequently smell of smoke and alcohol.

When asked about possible substance use, the teenager overreacts to question with explosive hostility.

This last group of signs is the most telling category. Two or three of these, and parents should take notice.

So when it comes to keeping a weather eye for substance use, what should you do? First, monitor the young person's decision making. Decisions that create persistent problems or cause serious trouble should catch your attention. Second, feel free to ask if substances were being used while troubling decisions were being made. And third, if your teenager assures you that no substance use was involved, before you close the door on the possibility, just run your son or daughter's recent conduct through the three categories of warning signs. When in doubt, check it out. Denial, whether by teenager or parents, is the enemy in hiding because it only enables further use. The teenager doesn't want to be found out, and parents don't really want to find out. Hope is the most common form of denial for them all. The teenager hopes that parents won't notice, and parents hope that by his denial the teenager is really telling them the truth, so that they don't have to face a family problem.

But just suppose parents identify sufficient numbers of general, overlapping, and nonoverlapping signs of substance use (maybe a few in each category), but their son or daughter refuses to answer questions they ask or tries to put them on the defensive. "Anything goes wrong," charges the teenager, "and all you think about are drugs! Well, I'm sick of not being trusted! Just leave me alone!" What should parents do now? The answer is, they use grounds for suspicion to look for harder evidence. "You searched my room? You took my stash! That's stealing! I could have you arrested! That's violating my right to privacy!" "No," explain the parents, "your privacy is a privilege earned by our trust; it's not a right. And when you abuse that privilege by using it to conceal destructive and unlawful behavior, we have the right to search and seizure, and that's what we've done. Now let's talk about what's been going on and what needs to be done."

And what needs to be done is to get the adolescent's substance use assessed by a qualified professional, such as a Certified Alcohol and Drug Abuse Counselor, to determine to what degree it may be a side issue or a contributing factor in the current array of problems going on. If it is a significant factor, substance abuse counseling or outpatient or inpatient treatment may be advised.

At the least, parents need to get themselves some help so that they don't, in ignorance and upset, enable what is going on and make matters worse. The most direct assistance, and free of charge, is Al-Anon, a self-help group available in most communities that provides support and guidance for family members when one of their number has become ensnared in substance abuse or addiction.

Of course, come late adolescence, teenagers are not just socially getting together for the purpose of using substances. Now there is more interest in developing dating and caring relationships. Social partnering is now of interest, but there is no formal training in how to manage these relationships in a healthy way. Young people must often learn from unhappy experience. In the process, parents can be of help.

## Caring Relationships

Significant dating most commonly begins in late adolescence (fifteen to eighteen), during the high school years. By "significant," I mean when young people want to experience a continuing relationship that involves more interest and caring than the casual socializing or friendship they have known before. They want to pair up, at least for a while, to experience what a more serious involvement is like. At this juncture, it can be helpful if parents provide some guidelines for evaluating the "goodness" of a relationship. To what degree is it constructed and conducted so that it works well and not badly for the young people involved? What should they expect in a relationship, and what should they avoid? Remember that in most cases, this relationship education is not addressed in the academic classes they take in school. It is a product of life experience.

Parents can begin by describing three components of a serious relationship: *attraction, enjoyment,* and *respect.* Attraction is how the relationship gets started. Typically it is based on appearance and personality, and it serves to motivate two people to want to spend some time together. Enjoyment is what keeps the relationship going. Typically it is based on compatibility and commonality that allow the couple to share experiences together. Respect is reflected by the sensitive and considerate manner in which the relationship is conducted. Typically it is based on keeping treatment of each other within limits that feel comfortable and safe for them both. Parents can declare: no matter how much attraction and enjoyment there is, if young people treat each other with a lack of mutual respect, then what they have is not a good relationship.

If a serious relationship becomes emotionally intensified by romance or even first love, then parents can suggest more specific factors for the young person to consider, because romantic and love relationships are the most intimately complex and challenging of all. Here are ten factors for the adolescent to check out:

1. *Freedom of speech*: "We each feel free to speak unguardedly and openly to the other about what concerns us."
2. *Quality of attention*: "We give and receive a full and fair hearing when there is something important each of us has to say."
3. *Assurance of sensitivity*: "We are considerate of each other's special needs and vulnerabilities."
4. *Safety in conflict*: "We manage differences and disagreements so that neither of us feels threatened or gets hurt."
5. *Goodness of word*: "We keep the promises and commitments we make to each other."
6. *Trust in truth*: "We can rely on each other to be honest and open."
7. *Sufficiency of independence*: "We each have enough freedom of time to be with our respective friends."

8. *Comfort with anger*: "When either of us feels offended or wronged by the other, our anger can be talked out in a constructive and harmless way."

9. *Equitable sharing*: "We divide out the giving and getting that it takes to maintain our relationship in a way that each of us considers fair."

10. *Reliable communication*: "We keep each other accurately and adequately informed about what we are feeling, thinking, and doing."

It takes a lot of work to create a love relationship in which both parties can answer yes to all these questions. It is not your job as parents to manage their relationships. It is your job, however, to provide your son or daughter with the important questions to ask. What you want is for your teenager to learn from significant dating, romantic, or in-love experiences what it means and what it takes to have a good relationship so that he or she is more likely, if so choosing, to make a well-functioning committed partnership later on.

## Romantic Breakups

In cases where the couple was deeply in love, parents must beware of *depressive or aggressive reactions* when their adolescent is the jilted partner in the breakup of a deeply attached relationship. They must be on the watch. The hardest lesson first love has to teach is that those we love the most can hurt us the worst. At issue is how the rejected party manages pain. Responding depressively over love's loss can lead a young person into feeling worthless, into believing that everything of value has been lost, into experiencing a depletion of the energy needed to maintain normal caring and accomplish normal tasks, into withdrawing from social involvement with friends and socially isolating, into becoming uncommunicative and deeply sorrowful. Parents have to monitor their son's or daughter's response to loss and feelings of rejection to make sure that adequate communication, caring, and connectedness to them and others are maintained during a painful but transitory period of sadness. If they see signs of a depressive reaction, getting counseling support for the young person is usually helpful so that he or she can learn from pain how to manage pain, and reflect on the lessons the relationship had to teach.

Responding aggressively, as some young men are prone to do, is turning pain into anger at rejection and retaliating with various degrees of violence. He can circulate lies to attack the girl's reputation, make verbal threats to intimidate her, vandalize her belongings to prove his angry intent, harass and stalk her to assert control, and physically assault her to exact revenge. To prevent such outcomes, parents need to set a watch over their high school–age adolescent to make sure the breakup does not lead to further hurt. Should they see a bad situation building, they must act to protect their daughter and restrain the jilted young man. They need to make sure their daughter keeps the relationship broken off and does not continue, often from feeling sorry, to send double messages that can lead him on: "I want to break off the relationship, but I still care for you and want us to be friends." They must communicate to the young man that all angry behaviors toward their daughter must stop. They need to get cooperation from the young man's parents if they can. And they should talk with the school counselor or assistant principal so that the school can put the young man on notice and also provide him some counseling help, if he is willing to accept it. If, despite all these actions, the aggressive behaviors toward their daughter continue, parents need to go to the police.

Parents of the jilted young man need to keep watch over him to make sure that he is able to talk out his feelings of hurt enough to reduce the risk of acting them out aggressively, defending against his pain by using anger to attack the young woman. Although an exceptional response and not the rule, it is frequent enough to warrant watching out for. Male retaliation and revenge inspired by anger at rejection harm everyone. Not only is the young woman at risk of injury from this response, but so is he when he is charged with the attack. He needs parents' emotional support to work through the loss, and encouragement to answer the question, "What else are you feeling besides anger?" For some young men, anger is the power emotion used to control relationships and cover up more vulnerable feelings of disappointment, rejection, failure, and hurt. In addition, young men are often more emotionally invested in first love because, unlike young women who are used to emotionally sharing with women friends, young men often do not have that emotional intimacy with anyone else, and certainly not with male friends. For an angry jilted young man, parents should get him counseling help so that he can talk out his pain and come to emotional acceptance of his loss.

## Sexual Experience

I believe conversation about sexuality, sexual feelings, and sexual behavior needs to start during early adolescence (ages nine to thirteen), when for most young people puberty begins and the age of sexual maturity soon arrives. Now, hormonally equipped, young people are physically fully capable of sexual reproduction. Psychologically, however, they are many years away from being mature enough to assume the responsibility that comes with making a baby, should that unintended consequence occur, or to cope with the possibility of contracting a sexually transmitted disease at such a young age, or to integrate sexual intimacy with emotional closeness to nurture a caring relationship. So most parents encourage delay in the hopes that a later onset of sexual activity will make such activity safer.

Reaching the age of dating and partying, the high school (late adolescent) years, dramatically increases the interest in and likelihood of sexual activity as more socializing between young women and young men is encouraged. According to a 2012 report on teenage sexual activity, *Facts on American Teens' Sexual and Reproductive Health,* by the Guttmacher Institute, "by their 19th birthday, seven in 10 female and male teens have had sexual intercourse." Thus parents need to understand that by the time young people enter the last stage of adolescence, trial independence (about ages eighteen to twenty-three), most have elected to have sex.

What frame of reference, what information, and what education to provide their adolescent about managing sexual interest and sexual activity largely depend on the particular values parents hold and their comfort in dealing with the topic. Parents vary widely in this regard. Of course there are a few who shy away from addressing the issue at all, or have "the talk" and rarely mention sex again. Mostly, however, what I hear of are parents who subscribe to three sources of persuasion: *expectation + discussion + instruction = prevention* and regularly attend to that mix.

In declaring their expectation, parents clearly state what they think is wise, appropriate, or right when it comes to having sexual intercourse. Some parents say, "Oh, my teenager won't listen to me." From what I have seen, that is not true. The young person will factor your opinions and convictions into his or her thinking and decision making. *Your beliefs and your values matter.*

By engaging in discussion, parents normalize the topic of sexual activity in the same way they would the topic of substance use or any other significantly risky adolescent behavior. When this discussion is accepting and nonjudgmental and two-way, the parent not just talking but openly listening too, the teenager can use parents as a sounding board and source of advice to deal with the complexities that begin when relationships become more sexually active. *Your knowledge can be helpful.*

By offering instruction, parents equip the young person with strategies for managing sexual feelings in relationships and safely using protections should the decision to have sexual intercourse occur. You don't have to agree with or approve of your adolescent's decision to become sexually active in order to provide information about contraception. *Your concern for safety is what counts.*

Most parents don't like it that they have to raise adolescents in a sexually active world any more than they like it that they have to raise adolescents in a drug-filled world, but that's how the world is. Although they cannot control the teenager's choice of sexual behavior, they can inform that choice, and they *should*, because the popular media are already romanticizing and glamorizing sex in very seductive and sensational ways. The media do not model sexual restraint, and adolescents are at an impressionable age. They are influenced by what they see, and what they see places a high premium on being sexually attractive as a young woman and as a young man, but offers very little guidance about how to manage sexual interest once it has been attracted or aroused. In addition, little distinction is made between lust and love, between conquest and caring, which can muddle much adolescent thinking already going on. For example, some boys, focused on performance and intent on proving themselves, see scoring sexual intercourse as a win for masculinity, a successful act of conquest. Or some girls, focused on relationship and intent on intimately connecting, see experiencing sexual intercourse as an affirmation of femininity, a statement that caring has been established. Thus there are implied arguments for intercourse that parents need to dispel: "If we truly care, that means we should have sex," "If we have sex, that means we truly care." No, both premises are false.

Becoming sexually active is complicated because the motivations for doing so vary, each leading to a different focus of discussion with your adolescent. So see if you can determine the context of sexual decision making. Some of the sexual circumstances I have heard reported include these:

1. *Having sex as a rite of passage.* A young person "does it" to be able to feel and say that he or she has now crossed this bridge into adulthood, certifying young manhood or young

womanhood. "I got it over with." (Having sex doesn't mean you are adult, prove that you're a man, or make you a woman.)

2. *Having sex because one was under the influence of alcohol or other drugs.* A young person insists on or allows what he or she would not if his or her sober judgment were intact. "I didn't know what I was doing." (Many first sexual experiences are affected by the use of alcohol or other drugs; sober dating is safest.)

3. *Having sex because one was swept away by romantic feelings.* A young person lets a magic moment make having sex feel desirable and right. "It was all so dreamy." (It's safer to plan to have sex than to let infatuated and excited impulse decide.)

4. *Having sex as an expression of caring.* A young person engages in sexual intimacy to enhance emotional intimacy. "Having sex together brings us closer." (If you truly care about each other, then care enough to use adequate protection.)

5. *Having sex because it is pleasurable to do.* A young person sees hooking up as a significant source of recreational experience. "It's just part of having a good time." (What seems casual for one person can be serious for another.)

6. *Having sex because it feels obligatory.* A young person feels he or she ought to have sex to meet commitments to the relationship. "I did what I felt I should." (Having been given a good time or having had sex with someone before does not oblige you to do so again, and love does not require having sex to prove that love is true.)

7. *Having sex because one is afraid to say no.* A young person submits to external pressure of persuasion out of fear of rejection or to internal pressure of insecurity out of fear of failing to measure up. "I didn't want to be criticized or lose

a relationship for holding back." (Never have sex when you are afraid not to.)

8. *Having sex because of coercion.* A young person is emotionally or physically forced to do what he or she doesn't want to do. "I gave in because I was made to." (To have sex against your will is rape.)

Having sex in adolescence is not a simple act, although it may feel simple to do at the time. In fact, it is a very complicated act, and parents can offer help sorting out what that complexity involves. For the adolescent, the value of feeling able to talk with your parent about sex is the same as the value of talking with your mom or dad about substance use. When you can freely discuss sexual issues with your parent, you get to think about those issues, you are no longer alone with them, you get to hear another perspective, you get to ask questions, you get to consider your decisions, you get to talk about your past experiences, and you get to plan about how to deal with those issues in the future.

The problem with peers is that they are a mixed blessing for your adolescent—simultaneously enabling and complicating growth, providing support and creating risk, and being a valued source of both information and misinformation. To get the good that peers have to offer and to moderate the bad, it really helps when parents can be friends with their adolescent's friends, or at least be friendly with them. The influence of peers can cause parents to feel relatively powerless, but this is not true. The next and final chapter describes what some of those powers are.

*Chapter Ten*

# The Power of Parents

"You can't make me and you can't stop me!" our teenager yelled the other night. She was really angry for how she was leading her life, blaming her troubles on us. I really think she wants us to save her from herself. But we can't make her decisions for her. Much as we wish it wasn't so, after we've told her what we believe is for the best and why, the final choice is always up to her, as she well knows. Is there nothing more we can do to keep her on a steady course? We feel so helpless!

Although it is true that they cannot control their adolescent's decisions, parents can do a lot to encourage the young person's constructive growth. Parents do control their own decisions, after all, and these can affect choices a teenager makes. So in this final chapter, I discuss the nature of parental influence, the impact of parental treatment, nurturing adolescent self-esteem, eight anchors to adolescent growth, managing life on the Internet, and the power of parental love.

## Parental Influence

Some parents subscribe to the input-output theory of parental influence and responsibility. Put in "good" parenting, and a healthy, successful child and adolescent will result. Effort equals outcome, they believe, because quality of parenting makes most or all of the difference in how a young person "turns out." This assumption is not exactly accurate. Parents who assume responsibility for everything that happens to their child become bound by a false equation: *parents = child*. This linkage ties adequacy of parenting to performance of the child, how well or badly a son or daughter does becoming a measure of the parenting received. Bound by this belief, when the child makes a bad choice, parents must fault themselves, asking "What have we done wrong?" Now they blame themselves for their adolescent's bad decisions. At worst, they even ask the young person, "What did we do wrong?" only inviting the young person to escape responsibility by blaming them. So their substance-abusing son goes for the opening: "If you hadn't divorced, I never would have gotten messed up with drugs this way." No, the young person must be held accountable for his choices. It's easy for a substance-abusing adolescent to mine excessive parental responsibility by playing on their guilt for manipulative gain. Better for parents to break this equation and maintain a realistic perspective instead. To that end, here is a mantra worth repeating all the way through your son's or daughter's adolescence. *When a child acts badly, that doesn't mean the child or the parenting is bad. Good parents have good children who will sometimes fall down (and fall away) during the normal step and stumble of growing up.*

In counseling with parents who feel bound by the parent = child equation, my first job, before I can even get to helping with the child's problem of concern, is to dispel them of these beliefs in "bad child" and "bad parents." Vilifying the child or blaming themselves does none of them any good. A bad adolescent choice just means that a mistake or a misdeed has occurred and that now parents have to help their teenager learn from the error of his ways and normalize conduct. And then everyone carries on.

Certainly parenting matters—the time and energy and loving dedication invested in one's mothering or fathering task. However, many other sources of influence over which parents have no control also shape the course of a child's growth. Parents don't control the larger society and the cultural messages the media send about what is desirable, fashionable, glamorous, and ideal. Parents don't control the child's innate capacities and inborn human nature that shape the boy or girl as a person. Parents don't make the child's decisions, which are always under his or her control. Parents don't control the child's life experience away from home and all the challenging circumstances to be encountered there. Parents don't control the company the child decides to keep and all the influences those peers can have. And parents don't control the play of luck in the child's life that can lead to helpful or harmful effect. Within the large array of significant influences affecting a child's growth and how a young person turns out, parenting is only one, and keeping that perspective is particularly important when traveling through the ups and downs of your son's or daughter's adolescence.

Because *parenting is a position of partial influence,* parents need to limit their sense of responsibility. They can never know enough. They cannot fully protect any more than they can fully prepare. They cannot do it all, and they cannot always do it right. Just like their teenager, they will make mistakes. Even when they are giving a full-faith effort, a mixed job is the best they can make of it, and a mix is mostly good enough. That mix is of knowledge and ignorance, sensitivity and insensitivity, good judgment and bad. And from this mix a child has to grow, partly because of and partly in spite of what parents were able to provide. Partly—that's the key, because parents don't control that much to begin with. So for those parents who tend to judge themselves harshly, it can be helpful to remember that not everything that happens in their adolescent's life, for good or ill, is to their credit or to their blame. Making a "good faith" effort is the key, and that's usually good enough. Parents don't have to be perfect for their son or daughter to come out okay. In fact, being a perfect parent isn't really a worthy goal, because the only way to be a perfect parent is to have a perfect child, and who wants to place that kind of performance pressure on their growing girl or boy?

Sources of parental influence come down to these: parents' human nature, the example they set, the instruction they give, the family structure they create, the family dynamics in play, and the treatment they give—this last deserving of more consideration.

## Parental Treatment

Most parents know that how they interact with their adolescent matters, but they often do not appreciate the many forms this influence can take. Ten aspects of the *psychology of social treatment*, as applied to parenting adolescents, are worth keeping in mind.

1. *How we treat others influences our social reputation.* On the basis of how the adolescent experiences living with us, they give us a rating or designation describing how we are to relate to. So when troubled or in trouble, the teenager tends to approach the "go-to" parent who has become identified with showing concern more often than the "keep at a distance" parent who has always been quick to criticize. *By reviews of our behavior we are known.* The question a parent may want to ask is, "Have I earned the reputation with my teenager that I want?"

2. *How we treat others is self-defining.* Treat others well, and we treat ourselves as a well-meaning person; treat them badly, and we treat ourselves as someone who is not. So when a parent regularly loses her temper at the teenager, that parent treats herself as an angrily explosive person. *How we act with others is how we treat ourselves.* The question the parent may want to ask is, "Do I like the person I become when interacting with my teenager?"

3. *How we treat others is how we encourage them to treat us.* People are imitative in relationships, often responding

back to each other in kind. So when a parent yells at the teenager to stop yelling or argues with the teenager to stop arguing, yelling and arguing are likely to be what the parent will get back, whereas acts of courtesy and consideration can beget courtesy and consideration in response. *Treatment given is often treatment received.* The question the parent may want to ask is, "Do I model the kind of behavior I want my teenager to return?"

4. *How we treat others influences how those people treat others.* People can pass on the kind of treatment they are given. So when parents send their teenager off to school with positive expectations, that young person may be more inclined to be optimistic in his dealings with others, just as an angry send-off can increase the likelihood of the young person's being hostile with others. *Treatment given can carry on.* The question the parent may want to ask is, "Am I treating my teenager the way I want him to respond to others?"

5. *How we treat others contributes to the pattern of treatment we practice.* People are creatures and captives of habit, automatically repeating patterns of behavior they have practiced before. Acting patiently or impatiently with their teenager increases the likelihood that parents will act that way again. *Present action shapes future behavior.* The question a parent may want to ask is, "Am I treating my teenager now how I want to keep on treating her later?"

6. *How we treat others shapes how they anticipate being treated.* Treatment we give now gives others grounds for what later treatment to expect. The teenager uses past parental behavior—being relaxed or tense around grades—to predict how they will respond when the next report card time comes around. *Experience influences expectation.* The question a parent may want to ask is, "Am I treating my

teenager in a way that is consistent with how I want him to anticipate my acting and reacting in the future?"

7. *How we treat one person in our group contributes to the social climate in which we all live.* Each act of treatment we give to one person in our community of relationships has an impact on them all. When parents come home after a tough day's work, it makes a difference to the entire family whether they take accumulated stress and irritation out on their abrasive adolescent, or simply declare that they have had a hard day and then calmly respond. *In a human system, no act of social treatment stands alone.* The question a parent may want to ask is, "Am I treating my teenager the way I want to impact the entire family?"

8. *How we treat others provides a model for others to follow.* Every act of treatment provides a lesson to others in how to act. When the parent commits a mistake with the teenager and admits it, apologizes, and makes amends, the teenager can learn to do the same. *By example, everyone becomes a leader.* The question a parent may want to ask is, "Am I demonstrating the kind of conduct in my life that I want my teenager to learn in hers?"

9. *How we treat others can affect how others evaluate themselves.* When parents continually criticize a teenager, that young person can become critical of himself; when parents continually appreciate the teenager's strengths, that young person can appreciate himself. Treatment acts like a mirror in which people can observe some aspect of their own image in another person's eyes. *In our response to others, they see a reflection of themselves.* The question a parent may want to ask is, "Am I treating my teenager in keeping with the way I want her to view herself?"

10. *How we treat others affects their feelings and our own.* Treatment has emotional impact both for the giver and the receiver. When the teenager feels falsely suspected by

the parent, who then realizes that the suspicion is unfounded, the teenager can feel hurt, and the parent can feel sorry. *Actions have emotional effect.* The question a parent may want to ask is, "Am I treating my teenager in ways that generate more good feelings than bad on both sides of the relationship?"

In the heat of the moment, parents can forget that how they interact with their adolescent has many levels of formative impact—on the teenager, on themselves, on the relationship, and on others. Because the treatment parents give is a matter of choice, it is worth keeping in mind possible effects of choices they are making. *Parental treatment matters.* One area in which parental treatment can be particularly helpful is in teaching their teenager, through the ups and downs of adolescence, how to manage and maintain strong self-esteem.

## Nurturing Self-Esteem

I see two major self-esteem drops during the normal course of adolescence. The first occurs at the outset in early adolescence (ages nine to thirteen), when the young person's separation from childhood creates a loss of contentment with being defined and treated any longer as just a child. In this process, many components of self-definition now considered "childish"—beloved interests, activities, and relationships that supported self-esteem—may be sacrificed for the sake of appearing and acting older. A lot of "kid stuff" of significant psychological value can be thrown away. Old toys and hobbies can be abandoned, and even cherished grandparents can be put at a distance. The second drop in self-esteem occurs during the last stage of adolescence, trial independence (ages eighteen to twenty-three), when the young person is confronted with the daunting reality of actual independence and feels overwhelmed and diminished by the unknown future ahead. Feeling not up to this challenge and sometimes acting this way, adolescents tend to feel disappointed in themselves, to get down on themselves, to be hard on themselves, and even to punish themselves, esteem falling in the process. "Here I am twenty-two years old, still messing up, and I don't know what I want to do with my life!" When it comes to maintaining self-esteem, the first and last stages of adolescence are often the hardest because in each case (transitioning from childhood into adolescence and from adolescence into adulthood), the field of life experience becomes much larger and more complex than it was before, and some old security of home and family is cast away.

So what is self-esteem? It is not real in the sense that it can be visually examined, physically touched, or directly observed. Similar to notions like "intelligence" or "conscience," self-esteem is an abstract psychological concept made up to describe part of a person's human functioning. Its existence and utility are inferred through actions and expressions considered evidence of its presence. Just as solving a problem may be considered evidence of intelligence, or acting in accord with one's ethical beliefs may be considered evidence of conscience, insisting on being dealt with fairly or respectfully may be considered evidence of self-esteem, the young person acting as though he or she is worth treating well.

More specifically, "self-esteem" is two words compounded into one. Separate them, and the meaning of the larger term comes clear. "Self" is a descriptive concept: By what specific characteristics do I identify who I am? "Esteem" is an evaluative concept: How do I judge the value of who I am? *Self-esteem has to do with how a person identifies and evaluates his or her definition of self.*

## Self-Esteem as Identification

When the adolescent commits his or her identity to just one part of life—to having friends, to competitive sports, or to high academic achievement, for example—then when friends are lost, when injury ends athletics, or when academic performance drops, esteem comes crashing down. "I'm nothing without my friends!" "I'm worthless without my sport!" "I'm a failure if I don't make straight A's!" To maintain relative constancy of well-being through the normal ups and downs of adolescence, it really helps to maintain multiple pillars of self-esteem. So parents need to encourage and enable teenagers to have many interests, involvements, relationships, and social circles. This way, if one pillar of self-esteem momentarily collapses, there are others to depend on for continuing self-worth.

### Self-Esteem as Evaluation

When the adolescent is routinely hard on himself or herself—insisting on perfection, criticizing failings, punishing mistakes—then when expectations are unmet, when flaws become apparent, or when human errors occur, esteem comes crashing down. "I'm so stupid!" "What's wrong with me?" "I can't do anything right!" To maintain constancy of well-being during the trials of adolescence, it really helps to treat oneself with tolerance, forgiveness, and understanding when life goes badly. Particularly in the response to a bad experience where impulsive or unwise decision making led to error, disappointment, or trouble, an adolescent can get into some pretty harsh self-evaluation, descending common steps that systematically lower self-esteem. He makes a bad choice, suffers hurt feelings, criticizes himself with blame, nourishes feelings of guilt, punishes himself for acting badly, treats this mistreatment as deserved, and spends more energy on penance than on recovery. Should a teenager proceed to beat up on himself for choosing unwisely or for life going badly, parents might suggest this to him: "When you do something that is wrong in your own or other people's eyes, you are not obliged to punish yourself, just to recover the situation and move on. To hurt yourself when you are already hurting only makes the hurt worse. When you're hurting is a time not to treat yourself badly; it is a time to treat yourself well. That way you can motivate yourself to do better."

So what might parents say to their adolescent about self-esteem? "The more narrowly you define yourself and the more negatively you evaluate yourself, the more at risk of lowered self-esteem you are likely to be. In that unhappy state, you may also be more at risk of treating yourself and others badly. Therefore, do yourself a favor. *To maintain positive self-esteem, define yourself broadly and evaluate yourself kindly,* and most of the time you will appreciate the value and enjoy the company of the person you are."

In addition to supporting strong self-esteem, what are some specific actions parents take to keep their adolescent anchored into family and on a constructive path as the young person grows?

## Eight Anchors for Adolescent Growth

Brief, but I hope to the point, are these descriptions of eight "anchors" that seem to steady a young person through the tumultuous teenage years. Over the course of counseling families with adolescents, I have repeatedly noticed this odd collection of eight practices that when consistently in place seem to stabilize teenage growth. Individually, each is helpful; but taken together, they provide significant anchoring power. After listing each one, I speculate about the contribution it makes.

1. *Completing homework.* Separate from any academic value, fulfilling this nightly study obligation provides *work ethic training.* By making himself get done what is in his best interests even when it is not what he wants to do, the young person develops strength of will. Adults are accustomed to routinely accomplishing much each day that they do not feel like doing; but the adolescent (who would

rather play than work) has to learn this habit of self-discipline. Regularly completing homework provides good practice for self-discipline to grow. Parents need to support this training by continuing to supervise the completion of homework until the adolescent becomes ready and able to assume this responsibility on his own.

2. *Cleaning up one's room.* The messy room is emblematic of the adolescent age. This increased personal disorder is partly a reflection of entering a larger, more distracting, more complicated world of experience, and partly an anarchic statement about being now entitled to live more independently at home. In addition to claiming control over personal space, adolescents often signify their growing presence in the family by marking further territory around the home. They do this by leaving belongings and disarray about in other rooms as well. It is by insisting on a regular room cleanup and on the adolescent's picking up after herself elsewhere that parents instill the value of personal order and fitting into family, and by doing so they assert the principle of *living on parental terms*.

3. *Doing household chores.* To maintain a well-functioning family takes a lot of work, most of that labor done by the resident powers that be, the parents, who do it for no pay. They do it out of love, through self-sacrifice, and for responsibility. Work they do for the family invests them in the family and affirms the connection they feel. However, if they do all the work, they can become resentful of an adolescent who does none. This is where teenage chores come in. Unpaid and in no way connected to receiving allowance, chores are routine investments of energy and effort that become *family membership requirements*. By investing effort in household maintenance, the adolescent becomes an active contributor. Now parents know that everyone, not just themselves, is pitching in, and

adolescents know that they have a working stake and value in the family.

4. *Joining in family gatherings and events.* It is easy for adolescents, preoccupied with their world of peers, to discount and neglect relationships at home, to prefer time with friends over time with family. It's not that they lose love for family, but they lose focus on the importance of family, which is why parents need to bring that focus back. Socially participating in events like family meals, significant observances, special celebrations, and extended family gatherings affirms the lasting value of this *primary social affiliation.* Such participation reminds the teenager of the abiding importance of family over the pressing (but usually passing) value of peers.

5. *Volunteering for community service.* Adolescence can be a very self-centered age. Thinking of self often trumps thinking of others. In addition, social awareness is often limited to one's social world with friends. Parents need to expand this world awareness so that the young person experiences the larger community of which he is a part, and then to get him to serve that community by helping others. Acting for larger social good shows *concern for those less well situated,* it socially exposes the teenager to concerned others as well as to others in need, and it supports self-esteem by demonstrating that the adolescent has a capacity for service that is worth offering.

6. *Saving money.* Money buys the power of choice to get something or to get to do something one would like. So money is of high value to adolescents. It creates the freedom to satisfy wants at an age when young people typically want a lot more. There can be extreme variation in how teenagers are inclined to handle this freedom. Some adolescents seem to be born *spenders* when it comes to managing money; others seem to be born *savers.* The

difference can be worth noting because of the psychological issues at stake. Spenders often have a hard time controlling impulse, resisting giving in to immediate gratification, and putting wants on hold. Savers can often exercise resistance in the face of temptation, set goals, and plan ahead to reach them. Parents can help a spender learn to conserve money for later use, and by doing so help the young person practice *delaying gratification* and use saving to increase capacity for self-restraint.

7. *Developing proficiency.* Developing a proficiency of knowledge or skill nurtures confidence that many adolescents sorely need. Those who feel that they lack any identifiable capability believe there is nothing they are particularly good at. Working hard to know or do something well builds a *sense of competence*, which becomes a powerful pillar of self-esteem. Because it's not automatically given to adolescents to find some activity or interest at which they want to work to develop proficiency, it's up to parents to act as door openers, helping the young person try out different possibilities in search of what may catch her interest and encourage her commitment.

8. *Relating to salient adults.* The power of peers lies in the adolescent's having a group of people the same age with whom to share the adventures of adolescence together and who provide each other an important measure of understanding and support. The problem with peers is that the effect they have on one another is an immature one because they are not yet grown up. This is why parents need to encourage some mature adult relationships for their teenager in order to provide a counterbalance to same-age companions. Enjoying this company of significant adults (members of the extended family, adult friends of the family, coaches and youth directors, activity leaders and adult mentors, for example) who are not one's parents

creates the opportunity for having *grown-up influential friends*.

Do I know for sure that these eight anchors will steady adolescent growth? No. But what I do know is this. A young person who never does homework, who never cleans up his room, who never does household chores, who never participates in family activities, who never contributes community service, who never saves money, who never develops any proficiency, and who never befriends salient adults will likely give parents a pretty rough ride through adolescence. So my advice is "strive for five." Consistently keep just five of these anchors in place, and your adolescent is likely to stay on a steady and responsible path of growth toward independence.

All this is assuming that you adequately deal with the "elephant in the living room," the Internet, and teach your adolescent to integrate online activities into his or her offline life in a healthy way.

## Managing Life on the Internet

Adolescents are adventurers. They want to experiment and explore the larger world for more experience to grow. And today the geography of that world, so different from that of their parents' youth, has dramatically expanded with the Internet revolution. Staying on the home computer or on a portable or cellular device, adolescents can go anywhere in this virtual world. They can search out all kinds of information, play computer games with people in faraway places, stream all manner of audio and visual entertainment, communicate in multiple ways, store and display a huge variety of data, shop for just about anything, create an online identity by which they are publically known, and join social networks through which they can keep in touch and stay informed. To put it mildly, "This isn't Kansas anymore." Computer travel on the Internet has vastly increased the adolescent's field of play, in the process vastly complicating the responsibilities of parents.

This said, the Internet is not the enemy of adolescence, nor does it change the nature of adolescence. It only creates a wider arena of experience in which adolescence can unfold. It becomes a major place to hang out and interact with friends, seek entertainment, acquire worldly knowledge, establish more independence from family, and grow oneself up. So what are parents to do with the "new normal" of the Internet? I believe they should have three goals for their adolescent when it comes to Internet use: acquiring *proficiency*, promoting *safety*, and maintaining *balance*.

## Proficiency

The online world is an extremely enriched, compelling, and empowering environment. And it is one adolescents need to become knowledgeable about and competent in because it is here to stay. The skills it takes to resourcefully access and navigate this virtual world will be essential to most educational, occupational, and social paths that lead into their future. To develop this proficiency requires practice, a lot of which takes place for most young people during adolescence. Practice takes time, and it is up to parents to determine how much is too much time, at the expense of other time, or a waste of time. Use of the Internet can create many conflicts with teenagers over the amount of time spent gaming, streaming entertainment, surfing, emailing, messaging, and social networking. Any use is practice, but not all use is otherwise beneficial. Whatever their reservations, parents do need to recognize that competence on the Internet is now an essential life skill.

## Safety

Technological change is usually embraced more quickly and enthusiastically by the young than by the old. Internet possibilities that excite adolescents often frighten their parents. Both adolescent and parents are asking the same question about online life: "What if?" However, for the teenager this is usually an expression of interest and curiosity, whereas for parents it is often a statement of worry and concern. What are they concerned about? "Free" as the Internet may feel for the freedom-loving adolescent, it is not free from risks, and parents need to help their son or daughter understand these risks. Consider a common few.

*The risk of exposure*: every click on the Internet allows you to be identified.

*The risk of linkage*: whatever you link to can link back to you.

*The risk of permanence*: what you post now is out there forever.

*The risk of exploitation*: your personal information can profit others.

*The risk of deception*: misinformation and misrepresentation abound.

*The risk of victimization*: other users can use you to your disadvantage.

*The risk of habituation*: repeated use can create patterns of dependency.

*The risk of isolation*: online connecting can substitute for offline socializing.

*The risk of impulse*: people may say on the Internet what they wouldn't say in person.

I believe that the Internet risks to adolescents go up as parental involvement goes down. Many teenagers, however, pleading their right to privacy, argue that parents should have no need to know what they do online. "I should be free to use the Internet no questions asked, no limits set, no supervision given." But consider the use of another piece of modern technology that gets adolescents out in the world and increases their drive for independence—the automobile. I have yet to meet a parent who says to their young driver: "Here are the keys. Your use of the car is private. Drive where you will. I will require no information, will do no checking up on you, and will set no conditions about where you go or what you do."

Just as parents have a need to know where in the physical world the teenager travels in the car, they need to know where in the virtual world he travels on the Internet. And because the home computer is a major portal to the Internet, they may want to prohibit certain destinations for the present, explaining why. For example, they may say that hate sites, pornographic sites, explicit violence sites, drug use sites, or gambling sites are off-limits. "Why?" asks the teenager. "Because," they reply, "we don't want that kind of content coming into our home and impacting our family." Rather than getting into an argument about privacy, parents should simply explain their need for some degree of participation in and communication about the adolescent's life in general, online activity just being another significant part, like social life, school life, or job life. It is normal and healthy for adolescents to want to be active on the Internet, and it is normal and healthy for parents to want to be involved.

## Balance

Of concern for parents should not just be the risks arising from commission (the influence and effect of what young people do on the Internet), but the problem of omission (the cost of what they give up doing by investing their time and energy on the Internet). It's easy to sacrifice physical exercise, face-to-face socializing, creative self-expression, family time, household chores, and homework for Internet activity. At issue is the balance between *how much of life is lived online* and *how much is lived offline*. A lot of offline living has to do with engagement with real-life challenges that develop real-life strengths. A lot of online living can take the form of escape, using endless possibilities for entertaining diversions to avoid the practicalities of self-care, work, and social participation.

At the extreme, there can be an online Internet retreat from the demands of offline reality. Online living can feel more pleasurable, secure, simple, and under control than offline living, which often feels more taxing, chaotic, challenging, and scary. The reality for many adolescents is that more social connecting and communication with peers is conducted online than offline and in person. Because much of this interaction is primarily written, it is *cue-less communication*. It lacks the nonverbal data provided by face-to-face talking—having access to the other person's physical posture and appearance, facial expression, and voice tone, for example. Sheltered from this more complete interpersonal exposure, some socially uncomfortable adolescents can prefer to be unseen and unheard when interacting. In the process, they may shy away from practicing and developing a full repertoire of communication skills that they will need to independently make their way in the world.

In the Internet age, parents must help their adolescent manage a healthy mix of online and offline life. To that end, here are three general guidelines to consider:

1. Explain how managing adult independence and mature relationships is going to require more offline capabilities than online skills.
2. Don't allow online activity to become so all-consuming that significant areas of offline functioning, such as commitments to family, school, self-care, and social growth, are neglected.
3. Use the adequacy of offline engagement, functioning, and responsibility as a guide for determining how much online activity to permit.

For good and ill, the Internet is a huge step in our social evolution. As parents, we want our adolescents to stay abreast of this technological transformation, learning to use it well as they grow forward in an ever-changing world, in which one life change, the process of adolescence, remains pretty much the same one generation to the next.

This leads us to consider another intergenerational constant, the presence of parents, and why their steadfast love matters as much as it does during the more turbulent adolescent years.

## Adolescence and the Power of Parental Love

The function of parental love is to secure the child. This is done in two ways. *Committed caring* is communicated to establish an *attachment* that can be depended on and trusted: "We will always be there for you, no matter what." And *unconditional positive regard* is communicated to establish absolute *acceptance* of individuality: "We will always value the person you are and who you become." These are the twin pillars on which secure parental love depends.

When the "teenage years" begin, both attachment and acceptance become harder for parents to provide. Adolescent separation and opposition for independence can strain attachment, particularly when they take the form of teenage rebellion against parental rules. Differentiation and experimenting with individuality can discourage acceptance, particularly when the adolescent adopts a lifestyle unfamiliar to parents. To maintain attachment, parents must keep reaching out so that they can stay connected to the young person as adolescence necessarily grows them apart. To communicate acceptance, parents must bridge developing differences between them with interest as the adolescent increasingly explores and expresses his or her unique interests and identity. A good example of how hard it is to do this parenting well was sent in as a response to a blog post I wrote about rebellion.

Please do not do what my husband and I did with our daughter. We did not give her enough space in the early and mid-adolescence period and paid for our error big time. At 16 and 17 she was in full blown rebellion (smoking, rough crowd, stealing, drugs, promiscuous sex, repeated traumas from various actions, rough boyfriends, and a stint of running away for 4 months to use drugs). We were shattered and needed to learn the skills we wished we had sought a lot earlier. We changed our communication to be more validating and empathetic, were firm with boundaries that affected us and our other kids, let her know she had our support when she asked for it, and let her live her life rather than us trying to steer it. I am happy to say one year later she is back at school going through the last stages described in your article, is off drugs, not stealing or doing reckless behavior, is calm and happy where she is studying, shares her hopes and dreams with us and is supported.

Managing to stay attached and accepting during this kind of adolescent passage was powerful for the parents to do. A young woman who rebelled against family rules and her own self-interests for freedom's sake remained anchored by parental love. With that security in place, she found her way safely back home after "breaking out of the barn" for a run on the wild side.

Parental love in adolescence must not be dependent on getting the young person you want, but in wanting the young person you get, most of all when you disagree with or dislike some of the changes in believing and behaving that start taking place. When parents fail in either expression of love, there are emotional costs for the adolescent to pay. When attachment is not maintained, the adolescent can feel abandoned and lonely. When acceptance is not maintained, the adolescent can feel rejected and estranged. In both cases, the outcome is likely to be more reliance on peers for the attachment and acceptance that are not forthcoming at home, creating less mature companionship more likely to lead to young person astray.

Parental attachment and acceptance do need to be constant, but they also sometimes need to be qualified by parental objection. Attachment does not mean automatic approval. For example, the attached parent says, "I am always ready to listen to whatever you have to say, but the language you use needs to be free of swearing and insults, both of which I find offensive and both of which get in the way of my hearing what you have to say." Acceptance does not mean automatic agreement. For example, the accepting parents says, "I understand your desire to dress the way your popular friend does, but I won't allow your doing so, because I believe it attracts sexual attention that would feel uncomfortable to you if it came your way." At these objection points, it may at first seem to the adolescent that parents are acting unlovingly, when in fact they are providing thankless parenting—taking stands for the young person's best interests against what she or he wants, and being criticized for their loyal efforts. Hanging in there with unappreciated acts of love is the toughest part of parenting adolescents who can act unlovingly when they don't get their way.

Love is perhaps the hardest emotion for parents to manage because under its influence, healthy limits with their increasingly self-centered adolescent become hard to set and maintain. Consider that specific and symbolic act that is most emblematic of parental love: *giving*. At first it seems like a good bargain: parents love to give to their teenager as a way of expressing their love, and the teenager loves being given to. However, from being constantly given to, the teenage taker may not be inclined to do much giving back, while the giving parents may feel taken, or at least taken advantage of, and feel exploited. Therefore, it's best to insist on mutual giving. That way parents feel that they are receiving some loving benefit in the relationship too.

For parents, what and how much to give to their teenager, under what emotional conditions to give, whether or not to give in, when to let go and give up, and how much giving should be expected in exchange can all be very complicated questions of love to answer. Parents who sacrifice themselves and give more than they can emotionally afford, parents who give with the expectation of a return from their adolescent that is not forthcoming, parents who give up under unrelenting adolescent pressure, parents who give in to avoid adolescent upset, parents who give to gain adolescent love, parents who are all give and no get with their adolescent—all put themselves at risk of feeling resentment in the name of love. But who said parental love with adolescents was meant to be easy?

During their child's adolescent passage, love is a challenge, one that parents must rise to meet. Just because the adolescent takes for granted most of what you give, and acts more unlovingly toward you than did the child, is no good reason for you to act more unloving in response. Although parents need to call the young person on any behaviors that are unmindfully or deliberately hurtful, so that they do not accept mistreatment and he or she does not learn that mistreating a loved one is okay, they must hold fast to their guarantee: "No matter how much you push against us or pull away, no matter how you change, our love for you is the same as it has always been and always will be."

The power of parents in the life of their adolescent is in the constancy of their caring, the loyalty of their concern, and the acceptance of all they don't control. Adolescents, even adult children, never happily give up the need for parents to communicate interest and to cheer them on. In this, the adolescent is no different from the little child who is ever hungry for parental notice and affirmation—"Watch me!" "Look at what I can do!" "Listen to what just happened!" "Care to know about me as I grow!" A reader of my blog put it best: "Parental love is the foundation of love. It is unconditional and infinite love....It is the best love in the whole world."

# Climbing Fool's Hill

I'll describe the path parents and adolescents take to you the way my grandfather once explained it to me many years ago, when at the proud age of ten, I stopped by to tell him that I was fed up with my parents, didn't need them anymore, and was going to run away from home.

Well, he didn't say anything at first. Just got out some bread and jam and soda, and then proceeded to feed me the way he always did.

"It's hard traveling on an empty stomach," he said at last. "And it sounds like you're ready to do some serious climbing."

"How's that?" I asked.

"Well, when I was your age, it was called 'climbing Fool's Hill,' and I guess that name is as good now as it was back then."

"I never heard of Fool's Hill, and I don't think that there really is such a place," I replied.

"Oh, there is, all right, and you're going to climb it, and it won't be easy. Most of the time you won't be able to see where you're headed. Just away from home and out into the world is all you'll know. Reason you'll be leaving is because you think your parents have changed and become too hard to live with. They're not so much fun to be around as they used to be, are making all kinds of unreasonable demands on you, and keep putting rules in the way of what you want to do.

"You'll think you're going one direction, but they'll say you're going opposite. Then there will be arguments about which way you should go, so you and your folks will disagree with each other a lot of the time. You'll tell them they don't understand, that you know best, and to let you alone to decide. But they'll tell you that you don't understand, that you're still their child, and they are responsible for getting you up that hill.

"Sometimes you'll go along with part or all of what they want, and other times you'll disobey, and some of those times you'll get in trouble from mistakes you make, which looking back on seem downright stupid. But you didn't know that at that time. That's when you'll feel like a fool and start wondering if you're ever going to make it to the top of that darn hill and grow up.

"Your parents will wonder about that, too. They'll criticize the path you've chosen to travel and who you're traveling with, and they'll decide that you can't get to where they want you to go from the way you're going. So they'll try to set you on a different path in different company. That's when things will really get hot between you.

"Then they'll tell you that they never did the darn fool things you're doing when they were your age. And that's true. They did different darn fool things. But they'll mean well even when you think they're just being mean. And you'll try your best even when they think you're not trying at all. And somehow, despite losing your way, backsliding, breaking a few bones and a lot of hopes and promises, you'll make it to the top of that hill. Then looking back down you'll see what a long way you've come.

"You'll see that in some ways your parents were right and that in some ways they were wrong about your path. In some ways they were a help to you and in other ways a hindrance. But you'll understand that at least they tried to do what was right even when it was wrong. And you'll know that at last you are on top of Fool's Hill because they're not interested in pushing at you anymore, and you're not interested in pushing back at them. Now you'll be able to climb something bigger and to climb it without their help."

"What's that?" I asked.

He laughed. "Well, I guess you could call it Fool's Mountain. But whatever you call it, you'll find enough triumph and trouble on your way up to last a lifetime. No matter how far you climb, you'll never get to the top. And no matter how well you climb, there will be times, after some stumbling steps from some stupid choices, that you'll wonder if you're still not back climbing that old Fool's Hill."

"You mean I'll never stop making mistakes?" I asked. "I thought going to school and listening to my parents were supposed to teach the stupid out of me!"

"Not exactly." He smiled sympathetically. "Not for you, not for your folks, not even for me. Everybody needs mistakes. I can testify to that. Education only makes you smarter. It takes learning from mistakes to make you wise."

# Recommended Reading

Buntman, Peter H., and Eleanor M. Saris. *How to Live with Your Teenager: A Survivor's Handbook*. New York: Ballantine, 1979.

Forward, Susan. *Emotional Blackmail: When People in Your Life Use Fear, Obligation, and Guilt to Manipulate You*. New York: HarperCollins, 1997.

Glasser, William. *For Parents and Teenager: Dissolving the Barrier Between You and Your Teen*. New York: HarperCollins, 2002.

Guiamo-Ramos, Vincent, James Jaccard, and Patricia Dittus. *Parental Mentoring of Adolescents: Current Perspectives for Researchers and Practitioners*. New York: Columbia University Press, 2010.

McIntire, Roger W. *Teenagers and Parents: 10 Steps for a Better Relationship*. (3rd ed.) Berkeley Springs, WV: Summit Crossroads Press, 2000.

Narciso, John, and David Burkett. *Relating Redefined: Discovering the New "Language" for Communicating*. (Rev. ed.) San Antonio, TX: Redman-Wright, 1994.

Pickhardt, Carl. *Boomerang Kids: Why So Many of Our Kids Are Failing on Their Own and How Parents Can Help*. Naperville, IL: Sourcebooks, 2011.

Pickhardt, Carl. *Keys to Successful Stepfathering*. (2nd ed.) Hauppauge, NY: Barron's Educational Series, 2010.

Pickhardt, Carl. *Why Good Kids Act Cruel: The Hidden Truth About the Pre-Teen Years*. Naperville, IL: Sourcebooks, 2010.

Pickhardt, Carl. *Stop the Screaming: How to Turn Angry Conflict with Your Child into Positive Communication*. New York: Palgrave Macmillan, 2009.

Pickhardt, Carl. *The Future of Your Only Child: How to Guide Your Child to a Happy and Successful Life*. New York: Palgrave Macmillan, 2008.

Pickhardt, Carl. *The Connected Father: Understanding Your Unique Role and Responsibilities During Your Child's Adolescence*. New York: Palgrave Macmillan, 2007.

Pickhardt, Carl. *The Everything® Parent's Guide to Children and Divorce*. Avon, MA: Adams Media, 2006.

Pickhardt, Carl. *The Everything® Parent's Guide to Positive Discipline*. Avon, MA: Adams Media, 2005.

Pickhardt, Carl. *The Everything® Parent's Guide to the Strong-Willed Child.* Avon, MA: Adams Media, 2005.

Pickhardt, Carl. *The Trout King.* Springville, UT: Bonneville Books, 2001.

Pickhardt, Carl. *Keys to Developing Your Child's Self-Esteem.* Hauppauge, NY: Barron's Educational Series, 2000.

Pickhardt, Carl. *Keys to Raising a Drug-Free Child.* Hauppauge, NY: Barron's Educational Series, 1999.

Pickhardt, Carl. *Keys to Parenting the Only Child.* Hauppauge, NY: Barron's Educational Series, 1997.

Pickhardt, Carl. *The Case of the Scary Divorce: A Jackson Skye Mystery.* Washington DC: Magination Press, 1997.

Pickhardt, Carl. *Keys to Single Parenting.* Hauppauge, NY: Barron's Educational Series, 1996.

Robin, Arthur L., and Sharon L. Foster. *Negotiating Parent-Adolescent Conflict: A Behavioral–Family Systems Approach.* New York: Guilford Press, 2003.

Schafer, Alyson. *Ain't Misbehavin': Tactics for Tantrums, Meltdowns, Bedtime Blues and Other Perfectly Normal Kid Behaviors.* Mississauga, Ont.: Wiley Canada, 2011.

Steinberg, Laurence, and Ann Levine. *You and Your Adolescent: A Parent's Guide for Ages 10–20.* New York: HarperCollins, 1997.

Sulloway, Frank J. *Born to Rebel: Birth Order, Family Dynamics, and Creative Lives.* New York: Vintage Books, 1997.

Schalet, Amy T. *Not Under My Roof: Parents, Teens, and the Culture of Sex.* Chicago: University of Chicago Press, 2011.

# Index

## A

*Abandoned youth* group, 207
Abandonment: emotional extortion over parents' fear of, 139; of parents by adolescent, 14–15. *See also* Loss
Academic benchmark: holding your adolescent to the selected, 181–182; identifying, 181
Acceptance: how adolescence challenges parental, 246–248; parental love function of providing, 245–246; understanding that automatic agreement is not required for, 247
Accessible listeners, 124
"Acting more grown up": differing parent and adolescent perceptions of, 50–51; older student pressure on younger students for, 50
Active resistance: description of, 34–35; father-son power struggles and, 95; opposition as pushing for more, 128–129
Adolescence: adjusting to the five realities of, 12–17; as age of social intolerance, 198–201; early adolescence (ages nine to thirteen), 22, 23–39, 179–184, 188, 233–234; eight anchors for adolescent growth during, 236–240; four necessary parental attitude changes about, 2–4; illusion of independence held by, 78–79; late adolescence (ages fifteen to eighteen), 23, 49–67, 106, 187–191, 218–220; life on the Internet during, 109–110, 240–245; limits to privacy during, 29–30; mid-adolescence (ages thirteen to fifteen), 22–23, 39–47, 184–187; overlapping signs of both substance use and, 214–215; parental influence during, 227–230; parental love during, 245–248; parents facing the reality of, 1–2; trial independence (ages eighteen to twenty-three), 23, 67–82, 233–234; when your dog becomes a cat metaphor for, 6–8. *See also* Puberty
Adolescence realities: abandonment by your adolescent, 14–15; conflict between parent and adolescent, 15–16; diminishing control over your adolescent, 15; estrangement of adolescent, 13–14; five parental adjustments to, 16–17; issues to consider regarding, 12–13; parental ignorance, 13
Adolescent daughters: complex process of claiming independence by, 101–104; father role as *salient male presence* in life of, 90–91; fathering, 88–91; modeling constructive conflict to, 103–104; mother-daughter conflict with, 86, 103–104; mothering, 100–104; similarities between mothers and, 102–103. *See also* Girls
Adolescent education: before-the-fact versus after-the-fact, 176; as coming from both informal and formal instruction, 175; early adolescent achievement drop enemy of, 179–184; escaping responsibility enemy of, 176–179; lacking self-discipline in college enemy of, 191–196; late adolescence procrastination enemy of, 187–191; mid-adolescence cheating enemy of, 184–187; trial independence challenge of furthering, 70
Adolescent growth anchors: cleaning up one's room, 237; completing homework providing work ethic training, 236–237; developing proficiency, 239; doing household chores, 237–238; joining in family gatherings and events, 238; relating to salient adults, 239–240; saving money, 238–239; volunteering for community service, 199–200, 238. *See also* Life skills
Adolescent secrecy: description of, 110; hide-and-seek game of, 110–111; keeping social cruelty from parents as part of, 206–207; partial truths revealed as part of, 113–116; as way to skirt authority, 110–112
Adolescent self-blame: performance-focused parenting and, 87; relationally focused parenting and, 87

Adolescent shyness: adolescent's ambivalence over fears versus, 108–109; alcohol used to self-medicate discomfort of, 106; four fears that contribute to, 107–108; how changes of puberty increase, 106; how social confidence in talking with grown-ups counters, 106; how spoken communication is impacted by, 105–110; how the Internet has impacted, 109–110, 244; strategies for overcoming fears and, 109–110; vicious circle of temperamental, 106–107

Adolescent sons: companionship between mothers and, 99; competition between fathers and, 93–94; father demands for similarity of, 95; father-son conflict and, 86–87; fathering, 91–95; mothering, 96–100; mothers as gender role-model for, 87–88, 99–100; need for father to *bridge adolescent differences with interest*, 92–93; need to create distance from mother, 96–98; paternal downsizing about their fathers by, 93; power struggles between fathers and, 94–95; sexism development by, 99. See also Boys

Adolescents: differing tolerance of conflict by parent and, 133–134; emotional extortion by, 138–140; lack of appreciation for parents by, 17–19; life on the Internet by, 109–110, 240–245; mutual disenchantment of parents and, 4–8; open questions policy between parents and, 119; parent shift from vertical to horizontal relationship with, 77–78; parental intolerance of changing tastes of, 148–149; parental treatment of, 230–233; public and secret lives of, 110–112; reciprocal giving between parents and, 171; resetting expectations of your, 8–12; shyness of some, 105–110; signs indicating social cruelty toward, 209–210; spoken communication between parents and, 105–126; starter list of essential competencies to develop in, 63–64

Adults: adolescent ability to relate to salient, 239–240; rebellion against authority of, 150. See also Parents; Teachers

Advice giving: mentoring rule on, 76–77; parental guidance on caring relationships, 218–219; parental guidance on sexual intimacy, 223–224

After-the-fact education, 176

Al-Anon, 218

Alcohol use/abuse: how decision making is impacted by, 212–216, 217; parental discussions about, 37–38; peer-group issue of substance abuse and, 211–218; self-medicating shyness with, 106; sexual intimacy under influence of, 225; uncharacteristic changes in behavior clues to, 213–214. See also Substance use/abuse

Alcoholics Anonymous, 72

Allowance: a measure of choice provided by, 60–61; money management skills taught through experience of, 62; spender versus saver mentality of managing an, 61–62; weekly versus monthly, 62–63; when to withhold an, 63

Ambitions expectations, 10–11

Ambivalence: of adolescent over independence, 79–80; over shyness versus fears, 108–109; of parents over adolescent independence, 81; procrastination as agent of adolescent, 80

Anger: caring relationships and healthy expression of, 220; caution against punishment made in, 162–164; punishment should be free of parental, 158; as warning sign of substance use, 216

Anger-prone parents: description of, 163; five characteristics of, 163–164

Appreciation, parent adjustment to lack of, 17–19

Arguments: emotional extortion as part of, 137–140; managing parental disagreement and, 140–145; parental conflict avoidance skills to stay out of, 136–137; treating it seriously, 135; understanding the dynamics of parent-adolescent, 134–137. See also Parent-adolescent conflict

Attachment: how adolescence challenges parental, 246–248; parental love function of establishing, 245–248; understanding that automatic approval is not required for, 247

Authenticity, 120–121

Authority: adolescent secrecy to skirt, 110–112; childhood structure and direction through parental, 153; compromises of adolescent obedience to, 152–153; father-son power struggles over father's, 94–95; five pillars of social, 44–45; gradual transference to adolescent of responsibility and, 153–154; loss of parental, 154; need for independence driving rebellion against, 151–154; parent-adolescent arguing over parental, 136; son's need to distance himself from mother's, 96–98. See also Rebellion

**B**

Bedrooms: chore of cleaning up one's, 237; conflict over messy, 27–29, 30; as expression of early adolescent's identity, 29

Before-the-fact education, 176

Behavioral expectations: ambitions type of, 10–11; conditions type of, 11; developing a realistic set of adolescent, 8–12; high cost of unpreparedness or unrealistic, 10, 11–12; middle school rules on, 208; predictions type of, 10; preparatory role played by, 10; psychological importance of, 9–10; recognition of adolescent for meeting, 158–159, 170

Behaviors: adolescent shyness, 105–110; nonoverlapping signs of substance use, 215–217; overlapping signs of adolescence and substance use, 214–215; secrecy regarding, 110–116, 206–207; social cruelty warning sign of observable changes in, 209; uncharacteristic changes indicating alcohol/substance abuse, 213–214. *See also* Mistakes; Risk-taking behaviors

Body image issues, 203–204

Boomerang kids: clarifications made to parents by, 73–74; clarifications to be made by parents to, 73; parental responses to, 72–73

Boys: body image issues by, 203–204; physical changes during puberty, 201–202; romantic breakups experienced by, 220–222; social and sexual stereotypes facing, 204. *See also* Adolescent sons

*Bridging differences with interest*: conflict management by parenting practice of, 145–148; fathers and adolescent sons need for, 92–93

Bullying: intimidate purpose of, 208; playing on fear of weakness, 208; social cruelty of, 205, 207

**C**

Car accidents, 212

Caring relationships: parental guidance on recognizing and developing, 218–219; romantic breakups of, 220–222; sexual experience issues in, 222–226; ten factors used to assess, 219–220; three components of serious, 218–219

Certified Alcohol and Drug Abuse Counselor, 217

Cheating: begun as an antiestablishment game, 184; emotional and personal costs of, 186–187; how the school should deal with, 185–186; internal ethical conflict creating by, 186; mid-adolescent nothing "wrong" perception and rationales for, 184–185

Child to adolescent, dog to cat analogy, 6–8

Chores. *See* Family chores

Clear-channel communication, 125

"Climbing Fool's Hill," 249–251

Closing the loop of responsibility, 177–179

Collateral of cooperation, 150

College: four academic responsibilities supporting true independence in, 194–195; lacking self-discipline in, 191–196; procrastination as key contributor to flunking or quitting, 188, 190, 191; where the final battle for independence is waged, 195. *See also* High school; Trial independence (ages eighteen to twenty-three)

Commitment and promises, 219

Communication: as always being the first consequence, 172; avoiding arguments by using declarative, not manipulative, 137; caring relationships and reliable, 220; clear-channel, 125; complexities of parent-adolescent spoken, 105–126; how conflict can change quality of, 122, 132–133; the Internet and nonverbal, 109–110, 244; middle school rules on treatment and, 208; open question policy by parents, 119; parental guidance through, 172; practicing clear, 120–122; regarding possible substance abuse, 216–217; *talking to* or lecture, 156. *See also* Language; Listening

Community volunteering activities, 199–200, 238

Companionship: between mothers and adolescent sons, 99; *talking together* and *doing together* creating, 109

Compliance: compromises of adolescent, 152–153; costs of yelling to get, 167–168; criticism as disincentive for, 167; patient insistence applied to get, 170. *See also* Resistance

Conditions expectations, 11

Conduct contract pact: to hold mid-adolescent to, 45–46; six articles of agreement in, 46

Conflict: caring relationships and safety in, 219; violence and, 133, 213. *See also* Parent-adolescent conflict

Conflict avoidance skills, 136–137

Consequences: clear rules are consistently supported by, 169–170; closing the loop of responsibility to take, 177–179; communication as the first, 172; confronting tendency to escape responsibility and, 176–179; expressing concern before giving, 171; what the adolescent learns from confronting natural, 177

Criticism: adolescent self-evaluation and, 235–236; better alternatives to, 166–167; how it can impact insecurities and self-esteem, 165;

name-calling, 164; negative consequences of parental, 164–165, 167; teasing as destructive form of, 165–166
Curfews: discipline related to, 160–161; substance use and continuous breaking of, 216

**D**

Dark poetry, 39
Dating. *See* Social dating
Daughters. *See* Adolescent daughters
Decision making: how alcohol and substance abuse may impact, 212, 216–217; for managing an allowance, 60–63; need for responsibility as driving, 129; parent-adolescent arguing over parental, 136; parental disagreement over, 140–145; respecting the adolescent's right to, 76, 171–172; trial independence challenge of increased range of, 69; various reasons behind parental, 136
Declarative communication, 137
*Declare Yourself* (Narciso), 138
Defamation fear, 209
Delayed gratification practice, 239
Deprivation: drawback as a corrective device, 161; grounding form of, 159–161; used as punishment, 159; reparation alternative to, 161–162
Developing proficiency, 239
Developmental intolerance, 199
Differences: *bridging with interest*, 92–93, 145–148; comparing mothering and fathering parenting, 83–88; parental intolerance of adolescent, 146–147; teaching adolescents how to manage relationship, 147. *See also* Resemblance; Social intolerance
Differentiation: as driving development of individuality/dependence, 128, 142; parental disagreement over adolescent, 142–143
Discipline: balancing instruction/approval and correction in, 150; conflict over adolescent resistance to authority and, 151–154; criticism as part of, 164–167; distinguishing between what works and what doesn't work, 173; grounding used as, 159–161; how anger interferes with, 162–164; how rebellion can increase under negative, 173; nature and goal of, 149–150; practices of effective, 169–173; punishment component of, 154–162; reparation and restitution used as, 161–162; yelling as part of, 167–169. *See also* Parent-adolescent conflict
Discipline practices: clear rules are consistently supported, 169–170; concern is expressed

before consequences are given, 171; constructive conduct receives positive recognition, 170; correction is nonevaluatively given, 170; the first consequence is always communication, 172–173; guidance is faithfully given, 172; individual choice is respected, 171–172; patient insistence is relentlessly applied, 170; speaking up is expected, 171; there is reciprocal giving, 171
Dishonesty: cheating in school, 184–187; how communication is derailed by, 115–116; how fear of being yelled at can result in, 168; how relationships are destroyed by, 115; substance use warning sign of continuous, 216. *See also* Truth
Distrust: emotional manipulation leading to, 140; of peer pressure by parents, 42, 197
Divided attention problem, 124–125
"Do no harm," 1
Doing together strategy, 109
Double punishment, 157
Driving: assessing readiness for, 54; high rates of car crashes and adolescent, 54; how substance abuse increases risk of accidents, 212; indication of responsible, 55; legal age versus readiness age of, 54; as transportation freedom, 53–55
Driving record, 55
Drug use. *See* Substance use/abuse
DWI (driving while intoxicated) charges, 176

**E**

Early adolescence (ages nine to thirteen): description of, 22; early experimentation phase of, 25, 36–39; initial parental reaction to, 23–25; limits of privacy during, 29–30; negative mind-set phase of, 25, 30–36; personal disorganization phase of, 25–30; procrastination installed as work ethic during, 188; school achievement drop during, 179–184; self-esteem drop during, 233–234
Early experimentation: alcohol and substance abuse, 37–38, 106, 211–218; appropriate parental response to, 36, 37–38; description of early adolescent, 36–39; function of early adolescent, 25; how fears are expressed in visual, 39–40
Education. *See* Adolescent education
Embarrassment fear, 108
*Emotional Blackmail* (Forward), 138
Emotional extortion: examples of different forms of, 138–139; parent-adolescent dynamics of, 137–138; parental response to, 139–140

Emotional manipulation: declarative communication versus, 137; description of, 137–140; distrust creating through, 140; holding firm in the face of, 139–140

Empathetic listeners, 124

Employment: late adolescence part-time, 59–60; trial independence challenge of finding and keeping, 69. *See also* Work ethic

Empty-house parties, 58

Ephron, Nora, 7

Equitable sharing, 220

Escaping responsibility: closing the loop of responsibility versus, 177–178; resisting temptation to help adolescents, 176; supporting mistake-based education instead of, 177

Estrangement of adolescence, 13–14

Ethical issues: cheating, 184–187; whistleblowing and reporting other students, 186

Evasion of responsibility, 43–44

Exclusion: to shun with rejection purpose of, 208; social cruelty of, 205, 207

Exit skills, 64

Expansion: driving development of individuality/dependence, 128, 142; parental disagreement over adolescent, 142–143

**F**

Fairness, 220

Family: boomerang kids returning home to the, 72–74; conflict is never an excuse to harm anyone in the, 133; gender differences in single-parent households, 85; how early adolescence independence changes the, 26; how five pillars of social authority support structure of, 44–45; primary social affiliation with, 238; sex-role models in the, 87–88, 99–100; trial education challenge of living apart from, 69

Family chores: learning to do household and, 237–238; messy room issue of, 27–29, 30, 237; supervision to overcome adolescent resistance to, 155

Family gatherings/events, 238

Family membership requirements, 237

Fatal car accidents, 212

Father-daughter relationship: father role as *salient male presence* in, 90–91; fathering in, 88–91

Father-son relationship: competition in, 93–94; performance focus of, 86–87; power struggles in, 94–95; sex-role modeling by father in,

87–88; teenager as opponent perspective of conflict in, 86

Fathering: an adolescent daughter, 88–91; an adolescent son, 91–95; comparing differences in mothering and, 83–88

Fathers: competition between sons and, 93–94; demanding son's similarity to, 95; how adolescents in pain respond to, 87; need to *bridge adolescent differences with interest*, 92–93; paternal downsizing process by sons about their, 93; performance-focused approach of, 84; power struggles between sons and, 94–95; as sex-role model in the family, 87–88; 20 percent of single-parent households headed by, 85

Fears: of abandonment, 14–15, 139; adolescent ambivalence over shyness and, 108–109; of attention, 107; of being inferior, 208; of being tongue-tied, 108; of being yelled at, 168; contributing to adolescent shyness, 107–108; early experimentation in visual expression of, 39–40; of embarrassment, 108; emotional extortion by adolescents and parental, 138–139; how social cruelty tactic play on, 208–209; of isolation, 208; parent empathy with adolescent's, 210; parental self-disclosure, 116–117; of persecution, 209; strategies for overcoming shyness, 109–110; of weakness, 208

Financial independence: delaying gratification practice of, 239; how part-time employment provides, 59–60; learning to save money as part of, 238–239; managing an allowance as, 60–63; spenders versus savers approach to, 61, 238–239; trial independence challenge of indebtedness, 70–71

Five pillars of social authority, 44–45

Forward, Susan, 138

Freedom: adolescent perception of messy room as personal, 27–28; caution against depriving adolescent of every, 159; dating as socializing, 53, 55–58; driving a car as transportation, 53–55; hide-and-seek game in effort to have illicit, 111–112; making money as financial, 53, 59–63; mid-adolescence importance placed on, 41–42; mid-adolescent conduct contract pact in return for, 45–46; protection of parental prohibitions through conditional, 47. *See also* Independence

Freedom of speech, 219

Freshmen (high school): challenges experienced by, 50–51; pressures of becoming seniors, 51

Future shock challenge, 71

## G

Gang recruitment, 40–41
Ganging up: purpose and fears played on by, 209; social cruelty of, 205, 207
Gay-bashing, 211
GED (General Equivalency Diploma), 191
Gibran, Kahlil, 145
Girls: body image issues by, 203–204; parental reactions to romantic breakups suffered by, 220–221; physical changes during puberty, 201–202; social and sexual stereotypes facing, 204. *See also* Adolescent daughters
"Govern thyself wisely," 2
Grievances: anger-prone parents' tendency to hold past, 164; reparation means letting go of past, 162
Grounding: used as deprivation punishment, 159; four guidelines for effective, 159–160; grounding in versus grounding out form of, 160–161

## H

Hide-and-seek game: by adolescents with parents, 110–111; by one parent with the other, 112
Hide-and-sneak game, 111–112
High school: accumulated pressures of, 51–52; benefits of socially mixing students during, 200; challenges experienced by freshmen in, 50–51; do not double punish in case of in-school suspension, 157; how middle school social cruelty may increase in, 211; increasing social speed of life in, 51; parental complaints of "lazy" teenagers during, 65–67; parental transfer of support responsibility to teenager during, 64–65. *See also* College; School achievement; Schools
Hobbies: conflict over giving up formerly loved, 33; self-esteem as identification through, 234–235
Homework: procrastination in completing, 188–191; work ethic training by completing, 236–237
Honesty. *See* Truth
Honor system, 186
Horizontal relationship: description of parent-child, 77; shifting from vertical to, 77–78
Household chores: learning to do, 237–238; messy room issue of, 27–29, 30, 237; supervision to overcome adolescent resistance to, 155
How to Live Life curriculum, 117

## I

*I Feel Bad About My Neck: And Other Thoughts on Being a Woman* (Ephron), 7
Identity: adolescent negative mind-set due to rejection as child, 31–33; allowing child's bedroom to reflect their, 29; redefining of adolescent's, 26; self-esteem understood as being adolescent, 234–235
Ignorance of your adolescent, 13
Indebtedness challenge, 70–71
Independence: adolescent daughters and complex process of claiming, 101–104; adolescent perception of messy room as, 27–28; adolescent rebellion driven by need for, 151–154; caring relationships and sufficient, 219; college as site for final battle for, 195; driving a car as transportation, 53–55; emotional benefits of conflict for adolescent seeking, 133–134; financial, 59–63, 70–71, 238–239; five psychological "engines" driving, 128–129; four kinds of academic responsibilities that support true, 194–195; mid-adolescence importance placed on, 41–42; mid-adolescent conduct contract pact in return for, 45–46; part-time employment empowering, 60; procrastination response to ambivalence over, 79–81; protection of parental prohibitions through conditional, 47; understanding the myth of, 78–79. *See also* Freedom; Social independence; Trial independence (ages eighteen to twenty-three)
Individuality: differentiation as driving development of, 128, 142–143; expansion as driving development of, 128, 142–143; opposition as driving development of, 128–129, 142–143; parental love function of acceptance of child's, 245–246; rebellion as asserting adolescent, 150–151; responsibility as driving development of, 142–143
"Innocent mischief," 38
Input-output theory, 227–228
Interests: *bridging differences with*, 92–93, 145–148; reversing the flow of interest from parent to child, 37
Internet: as adolescent temptation, 240–241; balancing adolescent use of, 243–245; developing proficiency with the, 241; how adolescent shyness has been impacted by, 109–110, 244; how social incapacity can be increased by using, 110, 244; safety issues related to the, 241–243; three general guidelines for adolescent use of the, 244

Intolerance: developmental, 199; social, 198–201

**J**

*Journal of College Retention*, 191

**K**

*Keys to Single Parenting* (Pickhardt), 138

**L**

Lack of appreciation, 17–19
Lack of self-discipline: during college, 191–196; how latitude may result in, 192–193; how parents can help adolescents change, 195–196; psychological drug dependency symptoms versus, 193. *See also* Procrastination
Language: how conflict is impacted by choice of, 122, 132–133; miscommunication due to unclear meaning of, 120–122; operational choice of words, 122. *See also* Communication
Late adolescence (ages fifteen to eighteen): caring relationships during, 218–220; description of, 23, 49; driving, 53–55; entry into high school, 50–53; everyday types of stress experienced during, 193–194; lacking self-discipline in college during, 191–196; managing an allowance, 60–63; parent versus adolescent perceptions of "act more grown up" during, 50–51; the parental agenda during, 63–65; parental complaint about "lazy teenagers" during, 65–67; part-time employment, 59–60; procrastination and school achievement during, 80, 187–191; self-medicating shyness with alcohol during, 106; social dating, 55–58
"Lazy" teenagers: adolescent's response to accusation of being, 65–67; parental complaints about, 65
Lecture (*talking to*), 156
Life skills: exit skills your child should have, 64; learning financial independence, 59–63, 70–71, 238–239; list of additional basic, 64; starter list of essential knowledge and competencies, 63–64. *See also* Adolescent growth anchors
Listening: by accessible listeners, 124; as act of valuing, 124; to adolescent about social cruelty, 210; to adolescent explanation for mistake or misdeed, 171; avoiding divided attention when, 124–125; clear-channel communication to facilitate, 125; during

conflict, 125–126; emotional overload and supportive, 125; by empathetic listeners, 124; importance of practicing, 122–123; message sent to adolescents by parents not, 123–124; *Pulp Fiction* (film) famous line on, 122, 126. *See also* Communication
Loop of responsibility, 177–179
*Lord of the Flies* scenario, 207
Loss: adolescent independence and parental feeling of, 81; of authority by parents, 154; early adolescence (ages nine to thirteen) and mutual feeling of, 24–25; mutual parent-adolescent disenchantment and pain of, 4–6. *See also* Abandonment
Love: power of parental love, 245–248; romantic breakups and end of, 220–222; trial independence as time for finding and losing, 70

**M**

Manipulative communication, 137
Media: alcohol/drug use portrayal in, 37–38; sexual stereotypes, 204
Mentoring. *See* Parental mentoring
Messy rooms: adolescent versus parental perceptions of, 27; appropriate parental response to, 28–29, 30; cleaning up one's, 237; as emblematic of early adolescent disorganization, 27
Mid-adolescence (ages thirteen to fifteen): cheating in school during, 184–187; conduct contract pact tied to granting freedom during, 45–46; description of, 22–23; evasion of responsibility during, 43–44; growing need for social independence by, 182; influence of certain friends during, 39–40; influence of friends during, 39–40; intolerance of restrictions by, 41–42, 44–47; more intense conflict characterizing, 40–41; as prime recruiting age for gangs, 41; protection of parental prohibitions during, 47; protective belligerence response by, 45; the shell of self-centeredness during, 42–43
Middle school: how parents can support their child during, 207–208; how social cruelty may increase in high school, 211; name-calling experience starting during, 206–207; setting classroom rules of communication and treatment in, 208. *See also* Schools
Mistakes: "climbing Fool's Hill" and learning from your, 249–251; consequences versus escaping responsibility from, 177; listening to your adolescent's explanation for, 171.

*See also* Behaviors; Risk-taking behaviors; Social violations

"Mommy's boy," 97

Mother-daughter relationship: as doubly close parent-child relationship, 101–102; importance of modeling constructive conflict in, 103–104; process of claiming independence and conflict in, 101–104; relationally focused approach to, 86; similarities component of, 102–103

Mother-son relationship: adolescent need to distance himself from mother, 96–98; companionship component of, 99; mothers as gender role model in, 87–88, 99–100

Mothering: an adolescent daughter, 100–104; an adolescent son, 96–100; comparing differences in fathering and, 83–88

Mothers: companionship between sons and, 99; complex process of independence by daughters and role by, 101–104; 80 percent of single-parent households headed by, 85; how adolescents in pain respond to, 87; how they deal with conflict, 86; relationally focused approach of, 84; as sex-role model in the family, 87–88, 99–100; son's need to distance themselves from, 96–98

Mutual disenchantment: complaints related to, 5–6; early adolescence (ages nine to thirteen) and, 24–25; loss and pain associated with, 4–6; when your dog becomes a cat metaphor for, 6–8

Myth of independence, 78–79

## N

Name-calling: by parents, 164; as social cruelty act, 206

Narciso, John, 138

Negative mind-set: adolescent rejection of self as child source of, 31–33; appropriate parental response to, 32; early adolescence (ages nine to thirteen), 25, 30–36; function of early adolescent, 25; multiply determined basis of early adolescent, 35–36; over parental restrictions, 33–34. *See also* Rebellion

*New York Times*, 54

Nonverbal Internet communication, 109–110, 244

Nurturing self-esteem: through early adolescence and trial independence self-esteem drop, 233–234; understanding self-esteem as identification when, 234–235; understanding self-esteem as self-evaluation when, 235–236

## O

Obedience. *See* Compliance

Open question policy, 119

Opposition: as driving development of individuality/dependence, 128–129, 142; parental disagreement over adolescent, 142–143. *See also* Rebellion; Resistance

## P

Parent-adolescent conflict: adolescent self-blame during, 87; emotional benefits for adolescent of, 133–134; emotional extortion and, 137–140; father-son power struggles, 94–95; over five pillars of social authority, 44–45; how emotions can impact spoken communication during, 122; importance of clear communication during, 122; over limits of privacy, 29–30; listening during verbal, 125–126; managing parental disagreement over, 140–145; over messy bedrooms, 27–29; mid-adolescence (ages thirteen to fifteen) characterized by, 40–41; mother and father differences in dealing with, 85–86; of mother-daughter struggles over independence, 101–104; mother-son and emotionally complicated, 98; mother's model of constructive dialogue to daughters in, 103–104; over parental restrictions during mid-adolescence, 41–42; performance focus of father-son, 86–87; protective belligerence response by adolescent to, 45; as reality of adolescence, 15–16; relationship focus of mother-daughter, 86; ten notions to consider when engaging in, 129–134; treating the teenager as an informant during, 86; understanding how conflict can create resemblance, 130, 131, 135–136; understanding how it impacts relationship, 127. *See also* Arguments; Conflict; Discipline

Parent-adolescent conflict notions: conflict can be instructive, 130–131; conflict can change quality of communication, 122, 132–133; conflict can create resemblance, 130; conflict can lead to violence, 133; conflict is cooperative, 129–130; conflict is how siblings get along, 132; conflict training in parent's family of origin, 129; cooperation can create conflict, 131–132; resemblance can create conflict, 131; tolerance for conflict can vary between parent and adolescent, 133–134

Parental agenda: during late adolescence (ages fifteen to eighteen), 63–65; starter list of essential competencies your child needs,

63–64; transfer of support responsibility from parent to teenager, 64–65

Parental attitude changes: accept that adolescence is a more combative age, 3; don't punish your child for acting adolescent, 2–3; don't take your child's adolescence as a personal affront, 2; understand that adolescence is meant to break the spell of childhood, 3–4

Parental attitudes: four important changes in, 2–4; mentoring and appropriate, 75–78; respecting adolescent's shyness and fears, 108–109

Parental disagreement: appreciating the benefits of, 144–145; managing, 140–145; origins and sources of, 141; over adolescent risk-taking behaviors, 142–144

Parental influence: input-output theory of, 227–228; need to limit sense of responsibility for, 229; for nurturing adolescent self-esteem, 233–236; other sources of influence in addition to, 228–229; sources of, 230

Parental love: adolescent passage challenges for, 246–248; complexity of *giving* to express, 247–248; establishing an attachment and acceptance function of, 245–246; the expressions and power of, 248

Parental mentoring: rules for, 75–77; shifting from vertical to horizontal relationship for, 77–78; trial independence and role of, 74–75

Parental mentoring rules: don't weight in with unasked for advice, 76–77; no parental disapproval or criticism, 75–76; respect adolescent's right to make decisions, 76, 171–172

Parental responses: to boomerang kids returning home, 72–74; conduct contract pact to hold mid-adolescent to, 45–46; to conflict by mothers and fathers, 86–87; of distrust or discomfort with new friend, 40; to early adolescent achievement drop, 179–180, 181–184; to early adolescent messy room, 28–29, 30; to early adolescent negative mind-set, 32; to early adolescent personal disorganization, 26–27, 28; to early experimentation, 36, 37–38; to emotional extortion by adolescent, 139–140; guidance on recognizing and developing caring relationships, 218–219; to helping student overcome procrastination habit, 190–191; to mid-adolescent self-centeredness, 42–43; normalizing discussion of alcohol and drug use, 37–38; to peers and peer pressure, 42, 197, 199–200; questions to ask about

healthy relationships and dating, 56–57; to romantic breakups experience by their adolescent, 220–222; to social cruelty directed toward child, 207–209, 210–211; supervision to overcome adolescent resistance to chores, 155; supporting adolescent self-discipline, 195–196

Parental restrictions: early adolescent negativity over, 33–34; mid-adolescence conflict over, 41–42, 44–47; mid-adolescence need for protection of, 47

Parental treatment: appreciating the emotional effect of, 233; psychology of social treatment applied to, 230–233

Parenting: adolescent daughters, 86, 88–91, 100–104; adolescent sons, 86–87, 91–100; *bridging differences with interest* practice of, 92–93, 145–148; comparing differences in mothering and fathering, 83–88; developing realistic set of expectations about, 8–12; input-output theory of, 227–228

Parents: adjusting to lack of appreciation by adolescent, 17–19; adjusting to the five realities of adolescence, 12–17; adolescent hide-and-seek/sneak game with, 110–112; ambivalence over adolescent independence by, 81; anger-prone, 163–164; assessing readiness of adolescent to drive, 54; coaching advice on dealing with mean teasing by, 210–211; conflict avoidance skills needed by, 136–137; differing tolerance of conflict by adolescent and, 133–134; facing the reality of adolescence, 1–2; five pillars of social authority instituted by, 44–45; hide-and-seek game played by one parent against the other, 112; How to Live Life curriculum taught by, 117; influence of, 227–230; initial reaction to early adolescence (ages nine to thirteen) by, 23–25; keeping social cruelty a secret from, 206–207; learning to reverse the flow of interest with child, 37; managing your adolescent's Internet use, 109–110, 240–245; mutual disenchantment of adolescents and, 4–8; open questions policy between adolescents and, 119; reciprocal giving between adolescents and, 171; resetting their expectations, 8–12; secrets kept by adolescents from, 110–112; self-disclosure by, 116–120; shifting from vertical to horizontal relationship with adolescents, 77–78; spoken communication between adolescents and, 105–126; who are intolerant of adolescent's changing tastes, 148–149. *See also* Adults

Part-time employment: developmental benefits of seeking, 59; independence empowered by, 60

Parties: empty-house, 58; overcoming social discomfort during, 57–58

Passive resistance: description of, 35; father-son power struggles and, 95; opposition as pushing for more, 128–129

Peer groups: *abandoned youth*, 207; alcohol and substance use as behavior related to, 37–38, 106, 211–218; emotional costs of belonging to, 199; emotional responses to puberty impacting relations with, 201–204; in-group allegiance demanded by, 200–201; social cruelty by, 204–211; social intolerance by, 199–201; "universal student" who are able to move between, 201

Peer pressure: to "act more grown up" by older adolescents, 50; high school and accumulated social and, 51–52; how parents can limit influences of, 199–200; parental distrust of, 42, 197; social discomfort during parties, 57–58

Peers: adolescent need for social independence and reliance on, 197–198; adolescent's determination to preserve social independence with, 207; alcohol and substance use as behavior related to, 37–38, 106, 211–218; emotional responses to puberty impacting relationships with, 201–204; how to help your freshmen adjust to high school, 50; influence during mid-adolescence (ages thirteen to fifteen), 39–40; learning about drugs from, 38; parental distrust or discomfort with new, 40; risk-taking social violations encouraged by, 38; social cruelty by, 204–211; substance use clues related to new, 214, 215; "universal student" who are socially accepted by all, 201. *See also* Relationships

Performance-focus parenting: father-son conflict centered around performance, 86–87; favored by fathers, 84; modeling behavior of both relationally focused and, 87–88

Persecution fear, 209

Personal disorganization: appropriate parental response to, 26–27, 28; developmental function of, 25; during early adolescence, 25; messy room symptom of, 27–28

Personal freedom. *See* Freedom

Physical punishment, 157–158

Pickhardt, C., 18–19, 129, 138, 205

Power struggles: father-son, 94–95; mother-daughter, 101–104

Pranking, 38

Predictions expectations, 10–11

Pressure of impulse, 51–52

Pressure of peers. *See* Peer pressure

Pressure of sensation, 51

Pressure of temptation, 51

Primary social affiliation, 238

Privacy: adolescent secrecy form of, 110–116, 206–207; parent-adolescent conflict over limits to, 29–30

Procrastination: "deadlines are made to be broken" lesson and, 189; developed as strategy of resistance, 188; installed as early adolescent work ethic, 188; as key contributor to flunking or quitting college, 188, 190, 191; late adolescence school achievement issue of, 80, 187–191; parental response to help student overcome, 190–191; Procrastinators Anonymous 12-step recovery program for, 188; relationship between stress and, 189–190; type-one versus type-two, 80. *See also* Lack of self-discipline

Procrastinators Anonymous 12-step recovery program, 188

Professional help: dispelling "bad child" and "bad parents" beliefs through, 228; substance use and abuse that may require, 217

Proficiency development, 239

Promises and commitment, 219

Protection of parental prohibitions, 47

Protective belligerence, 45

Psychological changes: a messy room as reflecting disarray of, 27; redefining one's identity as adolescent, 26

Psychological drug dependency, 193

Psychology of social treatment, 230–233

Puberty: adolescent shyness during, 106; body image problems during, 203–204; emotional responses to, 201–204; hormonal changes of, 26; intense adolescent transformation during, 203; psychological changes during, 26. *See also* Adolescence

*Pulp Fiction* (film), 122, 126

Punishment: administered when communication fails to teach lesson, 156; appropriate purpose and function of, 155; avoid double, 157; balancing with recognition of good behavior, 158–159; deprivation used as, 159–160; possible payback by adolescent to parents for, 154; should be free of parental anger, 158; spanking or other physical, 157–158; *talking to* or lecture as, 156; understanding the difference between supervision and, 154–155

# R

Rape, 226

Realistic expectations: developing a set of, 8–12; high cost of not having, 10, 11–12; predictions, ambitions, and conditions types of, 10–11

Rebellion: as act of dependence, 34; active resistance form of, 34–35, 95; against adult authority and noncompliance, 150; challenge as antidote to, 34; developmental function of, 35; early adolescent, 33–34; how parental negativity can lengthen period of adolescent, 173; mid-adolescent, 41–42, 44–47; parent versus adolescent perception of, 150–151; passive resistance form of, 35–95; social fitting in and nonconformity, 150. *See also* Authority; Negative mind-set; Opposition; Social violations

Reciprocal giving, 171

Rejection: anger by jilted young men suffering, 221–222; need for differentiation versus emotional costs of, 128; romantic breakups and feelings of, 220–222; shyness and fear of, 108

Relationally-focused parenting: conflict response by, 85–87; favored by mothers, 84; how dishonesty and telling lies destroys, 115; modeling behavior of both performance and, 87–88

Relationships: encouraging caring, 218–220; how partial truths and lies hurt, 114; how physical punishment impacts future, 158; psychology of social treatment and, 230–233; serious versus casual dating, 55–56; social dating, 53, 55–58; teaching adolescents how to manage differences in, 147; understanding how parent-adolescent conflict impacts, 127. *See also* Peers

Reparation, 161–162

Reputation: fear of defamation of, 209; how we treat others influences our social, 230; name-calling contaminating, 206; rumoring used to destroy, 205, 207, 209

Resemblance: arguments and imitation of others' tactics, 135–136; understanding how conflict can create, 130, 131. *See also* Differences

Resistance: active, 34–35, 95, 128–129; passive, 35, 95, 128–129; procrastination developed as strategy of, 188; supervision defined as parental persistence to overcome, 155. *See also* Compliance; Opposition

Respect: of adolescent's right to make choices by parents, 76, 171–172; of adolescent's shyness and fears by parents, 108–109; compliance

with parental authority to show, 152–153; as component of serious and caring relationship, 218–219

Responsibility: as driving development of individuality/dependence, 142; escaping, 176–179; goal of discipline to teach adolescent, 149–150; gradual transference to adolescent of authority and, 153–154; how true independence is supported by four kinds of academic, 194–195; lack of self-discipline instead of taking, 191–196; mid-adolescent evasion of, 43–44; need for parents to limit their sense of, 229; parental disagreement over adolescent, 142–143

Responsibility driving independence, 129

Restitution, 162

Risk-taking behaviors: alcohol and substance use, 37–38, 70, 106, 211–218; cheating at school, 184–187; hide-and-sneak game and, 111–112; how alcohol and substance abuse affects, 212; how peers encourage, 38; parental disagreement over adolescent's, 142–145; social pressures leading up to, 51–52; withholding an allowance when there is evidence of, 63. *See also* Behaviors; Mistakes; Social violations

Romantic breakups: parental reactions to their adolescent's, 220–221; special cautions for parents of jilted young man, 221–222

Roommate challenges, 70

Rumoring: playing on fear of defamation, 209; slander purpose of, 209; social cruelty of, 205, 207

# S

Safety issues: guidance regarding caring relationships and, 219; the Internet, 241–243; related to jilted young man, 221–222; sexual intimacy and, 223–224

Salient male presence, 90–91

Savers, 61, 238–239

School achievement: cheating in mid-adolescence and, 184–187; completing homework to provide work ethic training, 236–237; early adolescent drop in, 179–184; late adolescence procrastination and, 80, 187–191. *See also* High school

School achievement drop: behaviors leading to, 180–181; early adolescence, 179–184; how parent react to, 179–180, 181–184; identifying academic benchmark to hold student accountable for, 181–182; late adolescence procrastination and, 80, 187–191

Schools: benefits of socially mixing students in, 200; college-level, 188, 190, 191–196; "deadlines are made to be broken" lesson learned in, 189; honor system set up by, 186; how they should deal with cheating, 185–186; social cruelty sign of unexplained anxiety about attending, 209. *See also* High school; Middle school

Secrecy. *See* Adolescent secrecy

Self-blame: performance-focused parenting and adolescent, 87; relationally focused parenting and adolescent, 87

Self-centeredness, 42–43

Self-discipline: college and lack of, 191–196; how latitude may result in lack of, 192–193; how parents can help support adolescent, 195–196; psychological drug dependency symptoms versus lack of, 193

Self-disclosure: being prepared to listen to adolescent's, 122–126; parental, 116–120; similarity connections between parents and adolescents revealed by, 118

Self-esteem: adolescent activities as pillars of, 33; do not use deprivation that takes away from, 159–160; how cheating lowers, 186; how parental criticism can impact adolescent, 165; parental nurturing of adolescent, 233–236; social cruelty and observable drop in, 209; understood as identification, 234–235; understood as self-evaluation by adolescent, 235–236

Self-evaluation, 235–236

Seniors (high school): challenges faced by freshmen as they become, 51–52; social pressure placed on freshmen by, 50–51

Sense of competence, 239

Sensitivity, 219

Separation: adolescent son's need to distance himself from mother, 96–98; disagreement between parents over adolescent, 142–143; driving development of individuality/dependence, 128, 142

Setting expectations. *See* Behavioral expectations

Sex-role models: how parents provide dominant, 87–88; of mothers to adolescent sons, 99–100

Sexism, 99

Sexual intimacy: complicated motivations for, 224–226; late adolescent and likelihood of, 222–223; parental expectations regarding, 223; parental instruction on beliefs, values, and safety of, 223–224; rape or forced, 226; serious dating and likelihood of, 56; under the influence of alcohol or substance use, 225

Sexual misadventure, 212

Sexual stereotypes, 204

Shoplifting, 38

Shyness. *See* Adolescent shyness

Siblings, 132

Single-parent heads of household, 85

Social authority pillars, 44–45

Social cruelty: bullying as, 205, 207, 208; committed by good kids acting badly, 205–206; description of five types of, 204–205; exclusion as, 205, 207, 208; ganging up as, 205, 207, 209; how parents can provide help in case of, 207–209, 210–211; *Lord of the Flies* scenario of, 207; psychological forces in play during, 208–209; rumoring as, 205, 207, 209; six signs to look for, 209–210; teasing as, 165–166, 205–208, 210–211

Social dating: "being in love" and serious versus casual, 55–56; empty-house party, 58; encouraging caring relationships as part of, 218–220; as freedom, 53, 55–58; questions to ask about healthy relationships and, 56–57; romantic breakups, 220–222; sexual experience element of, 222–226; social discomfort when attending parties, 57–58. *See also* Relationships

Social independence: adolescent reliance on peers as part of, 197–198; adolescent's determination to preserve it with peers, 207; dating as, 53, 55–58; mid-adolescent growing need for, 182

Social intolerance: adolescence as time of, 198–201; developmental intolerance toward self form of, 199; by peer groups, 199–201; puberty changes which may affect, 201–204; "universal students" who seem to be immune from, 201; watching for signs in your adolescent, 199–200. *See also* Differences

Social speed of life, 51

Social treatment psychology: actions have emotional effect on others, 232–233; experience influences expectation of treatment, 231–232; how we treat others affects how they see themselves, 232; how we treat others is self-defining, 230; no act of social treatment stands alone, 232; our reputation for treating others, 230; parental treatment matters, 233; present action shapes future behavior, 231; providing a treatment model for others to follow, 232; treatment given can carry on, 231; treatment given is often treatment received, 230–231

Social violations: alcohol and substance abuse, 37–38, 106, 211–218; encouraged by peers, 38; how substance abuse can increase risk of, 212; pranking, 38; shoplifting, 38; vandalizing, 38. *See also* Mistakes; Rebellion; Risk-taking behaviors

Sons. *See* Adolescent sons

Spanking, 157–158

Speed of life: high school and social, 51; speed-of-life crashes, 52; speed-of-life decisions, 52

Spenders, 61, 238–239

Spoken communication: adolescent secrecy impact on, 110–112, 207; adolescent shyness impact on, 105–110; as always being the first consequence, 172; avoiding arguments by using declarative, not manipulative, 137; caring relationships and reliable, 220; complex nature of, 105, 126; how conflict can change the quality of, 122, 132–133; how to best clarify and create authentic, 120–122; importance of listening to, 122–126; middle school rules on treatment and, 208; open question policy by parents on, 119; parental guidance through, 172; practicing clear, 120–122; regarding possible substance abuse, 216–217; selective truths revealed by adolescents during, 113–116; self-disclosure reluctance by parents impact on, 116–120; *talking to* or lecture, 156

Sports: conflict over giving up formerly loved, 33; self-esteem as identification through, 234–235

*Stop the Screaming* (Pickhardt), 129

Stress: last-stage adolescents and everyday types of, 193–194; relationship between procrastination and, 189–190; as trial independence, 71

Substance use/abuse: college challenges related to, 70; discussions with adolescent regarding, 217–218; five progressively serious levels of, 212–213; hearsay from peers about, 38; how decision making is impacted by, 212–216, 217; nonoverlapping signs of, 215–217; overlapping signs of both adolescence and, 214–215; parental discussions about, 37–38; as peer-group issue, 211–218; sexual intimacy under influence of, 225; uncharacteristic changes in behavior clues to, 213–214. *See also* Alcohol use/abuse

Supervision: to counter the mid-adolescent achievement drop, 182–184; defined as parental persistence to overcome adolescent resistance, 155; understanding the difference between punishment and, 154–155

**T**

*Talking to* (lecture), 156

Talking together strategy, 109

Teachers: adolescent keeping social cruelty a secret from, 207; benefits of socially mixing students up, 200; coaching advice on dealing with mean teasing by, 210–211; ignoring social cruelty toward students, 206. *See also* Adults

Teasing: classroom rules on, 208; coaching advice on how to combat, 210–211; used as criticism by parents, 165–166; humiliation purpose of, 208; name-calling form of, 164, 206; parent and teacher help to diminish, 208–209; as social cruelty act, 205–208

Teenage rebellion. *See* Rebellion

Temperamental shyness: description and circle of, 106–107; social and emotional costs of, 107

"Thankless Parenting" (Pickhardt), 18–19

Treatment of people. *See* Social treatment psychology

Trial independence (ages eighteen to twenty-three): ambivalence and disillusionment emotions during, 79–80; assuming self-reliance to achieve independence outcome of, 80–82; boomerang kids, 72–74; caution against comparing your child to others, 72; challenges of, 68, 69–72; college as site for final battle for, 195; description of, 23, 67–68; getting ready for the *Big R*–reality), 67; life challenges to face during, 69–71; the myth of independence and, 78–79; parental mentoring during, 74–78; risks of parties and social gatherings, 68; self-esteem drop during, 233–234. *See also* College; Independence

Trial independence challenges: emotional disturbance, 71; finding and keeping employment, 69; finding and losing love, 70; further education, 70; future shock, 71; indebtedness, 70–71; living apart from family, 69; living in a drug-filled world, 70; living with roommates, 70; more range of choice, 69; stress, 71

Truth: adolescent's secrecy and partial revelations of, 113–116, 207; caring relationships and ability to be honest, 219; confession versus self-incrimination of, 113; how relationships are hurt by partial, 114. *See also* Dishonesty

Type-two procrastination, 80

**U**

"Universal student," 201
Unrealistic expectations: emotional consequences for parents of, 11–12; high cost of having, 10

**V**

Vandalizing, 38
Vertical relationship: description of parent-child, 77; shifting to horizontal from, 77–78
Violence: how conflict can lead to, 133; how substance abuse can increase risk of, 212; by jilted young man, 221–222; of rape, 226
Violent drawings, 39
Volunteering activities, 199–200, 238

**W**

When your dog becomes a cat metaphor, 6–8
Whistleblowing, 186
*Why Good Kids Act Cruel* (Pickhardt), 205
Work ethic: how completing homework provides training, in, 236–237; procrastination installed as early adolescent, 188. *See also* Employment

**Y**

Yelling: breaking the pattern of, 169; resisting the temptation for, 167; understanding the costs of, 167–168